STATE *of* READINESS

PRAISE FOR STATE OF READINESS

"Joseph F. Paris' *State of Readiness* offers an engaging and provocative look at effective strategies to prepare businesses for the harsh realities of the twenty-first century. He artfully challenges the core belief that eliminating waste and optimizing processes are still the main factors of operational excellence, as they were in the last century. Paris shows how companies now also require quick decision-making processes, effective communications, and a thorough understanding of cultural differences (both internal and external to the corporation) in order to survive and then to thrive. High-performing companies will be those that use operational excellence in a proactive manner, who don't wait until the next crisis is already knocking at the door. They will need to develop the capability to identify and react to challenges quicker than ever before. Whether a C-Suite executive or an operations manager, *State of Readiness* is a great way to help determine if your company is ready to face the new business climate that lies ahead."

—Robert J. Szczerba, senior fellow emeritus
at Lockheed Martin

"*State of Readiness* looks beyond the traditional Lean process improvement to enterprise-wide strategy in system performance. This is next-level thinking, moving from isolated standards and abnormalities, to creating a proactive organization that is developing predictive-outcome systems. With the Fourth Industrial Revolution upon us, Joseph Paris has taken operational excellence to a new level, and leaders who are serious about competitive advantage need to do more than smart manufacturing and create a *State of Readiness* in their company."

—Jonathan Taurman, director of global Lean/ops excellence
at GE Healthcare

"Want your company to be a high achiever, nimble enough to handle new opportunities or threats? Or are you that high performing nimble company now? If you need to improve, *State of Readiness* will help climb to the top. If you're at the top, it provides a thought-provoking check to ensure you retain your pinnacle of performance."

—**Bob Summers,** brigadier general (retired) in the US Air Force, former deputy director of operations of Air Force Space Command

"*State of Readiness* is a must-read for any serious continuous improvement professional involved in the deployment of operational excellence! Joseph Paris questions why so many experts in operations management tend to 'glorify the supposedly unmatched performance of Japanese companies and their management techniques' and provides compelling evidence and a fresh perspective as to why this might not be as true as generally believed. In doing so, he explores the lessons learned from the past and how organizations of today need to go beyond what is known toward designing and building world-class operational excellence programs in order to truly become a high-performance organization in the twenty-first century—providing a template and roadmap for organizations to evolve beyond the traditional emphasis on processes to an emphasis on systems thinking."

—**Paul O'Brien,** director of business excellence at eBay

"Joseph Paris is your operational excellence Sherpa, and his book *State of Readiness* will passionately inform and challenge you as it seeks to help you guide your organization's transformation from disjointed pockets of processes to an integrated sea of systems. Timely yet timeless, it is a thought-provoking read and will often challenge what you think you know. Paris does not set goals that are lofty and theoretical states that are intangible and largely unattainable. Rather, he explains why a state of readiness is vital to an organization and offers visionary insights, balanced with pragmatic approaches—with ample storytelling and often light-hearted content that will keep your attention. For some, it will serve as an introduction to operational excellence and its importance; for others, it will be a how-to book, and still others will find it a regular reference as you endeavor to transform your organization to face the challenges of today. Whether you are in operations or an executive of a global conglomerate, this book hits the mark and will appeal to a diversity of readers—and providing this book to key team members will certainly derive beneficial results."

—**Donna O'Leary,** chief information officer of the New Hampshire Department of Health and Human Services

"Joseph Paris's *State of Readiness* is an entertaining and educational book that creates a path to understanding what is necessary to become a high-performance organization. There are many examples drawn from personal and professional perspectives that help make the insights inside the book tangible, vivid, and a real guide to creating a business operating system. Throughout the book, Paris clearly demonstrates that the whole of an organization is greater than the sum of its parts: customers, employees, associates, suppliers, partners, society, and shareholders. And if the organization knows and hones its capabilities and capacity—if all these parts are synchronized and aligned across the business smokestacks toward a clearly communicated vision—there will exist a state of readiness that is a requirement to becoming a high-performance organization. You got the right things right, Mr. Paris. In the end, as Shakespeare put it in *Hamlet*, 'The readiness is all.'"

—Jonathan Escobar Marin, director and global head of
Lean management at HARTMANN GROUP

"From beginning to end, *State of Readiness* educates and entertains through a lively narrative. Joseph clearly differentiates *operational excellence* from *continuous improvement*, yet aligns both toward establishing a state of readiness in an organization as it pursues its vision. Whether you are a wizened expert or just beginning your professional journey, this book is a must-have for your professional library. You could wait until tomorrow to get started, but as JP challenges, 'How many tomorrows do you have?'"

—Jeff Naglestad, director of operational excellence at Sanofi

"In *State of Readiness*, Joseph Paris skillfully shares his experiences and wisdom in enterprise transformation and leadership. His uncommonly visual language conjures vivid mental images and makes the book such a tangible and rewarding experience for the reader. Threaded throughout are many examples and anecdotes that are common sense but, at the same time, demonstrate that, as Voltaire said so many years ago, "Common sense is not so common." The book strikes a perfect balance between enterprise-wide and line-of-business, and every reader will come away blessed with a vision of what operational excellence is and the indelible and positive impact it can have on a business and those who work there. It is a must-read for every executive and manager who aspires to sustainably change the operational performance of their company."

—**Donald Kuk,** vice president
of global business transformation at AIG

"Joseph Paris clarifies and defines what *operational excellence* means in the real world. His book *State of Readiness* is a good read and resource for those striving to understand their business as a single system based on a common culture and the use of methods and goal alignment. Sometimes amusing and sometimes blunt, JP pulls no punches in offering a solid review of concepts and tools for performance improvement. He includes many anecdotes and historical examples of companies that were ready for change and others that were not. If you want your business to be ready and able to meet future challenges successfully, then this book is for you."

—**Helmut Welke,** material flow design manager
at Deere and Company (retired)

"An exceptional book encompassing all areas of the OPEX discipline, this is a great starting place for leaders when embarking on their OPEX journey. From Lean Six Sigma to Hashin Kanri, Paris provides an excellent and comprehensive OPEX guidebook for all types of organizations. *State of Readiness* is a must-read for leaders who want to become true OPEX practitioners and leaders of high-performance teams."

—Jamie "Jay" Guttenberg, PhD (ABD),
director of operational excellence at
Blue Cross Blue Shield of Minnesota

"*State of Readiness* describes in an exact—but also an easy to read—way what is meant by the term *operational excellence*. It will be obvious for anyone who reads Paris's book that achieving operational excellence is not about following one set of tools or considering one single improvement approach as a bible for achieving substantial improvements in an organization. In reality, achieving operational excellence is as about the joint focus on creating a culture of leadership, processes, people, technologies, and behavioral change—and using the appropriate tools and methods from Kaizen via Lean Management to Six Sigma as warranted—but always with a mindset of building capacity and capabilities to create readiness. JP offers excellent examples of what happens to a company if it is following one way of achieving improvements but is not ready for (or willing to) change. They simply fail."

—Carsten Hurth, global director of
operational excellence at Gerresheimer

"Joe Paris has produced a kind of atlas of operational excellence thinking, infused with his own characteristic humorous, insightful, and enthusiastic style. It gives a solid and grounded overview of the history and current state of the field, taking in everything from individual responses to change to historic comparisons between nations. And it adds JP's own sometimes surprising sayings, reflections, and inspiration. I recommend this to any established or aspiring manager or change expert; it's like having a wise and friendly old uncle, full of energy and mischief, as your personal adviser and consultant."

—**Benjamin Taylor,** chief executive at the
Public Service Transformation Academy

"Reinvigorating the industry's view of operational efficiency with a witty and charming narrative, *State of Readiness* outlines key components that should be addressed to become a high-performing organization. The reader will also come away with a ton of business analogies that will help in their communication of complex ideas and hold court in any professional environment."

—**Pavle Sabic,** global financial risk manager for
Fortune 500 companies

"Joseph Paris is a strategic thinker and process improvement expert extraordinaire, and his *State of Readiness* is nothing short of groundbreaking. In this well-researched guide, JP questions the wisdom of all-things-process and offers keen insights into the achievement of true operational excellence."

—**David Deutsch,** president of
David N. Deutsch & Company

STATE *of* READINESS

OPERATIONAL EXCELLENCE

as PRECURSOR *to* BECOMING *a*

HIGH-PERFORMANCE ORGANIZATION

———

JOSEPH F. PARIS JR.

GREENLEAF
BOOK GROUP PRESS

This publication is designed to provide accurate and authoritative information in regard to the subject matter covered. It is sold with the understanding that the publisher and author are not engaged in rendering legal, accounting, or other professional services. If legal advice or other expert assistance is required, the services of a competent professional should be sought.

Published by Greenleaf Book Group Press
Austin, Texas
www.gbgpress.com

Distributed by Greenleaf Book Group

For ordering information or special discounts for bulk purchases, please contact Joseph F. Paris Jr at PO Box 2554 Jackson, WY 83001, 607.765.6634 JosephFParisJr@gmail.com.

Design and composition by Greenleaf Book Group and Kim Lance
Cover design by Greenleaf Book Group and Kim Lance

Cataloging-in-Publication data is available.

Print ISBN: 978-1-62634-311-5

eBook ISBN: 978-1-62634-312-2

Printed in the United States of America on acid-free paper

17 18 19 20 21 22   10 9 8 7 6 5 4 3 2 1

First Edition

To my family, my wife, Beata, and my sons,
Jonathan and Anton, who have supported me and
loved me through thick and thin over all these years.

To my parents, Joseph and Shirley, for often not understanding
me or how I think but supporting me unreservedly.

To Rick Hulse, my wingman, my other brother,
for helping me get where I am and giving clarity.

TABLE OF CONTENTS

FOREWORD

We have all heard the horror stories of change and continuous improvement efforts failing. But we need to ask ourselves *What is driving us to challenge the status quo? What is it that we want to achieve? How can we gain alignment and build momentum throughout the entire company? How can we achieve more, faster? How can a fixation on the tools detract from what is important? Personally, will the legacy of our efforts leave us fulfilled with what we have achieved? And how do we avoid these same pitfalls?* The key is to make the effort to build a culture for success as a cornerstone of your company so that you can more readily recognize when an alternative approach is necessary and respond more decisively.

There are many books available to help us answer these questions as we embark on our journey to achieve the highest level of operational performance possible. Each will illuminate the various methodologies, the relevant tools you should be aware of, their appropriate use, and which to pull from your kit when and under what circumstances.

The present book is a definitive work on the discipline of operational excellence. In it, Joseph Paris gives a retrospective on how management approaches to business operations came to exist as they are today and offers a definition and paints a picture of what operational excellence is and its strategic and tactical importance to your company. He offers insight as to why a culture of leadership and accelerated decision-making will be the competitive advantage for companies in the twenty-first century. He does a deep dive into the nuanced and often neglected soft skills of communication, debate, and motivation that establish team-building and foster alignment. He discusses the arsenal of tools available and how they should be used for maximum benefit. And he offers guidance and a framework for building an operational excellence program and illuminates the tell-tale signs as to whether your program is on the right track or not.

Having worked at BMW as the vice president of manufacturing for the Mini Cooper and now at SpaceX in their manufacturing operations, I have experienced how the differing cultures of the United Kingdom, the United States, and Germany, among others, can complement one another and become a force multiplier instead of a hindrance. What is necessary is the opportunity and desire to align the energies and efforts of all with a shared purpose and goal that is known and understood by everyone. Approaches will naturally differ, but people like to win. And when shared beliefs exist, effort, obstacles, sacrifice, and hardship are no longer measures of the challenge but, instead, rallying cries to come together and deliver as a high-performance team.

Now, you may be asking how I can possibly compare the achievements and approach of an automotive powerhouse like BMW, with its long history, with that of an impressive new entrant into the space industry like SpaceX? The one quality that is shared by the two—a competitive advantage in each of their respective industries—is that both companies have leadership cultures that create organizational alignment rarely experienced in most organizations. And they both have an inherent belief that people's abilities are, more often than not, underestimated.

SpaceX has the grand ambition of inaugurating interplanetary life as a reality, with plans to establish transport solutions to and from Mars. And although BMW's transport goals are a lot closer to home, both companies harness more of the human potential within their organizations than most others. There is no shortage of challenges placed on the teams to resolve problems, as well as the natural pressure and sensitivity to the timeliness of results, but when walking the floor in either company, you feel a sense of purpose, camaraderie, and a desire to win.

So consider whether you really have an open culture for feedback. Do you allow a new intern to freely ask questions or make suggestions in the first meetings they attend? Do you actually provide adequate support and a role with immediate accountability, or do you have them "shadow" other team members through fear of their inexperience and potential failure? Is every meeting simply a matter of an agenda and minutes, or can someone's great suggestion turn the agenda a full 180 degrees from its original intent?

If you want to inspire innovation at a pace that is unrivalled, then you need to encourage creativity, and this requires that organizational leaders at all levels and everywhere in the company be responsible and supportive, especially when lessons are inevitably learned by individuals seeking to achieve stretch goals. When mistakes are made, they must be shouldered by both the individual who made them (to prevent a repeat), and the leader, who assumes accountability for both the result and maintenance of the culture for change. The fear to stretch beyond your comfort zone and ability is born of a previous mistake that was punished. The result is that a culture of fear is the culture of the company. Don't be that company.

Many organizations seeking to achieve operational excellence and become a high-performance organization fail at the fundamentals: to train and coach their leaders as to what real leadership is and to unlock and unleash the talents and full potential within their teams. Poor-performing organizations will focus their efforts on "building belts" and will concentrate their training efforts solely on the tools and how to view existing processes and value streams from the usual perspective. What if the team responsible for delivering the results was able to examine the challenges from an entirely different viewpoint and ensure all the leaders within the organization were constantly available as an extension to the team's problem resolution process? How many more challenges would be resolved, and how empowered would the team feel with regard to making a difference? A sense of ownership and pride in a job well done matters.

So although the various methodologies and tools associated with continuous improvement are useful in their own right, there is much more required to achieving the high performance desired by so many. In this book, JP provides clarity on how to push beyond these methodologies and tools and to incrementally and deliberately progress toward the realization of your organizational potential.

People become very anxious with the thought of change—not to mention transformational change. Even when faced with great peril or opportunity, human nature is to resist change. Too often, they wait too long, and their control of the circumstances diminishes; the result is a negative impact on the outcomes. It is therefore important to invest the time and effort up front and to communicate with clarity the form, substance, and intent of the change so that this fear is minimized.

State of Readiness provides meaningful guidance for creating a culture of leadership and innovation within your company. It shows how to accelerate the decision-making process so that iterative progress toward company objectives occurs faster and the missteps are less costly, how to build high-performance individuals and how to form high-performance teams from these individuals, and how to ensure that all the efforts and resources across your value chain are aligned for the pursuit of your company's strategies.

If you want to be the next greatest disruptor within your industry, to gain the maximum market share, to increase profitability, or to simply remain relevant and prevent bankruptcy, then this strength of purpose has to be shared within and across your organization. JP helps you with his experiences globally and offers an approach and framework to eliminate the bureaucracy that stifles creativity, to transcend cultural differences and make diversity an asset, to focus everyone's efforts toward what is important, to have a superior understating of your company's capabilities and situational awareness, and to individually and collectively make a lasting positive and indelible difference within your organization.

I am excited that this book provides the substance and context that has eluded so many other works in the past. I am certain that those who read it will be better prepared to enable their business and leaders to accomplish much more in less time than can be accomplished by simply having knowledge of tools and techniques. Leadership, the understanding of what motivates people, their native knowledge and culture, an understanding of their circumstances in context, and a clear vision for the future that is unmistakably communicated will result in an environment where true transformational change is the norm and not the exception.

I gained some keen insights from this book on what it takes

to build a successful operational excellence program and become a high-performance organization, and I am sure you will too.

Andrew Lambert, FIET
Vice President, Production & Supply Chain
SpaceX

INTRODUCTION

"Perfection is not attainable, but if we chase
perfection, we can catch excellence."

—Vince Lombardi

The ways and means of businesses operating around the world have been increasingly optimized over time, even while supply chains and finance have become more complex and stretch further around the globe—in pace with advances in transportation and technology. Today, we think nothing of going to the grocery store and purchasing a pint of fresh strawberries, regardless of the season. But what has really changed in business—and even in our own lives—is the incremental, relentless compression of time. More specifically, that we and our companies need to accomplish more in order to remain competitive and relevant—even viable—in a continually decreasing amount of time.

How does a company accomplish more in less time and not spin out of control? The challenge is increasing efficiency while also increasing effectiveness. We have to manage multiple (often competing) priorities. We need to recognize opportunities and threats to our strategies, and we must formulate and deploy effective countermeasures to maintain control over our own narrative. We need to make sound decisions quickly. And we need to do all of this in real time.

This is the nature of *operational excellence* and the essence of its importance: The organizations that pursue operational excellence will achieve a *state of readiness* to quickly identify and decisively engage opportunities and threats and more rapidly develop and execute their strategies. In doing so, they will become a *high-performance organization.*

I have had the opportunity to work with countless companies and people within those companies all around the world. Even with two sets of additional pages, my passport is almost full, with a full four years before it expires. Most of my experiences have been very positive. I consider the relatively few experiences that were not positive as paying tuition to the University of Life.

Who might be interested in, and benefit from, reading this book?

You are an executive in a company—perhaps even in the C-suite—who needs to accelerate the realization of your vision for the company and recognize you need the help of others to accomplish this. And you could do this, *if only* . . .

Or . . .

You are in operations or part of the continuous improvement efforts within your organization and feel you are not getting the proper attention and support from the executive leadership. And you could do so much more, *if only* . . .

If only what?

The answers to that are why I wrote this book—to share my observations and experiences, developed over more than thirty years, of how things are, how they could be, and what it takes to get from where you are to where you want to be. We'll discuss things to avoid, things to embrace, and how to see the signals within your organization that foreshadow its future state. I want to share what I have learned with you so you might not have to pay as much tuition to the University of Life as I have.

I am not going to say it's easy. There is no button to push or pill you can swallow that will make it easier or faster. It's damn hard work, and it's going to take time, effort, investment, gumption, and perseverance. And if you think it can be otherwise, you need to put this book down right now and walk away—because it's definitely not for you.

But if you want your company to become a high-performance organization and believe in moving the ball down the field in a deliberate, continual, pragmatic, and measured manner—day by day, week by week, month by month, and year by year—then this book will offer some keen insights that will help you on your journey and may even prove invaluable.

PART 1

OPERATIONAL EXCELLENCE

"The epitome of an elegant design is *not*
when nothing else can be added but, rather,
when nothing else can be taken away."

—Antoine de Saint-Exupery

What do you want to be when you grow up? We have all heard this question since our childhood. For many of us, it might be the very first memory we have.

From the moment we realize we can become what we dreamed of becoming, we embark on the journey to realize that dream. Most of the time, these early dreams are replaced with other dreams. For instance, when I was younger, I wanted to be a pilot, an astronaut, a scientist, and a photojournalist, among any number of other professions. What was specifically not on that list is who I am today: businessman, entrepreneur, writer, teacher. Who'd a thunk. . . .

But at some point in our lives, we snap into focus some image of our future self; we create *a vision of our future state.* Once we create this vision, how do we pursue it? What does it take to achieve it? And, not to confuse a future state with an end state, once we are there, how do we continue on? Is reaching that goal the end of the road?

Can we do it alone? I've never heard of anyone achieving greatness by working alone in a vacuum. All along life's path, we are being nurtured, coached, and taught by our parents, our extended family, and our community. Our teachers instill in us vast amounts of knowledge and information during our years as students. Our mentors in our professions and our businesses offer us guidance based on the wisdom they have gained over their years. And we certainly learn a lot from the mistakes we make on our journey.

We have also had to call on the expertise of others to facilitate us on our journey. Perhaps there were doctors who treated our injuries, or we hired a tutor or joined a study group to help us with a subject in school that was giving us difficulty. Even in the position we hold at work now, how many people do we routinely rely on for help?

When faced with a challenge—when the going gets tough—do you possess a state of readiness? Do you go it alone, or do you summon the help of those around you so that you can face the challenge together? Do you at least seek their sage advice before you make a decision and respond?

The same holds true in businesses and organizations. Your desired future state may change, and your means of getting to it may change. You will be faced with challenges—some anticipated and some not—but a constant state of readiness will increase your chances of successfully achieving that future state.

CHAPTER 1

WHAT IS OPERATIONAL EXCELLENCE?

"Desire is the key to motivation, but it's the
determination and commitment to unrelenting
pursuit of your goal—a commitment to excellence—
that will enable you to attain the success you seek."

—Mario Andretti

Operational excellence is a term you've probably heard a thousand times. There are centers for excellence and even prizes and certifications awarded for various forms and manifestations of it. But what does it *mean?*

Let's start by differentiating *operations* from *operational*. *Operations* refers to processes, whereas *operational* deals with systems—even entire enterprises. Accordingly, there must be a difference between *excellence in operations*, or process excellence, and *operational excellence*. Simply put, excellence in operations is efficiency, doing things right, but operational excellence is effectiveness, doing the right things.[1]

For instance, when the United States Navy determines that a carrier group is *operational*, it means the carrier group, as an entity, is in a *state of readiness* to fulfill its intended purpose. And all of the nearly infinite number of individual processes that determine how the operations of the group are conducted are optimized and configured into systems that govern how the carrier group performs. When that state of readiness is achieved, the carrier group acts as a *high-performance organization*.

Let's look at another example.

In the early days of the Great Depression, one of the most ambitious builds in modern history started in Midtown Manhattan—the Empire State Building. At the time, and for some time afterward, it was the tallest building in the world. Excavation of the site started on January 22, 1930, and the ribbon-cutting ceremony took place on May 1, 1931. From start to finish, it took only one year, three months, and nine days—464 days in all to build the 2,248,355 square feet of floor space.

Even more impressive is that all of this was accomplished with 1930s technology and infrastructure, when there was little in the way of automation and a lot of manual labor. There were no highways, only waterways and steam rail. Yet the materials came from Bethlehem and Pittsburgh (one hundred and four hundred miles away respectively), and all the limestone block for the edifice came from Indiana (eight hundred miles away).

Compare this with the construction of the Freedom Tower, which replaced the World Trade Center. After all of the legal and financial hurdles were overcome, construction started on June 23, 2006, with excavation of the foundation. The tower finally opened on November 3, 2014—a full 2,690 days later—with 3,501,274 square feet of floor space.

The floor space of the Freedom Tower was only one and a half times that of the Empire State Building, and it took almost six times as long to build. With all our technological advances in the prior seventy-five years, how did it take so much longer?

When I think about the story of the Empire State Building—all of the companies and workers involved in the project, the supply chain and the coordination required, the logistics necessary, the clarity of purpose held by all those involved—I think about operational excellence.

Let's examine one more.

During World War II, at peak production in 1943, the United States produced[2] 1,238 Liberty ships (over 3 per day), 16,005 landing vessels (44 per day), 9,393 four-engine bombers (26 per day), 21,743 single-engine fighters (60 per day), and 29,497 tanks (80 per day). And we mustn't forget the supply chain and logistics necessary to support this level of production.

The industrial world of the twenty-first century certainly outproduces what it did in the 1940s, but that is not what I find remarkable. We *should* be outproducing ourselves eighty years later. What I find remarkable is the *pace* of improvement in production over a very compressed period of time during the 1940s. The GDP of the United States doubled in three years (from 1940 to 1943; 33 percent per year on average). Compare that pace with what we consider healthy growth today (2–3 percent). Whatever inefficiencies might have existed were overcome by effectiveness—a key competitive factor of operational excellence.

When I think about the rapid scaling and transformation of industry in the United States in the 1940s—the reduction in time from thinking about the product to its being manufactured, the supply chains and logistics necessary for the raw materials to be manufactured and for the final product to get to the field, and all of the people involved, all working in concert—I think about operational excellence.

The motivation driving the Empire State Building was commercial, and the motivation driving the industrialization in the early 1940s was certainly national, but that only demonstrates that operational excellence—achieving a state of readiness and being a high-performance organization—transcends the source of motivation.

So what is operational excellence, and why is it important? If I were to stub my toe on it, what would it look like? We need to fully understand the term before we can pursue it as a strategy. I propose the following definition:

> *Operational Excellence is a state of readiness attained as the efforts throughout the enterprise reach a state of alignment for pursuing its strategies—where the corporate culture is committed to the continuous and deliberate improvement of company performance AND the circumstances of those who work there—and is a precursor to becoming a high-performance organization.*

When a company reaches a **state of readiness**, it **attains** a situational awareness and command of its capabilities—the ability to see and anticipate opportunities and threats. Along with it comes the ability to react in a meaningful and expeditious manner to any such challenges that may present themselves—keeping in mind this awareness will never be perfect and will need to be perpetually refined. As Mike Tyson famously said, "Everyone has a plan, until they get punched in the mouth." That is to say, even though you are talented, trained, professional, and on the offensive pursuing your plan, the business that is better prepared to identify and engage an unforeseen challenge more quickly than its competition has a strategic and tactical advantage.

The efforts throughout the enterprise—from the vendor's vendor to the customer's customer, every calorie expended and every bit of treasure invested, from inception through execution and even after action, all activities from all resources and assets in any capacity—must be dedicated to these endeavors.

The business needs to practice transparency and communicate its ambitions and vision of the future in a clear and concise manner so that all of this energy, efforts, and available assets *reach a state of alignment*—a unity of purpose and action throughout the enterprise—*for pursuing its strategies*.

There should demonstrably exist—through its effective leadership, stewardship, mentorship, and followership—an ethos throughout the enterprise *where the corporate culture is committed* and everyone is unreservedly devoted to the effort.

When the highest level of alignment and commitment is achieved, the enterprise is prepared for action and *for the continuous*—meaning never-ending—engagements it needs to perform to become and remain best in class. But the enterprise is not only continuously moving, it is also moving in an intentional, calculated, engineered, *and deliberate* manner with not only a sense of purpose but purpose itself. Operational excellence can only be achieved by design and implemented in an engineered manner—not by accident or coincidence.

The *improvement of company performance* simply means to improve profit in a sustainable manner—the bottom line, EBITDA (Earnings Before Interest, Taxes, Depreciation, and Amortization), shareholder value, and whatever metric you

might use to measure performance. There are many ways to facilitate increased profits, but make no mistake, businesses exist to
make profits, and their improvement efforts must yield greater
profits. And not just by engaging in the pursuit of short-term
opportunities but also by keeping an eye on the long term, so the
viability of the enterprise is ensured for the ages.

The efforts to improve company performance should ensure
the company is always innovative and competitively positioned
in its value proposition to its present and future customers to
drive both short- and long-term value. These efforts include
the following (but by no means should this list be considered
exhaustive):

⇨ Being the innovation company—the company that creates demand and marketplaces and not a company that
   just satisfies a preexisting need

⇨ Aligning the company's offerings to the desires of the
   marketplace and ensuring the messaging and sales efforts
   are effective

⇨ Making sure the finance and equity structure are optimal
   for supporting the strategies of the company

⇨ Validating the efficiency and effectiveness of the supply
   chain

⇨ Considering all other influences, including those involving operations, such as Lean Six Sigma[3] (LSS), the Theory of Constraints (ToC), Total Quality Management
   (TQM), Enterprise Resource Planning (ERP), and the
   entire alphabet soup of management methodologies—
   yes, even flow

In addition to improvements in company performance, *the circumstances of those who work there*, who are instrumental in making the company successful, must be equally considered. I don't necessarily mean *pay* or *compensation*, because it's been my experience that what is important varies with each individual. Most people will not leave a company over a 5 or 10 percent increase in pay, but they will leave if they feel disenchanted, disrespected, detached, undervalued, or have no potential for personal or professional growth. They want a sense of pride in ownership. They want their lives to be more joyous, and they want to look at their job as a means to that joy. Company leaders who understand this will reap great rewards, both professionally and personally.

It is a colossal mistake for companies to believe they can improve company performance just by heaping more and more on the backs of their employees. It's unsustainable, and a breaking point will eventually be reached. You need to set the company's pace for a marathon, not a sprint, and there needs to be enough energy in reserve for a kick when it is needed.

All of this *is a precursor to becoming a high-performance organization*, which is the ultimate goal. Your company cannot become a high-performance organization without alignment, commitment, and effort—a lot of effort—or without improvements in performance and in the lives of the people who work there, or with a culture that is not committed to achieving a state of readiness. Your company cannot become a high-performance organization without operational excellence.

Becoming a high-performance organization is the ultimate goal—a business that is best in its class and is more innovative and successful than its competitors in areas such as strategy development and execution. It should be an efficient and effective organization with clear roles and accountability, delivering superior customer service and maintaining the best vendor relationships, utilizing and maintaining its assets so they reliably produce more, and consistently and sustainably generating more profits.

This is a never-ending race without a finish line.

MISSING THE POINT

Defining *operational excellence* as continuous improvement and Lean Six Sigma is like defining a vehicle as an automobile: The latter of each is a subset of the former but does not represent the entire meaning of the term. Over the past few years, I have increasingly seen a great many organizations (companies and in academia) and professionals (practitioners and consultants) attempt to hijack the term *operational excellence* in an effort to rebrand the disciplines of Lean Six Sigma or continuous improvement. Admittedly, some programs do try to build a differentiator by sprinkling some soft skills, such as leadership or culture change, into their program. But this is merely window dressing and not what operational excellence is truly all about.

Take, for instance, the advertisements I receive for conferences that supposedly address operational excellence. Although the conferences appear to offer considerable value for those interested in Lean Six Sigma and continuous improvement, they fall very short of anything resembling what I would argue is operational excellence. If you were to look at the abstracts for the talks, each has an emphasis on some *tool* of Lean Six Sigma, but almost none of them speak to a business's efforts outside of production, supply chain, and delivery. Why not just title the conference "Lean Six Sigma" or "Continuous

Improvement" or even "Process Excellence"? Would anyone notice the difference?

I have recently seen conferences on operational excellence within functional *smokestacks*[4] of the business—such as in customer service, sales, or human resources—and some that are industry specific (almost always with a focus on production alone), such as those for oil and gas, insurance, and so on.

But where are the conferences that address a business as a single system, involving multiple dimensions of an enterprise's efforts? Certainly, I often see C-level speakers at these conferences (often because they are sponsors of the event). But might this lack of strategy discussion be why I rarely see C-level delegates *in the audience* and, instead, usually find mid-level managers?

In a Google search for *operational excellence*, there is a dearth of significant detail prior to 2002, and what exists is very thin. In 2002, the American Society for Quality (ASQ) published an article entitled "How to Achieve Operational Excellence,"[5] and the keywords included *business plans, commitment, communication, continuous quality improvement, performance objectives, cost management, goals*, and *quality management*. It is interesting that there was no mention of Lean Six Sigma or any of its associated buzzwords. It's as though ASQ knew operational excellence was different than Lean Six Sigma.

In 2003, the United States Coast Guard (USCG) initiated an operational excellence program in which the criteria was to "provide Coast Guard Auxiliary boat crews with a challenging opportunity to highlight their proficiency and skills, foster teamwork, and encourage fellowship among operational members."[6] To the USCG, operational excellence was all about performing as a team with an exceptional level of proficiency in completing the tasks necessary to result in mission success. In my opinion, this program embraces the spirit of operational excellence.

In November of 2003, the Economist Intelligence Unit (a sister division of *The Economist* magazine) published a report commissioned by Celerant Consulting called "Strategy Execution: Achieving Operational Excellence."[7] It surveyed 276 executives in North America, with 50 percent of the respondents being from the C-suite across various industries.

The interesting thing about this analysis is that its intent was to measure the importance and impact of operational excellence, but nowhere does it state what operational excellence might be. It's obvious from reading the questions that there was a spin for leveraging technology as some means of achieving operational excellence. However, the only clear description was that top performing companies have "more committed management, make better and more frequent use of performance data and management mechanisms, and have stronger communication channels to link senior management with frontline employees."

I read that and couldn't help but think, *Duh—no kidding*. But again, there was no clear definition of operational excellence and no clear connection with Lean Six Sigma.

By far, one of the more interesting position papers I came across was a paper from DuPont from 2005 entitled, "Delivering Operational Excellence to the Global Market: A DuPont Integrated Systems Approach."[8] It's a fairly detailed document, but after reading it a few times, I came away feeling it was disconnected and incomplete.

Although the document spoke to operational excellence and its achievement, it never defined it. How can you know whether you have achieved operational excellence (or are even on the right path) if you don't know what it looks like?

There seemed to be a conflict in messaging: The philosophies were presented graphically and never addressed, but what was addressed were the details of the approach with no reference to the philosophies. This left me feeling that the graphics were created and presented by the strategists at DuPont, but the verbiage describing the program was created by the tacticians who implemented it, as is demonstrated by the following:

> "Taking the journey toward operational excellence typically begins with making an initial step-change improvement, followed by a continuum of incremental enhancement. Installing a culture of operational excellence results in a significant and sustained competitive advantage." (p. 2)

and

> "A study by the Board of Manufacturing and Engineering (formerly the Manufacturing Studies Board) of the US National Research Council showed that the companies that effectively implemented world-class manufacturing systems achieved improvements in asset productivity performance." (p. 3)

Although I thought the graphics went a long way toward illustrating the concepts of operational excellence, the content spoke more to continuous improvement and, in fact, emphasized "world-class manufacturing systems." This seems to be a conflicting message; it makes the message unclear and confusing. How are the two related? DuPont doesn't explain.

However, DuPont did demonstrate that it felt operational

excellence had three aspects: asset productivity, capital effectiveness, and operational risk management. In any case, DuPont makes no mention of Lean Six Sigma being a component of the program, and this indicates that DuPont feels there is a difference between operational excellence and Lean Six Sigma.

Storebrand (a Norwegian finance and insurance company) described a model for operational excellence[9] that is very nearly identical to the one described by DuPont. The major difference between the two models is that Storebrand lists the customer first, whereas DuPont does not list the customer at all. There is little mention of Lean Six Sigma (except for the term *Lean Project*), and it is apparent that Storebrand differentiates operational excellence from Lean Six Sigma.

The approaches used by the American Society for Quality and the description used by the USCG in their operational excellence program approach my definition of operational excellence, but the other definitions are inconsistent, even among and within the companies that embrace it, and most of these individual definitions are also incomplete—if they bother to define it at all. And, I swear, if I read one more definition of operational excellence that describes it as being only about production "flow," I am going to retch. Although important, and you will not achieve operational excellence without efficient and effective production flow, operational excellence does not begin with it or end with it.

Product design and development, sales and marketing, facilities management, logistics, finance, human resources, as well as the other functions of the business are all interdependent, integral functions of a business. Since an event that initiates an action could come from anywhere, all business functions must be considered and included in defining—and then achieving—operational excellence. Accordingly, the definition of operational excellence must embrace the entirety of an organization, as the one I've proposed does.

ORGANIZATIONAL CONSIDERATIONS FOR OPERATIONAL EXCELLENCE

Operational excellence isn't just about customers, capital and assets, processes and operations, people, flow, or any given approach, such as Lean Six Sigma. Following is an extensive (yet incomplete) list of questions about the business requirements and functions whose answers must be integrated into any true operational excellence program:

⇨ **The Business.** What is the best type (sole proprietorship, limited liability company, partnership, corporation) and structure for the company (investor terms and conditions)? Where is the best place for the entity to be formed (e.g., the state where company holds office)? Where should the production and logistics facilities be located? The decisions made here cannot be taken lightly and can very well determine the future of the company.

Take the story of Apple at its inception, for example. You might not know there was a third founder of Apple—Ronald Wayne. Being older and (supposedly) much more experienced in business, Wayne's role was to be the "adult" to the much younger and inexperienced Steve Jobs and Steve Wozniak. Wayne designed the Apple logo and drafted the original partnership agreement. But whereas Jobs and Wozniak had nothing to lose, no assets other than the company, Wayne did. The nature of partnerships is that each partner has unlimited personal liability. If something went wrong in the company—bankruptcy, for instance—Wayne's personal assets could be included in the settlement. This made Wayne uneasy, and he sold his 10 percent stake in the company back to Jobs and Wozniak for $800 (he later received an additional $1,500 to quit any claim against the company).

If Wayne had the business experience he claimed, he would have realized that creating a corporation would have been the much better path. He could have shielded his personal assets from attachment while still having an equity stake. And today, he would be stinking rich for making that decision. For you to become a high-performance organization, you need high-performance teams, each experienced experts in their respective disciplines, such as—

⇨ **Professional Services.** Who are the legal eagles, accountants, and financial advisors for the company, and what are their respective areas of expertise? Does their expertise support the requirements of the business?

⇨ **Finance.** What is the best capital finance structure for the organization? Are the investors strategic, and what is their exit strategy? How much equity does the company carry relative to debt? What is the collateralization of the debt, and what are the covenants associated with the loans?

⇨ **Development (Design Engineering).** Who is the principal designer of the service or product offerings? What do they need to get to market and then perpetuate the value?

⇨ **Facilities and Production Assets.** Where are the production facilities to be located, and what characteristics are required for the facility site (e.g., existing talent pool, roads, Internet, airport, utilities, taxes)? What is needed to produce the product or service?

⇨ **Human (Talent) Resources.** I dislike the term *human resources* and prefer *talent resources*. In any case, what talent is required to produce, deliver, and service the offerings? How do you find them, and how do you effectively onboard them?

⇨ **Marketing.** Let's assume you have something people will want. How do people know? Who is your customer, how do you reach them, and what's your messaging? Are you sure that is the message they want to hear?

⇨ **Sales.** Hurray! They like your messaging! Now, how do you get them to turn that attraction into a transaction, to monetize your offering? You do realize that without this transaction there is no need to worry about "pull" or "flow," right?

⇨ **Front-Office Operations.** We need to make sure the business entity is running smoothly and that the transactions (and all related details) are moving through the entity with as much accuracy and velocity but with as little friction as possible. Is that happening?

⇨ **Supply Chain.** Do your suppliers know what you need (product or services), to what specifications, the quantities you need, and when you need it by? How do they know all of this? How do *you* know all this?

⇨ **Production (Whether a Product or Service).** How do you generate the product or service in the most efficient and effective manner?

⇨ **Logistics and Delivery.** How do you efficiently and effectively convey the ownership of your product or services from you to the customer?

⇨ **Post-Sale Service.** Once you convey your product or service to the customer, how do you keep them happy with having placed their trust in you?

⇨ **Reliability and Uptime.** What programs and policies does your company have in place to ensure the assets and resources (facilities, machinery, equipment—even personnel) consistently perform in a predictable and optimal manner with the minimum of unscheduled interruption.

———

In the end, it's about improving the way people in an organization think and act. If we design and implement a program that enables a tighter alignment of the efforts of the various individual business functions with the top-level strategies of the company and facilitates and accelerates the achievement of those strategies (but not so rigidly that it stifles innovation and agility), the company will obtain the ability to quickly and decisively react to opportunities and threats as they are identified and even learn to anticipate and seek them out. This is operational excellence.

It has taken me a very long time to develop this definition (with many revisions), and I am sure many will disagree with me. However, discourse and debate is fair and welcome. After all, even its definition should be subject to operational excellence. Refusing the opportunity to improve on it would be hypocritical.

This definition, applied throughout an organization and its value chain—from its vendor's vendor to its customer's customer—is the *manifesto of operational excellence* and, if pursued with vigilance, will result in your company becoming a high-performance organization.

But understanding or saying this, even writing it down or making a plaque, will not make it real. You have to embrace operational excellence as part of your corporate culture, as part of your DNA, for it to become real. So where do we start?

CHAPTER 2

CONTINUOUS IMPROVEMENT: THE TPS, LEAN, AND SIX SIGMA

"The thing is, continuity of strategic direction
and continuous improvement in how you do
things are absolutely consistent with each
other. In fact, they're mutually reinforcing."

—Michael Porter

When people refer to continuous improvement, they usually mean the overarching title given to all efforts of a business to better its efficiencies and overall effectiveness. Most of these benefits will be realized incrementally by executing a series of projects, with very few being transformational in nature, changing the entirety of how a company organizes and conducts itself.

It is important to not minimize the significance of the word *continuous* in this title, because it holds considerable meaning and gravitas. An organization can never be perfect, so it must continuously strive for improvement. Therefore, to remain competitive—even *viable*—a business must make a conscious effort, with words backed by deeds, to improve its level of performance each and every day.

The phrase *continuous improvement* as we use it originates in the Japanese word *kaizen*—from *kai*, meaning "change," and *zen*, meaning "good." Together, it means "change for the good," or "improvement," and this is where a continuous improvement effort all starts. In practice, it means to take your enterprise apart, piece by piece, and put it back together again in a better way.

As such, a continuous improvement initiative realizes its improvements through a series of activities called *kaizen events*. Kaizen events are not normally massive projects (although they can be) but, rather, the identification of an opportunity for improvement and the realization of improvement through appropriate action. Each kaizen event is definable and quantifiable and can be considered an incremental step in the larger continuous improvement program.

Although there are many methods, tools, and doctrines, over the last several decades, companies have come to merge a variety of approaches and have largely settled on the operations-management disciplines collectively known as *Lean Six Sigma*.

THE TOYOTA PRODUCTION SYSTEM AND LEAN

Historically, creating a production line in Western companies (i.e., in Europe and North America) during the Industrial Revolution involved a considerable amount of design and engineering up front. The executives and engineers set up a production line, and that was the way production was to run from that point forward. Once it was in place, the production line was rarely updated (certainly not to any significant degree). It usually remained in a static state until the model being produced evolved or was discontinued. There was little scope or consideration for suggested improvements with the more autocratic management style, which was pervasive in Western companies. What was most important was a level of predictability and maintaining the status quo. Through the mid-1900s, perhaps even until the Organization of the Petroleum Exporting Countries (OPEC) oil embargo of 1973–1974, the management approach was command and control.

Contrast the development of manufacturing processes and corporate culture in the West with what was occurring at the same time in the East, particularly in Japan, where the origin of many of the differences between the developments of company operations can be found in the social and cultural differences between the West and the East. For instance, whereas Western society was more autocratic and oriented toward the individual, Eastern society was oriented toward the community and collaboration. In the West, decisions were mostly made by a single person; in the East, decisions were the result of a consensus that had to be built.

The history[1] of the Toyota Production System (TPS) starts with Sakichi Toyoda (1867–1930), a Japanese inventor and industrialist who had a particular fixation on continually improving his products and his business's ability to execute. He was known for his advances in the textile industry through his design and production of weaving devices and looms. After several years in the industry, in 1926, he founded Toyoda Automatic Loom Works. Sakichi worked relentlessly to eliminate waste in the processes involved in operating his machines and the manufacturing of the machines themselves.

The emphasis on the elimination of waste was carried forward by Sakichi's son, Kiichiro Toyoda (1894–1952), among others. In 1935, Kiichiro started a business unit within Toyoda Automatic Loom Works, which spun-off as a separate entity in 1937 as Toyoda Motor Company—now known as Toyota Motor Company.

Sakichi, Kiichiro, and Sakichi's cousin, Eiji Toyoda (1913–2013), began the development of a business operating system. Others would help to evolve the system over time, including the adoption of many methods then deployed at the Ford Motor Company; the contributions of industrial engineers Shigeo Shingo (1909–1990) and Taiichi Ohno (1912–1990); the works of Kaoru Ishikawa (1915–1989); and the quality-control practices of William Edwards Deming (1900–1993)[2] and Joseph Juran (1904–2008).[3]

The ethos of the business operating system was collaborative (reflective of the Japanese culture) and took into account not only the technical aspects of the production process but also the human dimension, whereby everyone involved in the process is encouraged to offer suggestions for improvement. The end result is a business environment where the workforce is encouraged to suggest improvements and the leadership is conditioned to consider and engage the workforce. As such, the purpose of the business operating system is to support the execution of Toyota's corporate strategy.

Initially called *Just-in-Time Manufacturing*, it would not be until about 1965 when the team at Toyota formalized their thoughts and created a management system. In essence, this was an integrated sociotechnical system that comprises a set of management philosophies and practices, which was to become known as the *Toyota Production System* (TPS). Later still, the

TPS served as the basis for the philosophies, tools, and methodologies of *Lean Manufacturing*[4] specifically and then just *Lean* for its general application outside its origin in manufacturing.

In the years since, the principles of the TPS and Lean have been common and widely adopted to other industries, although with varying degrees of completeness and success. As such, it is important to always keep in mind Lean is a journey, not a destination: When I am speaking with someone and they tell me they are already "lean," indicating they have already completed the implementation of Lean, I know for certain they are not.

LEAN IS ABOUT PROCESS VELOCITY

Several years ago, I was working on an implementation of an *Enterprise Resource Planning* (ERP) system at a large manufacturer and distributor of medical products. We were in the conference room pilot and had reduced the order-to-cash process to seven steps. While we were proving out the process, someone asked how an exception (which had not been discussed to date) would be handled. Looking at the challenge, I realized it was going to add another five steps to every order.

I asked, "How is it possible we didn't hear of this variant before?"

The response was "Because it doesn't happen too often. Our old system didn't handle it either."

I followed up with "How often does it happen?"

And the response was "A couple of times a quarter."

I put my stake in the ground and said, "We are not going to add five process steps to each of the six hundred orders you get every day so we can accommodate the few orders per quarter that may or may not

(*Continued . . .*)

actually happen. That is a colossal amount of friction and waste that will only slow the process and add to overhead. If it happens again, however you handled it according to the old system is how you will handle it in the future."

Persuing Lean is not difficult. Keep it simple; complexity kills.

SIX SIGMA

Six Sigma is a highly disciplined approach focused on delivering near-perfect products and services by minimizing the variants within a process and identifying the causes of defects. Within Six Sigma is a framework with a collection of tools and techniques used to improve the quality and effectiveness of processes. This is accomplished by collecting significant quantities of observed data that is then analyzed by statistical methods to detect the causes of defects or errors.

The origin of Six Sigma is much cloudier than TPS, with many individuals contributing to its body of knowledge over centuries. Did you ever wonder why it's six and not five or seven sigma? After all, the expected result of achieving Six Sigma is three or four defects per million, meaning there is opportunity to achieve a greater level of perfection. Perhaps it's simply marketing, that *Six Sigma* rolls off the tongue easier.

Since Six Sigma is based on statistics, the discipline goes back as far as the origin of statistics itself. Carl Friedrich Gauss[5] introduced the concept of the normal curve to represent variants, results, and impact. In the 1920s, Walter Shewhart[6] hypothesized three sigma from the mean was a point where a process required corrective action. Joseph Juran came across the work of Vilfredo Pareto[7] and evolved the Pareto Principle to quality issues. Homer Sarasohn,[8] along with Edwards Deming, introduced these works to Japanese companies starting around 1954. Then Bill Smith,[9] Bob Galvin,[10] and John Francis Mitchell,[11] all with Motorola, made the determination that if three sigma was good, six sigma was better (and Motorola decided to register *Six Sigma* as a trademark). And soon other companies began adapting Six Sigma as a demonstration to their commitment to quality.

SIX SIGMA IS ABOUT THE QUALITY OF THE PROCESS

When I lived in the United States, we would hang icicle-shaped Christmas lights on the house for the holidays. I knew I needed three lengths of fifty feet of lights to accomplish what I wanted to achieve. Because the lights came in lengths of twenty-five feet, I needed six strands. But I would always buy eight strands, because I knew from experience that one of the strands would be defective, and I didn't want to come down from a frozen roof midtask to go back to the store to exchange it; I just wanted to finish the job.

But I was only paying four dollars a strand. How much would they cost if they were manufactured to Six Sigma standards? Would I be willing to pay that price? Obviously, the light manufacturer's management decided that the extra effort to avoid that defective strand was not worth the additional cost and that the consumer was not willing to pay for that improvement. I found it ironic that the manufacturer of the lights was a company who proudly professed their embracing of Six Sigma as a core tenet of their business operating system.

The moral of the story is this: Although the underlying mantra of

(Continued...)

Six Sigma is *zero defects*, there must be sound business and economic reasons for pushing for perfection beyond just the pursuit of perfection itself: pragmatism over ideology.

LEAN SIX SIGMA: SIMPLIFY THEN PERFECT

When I was first introduced to Lean and Six Sigma (separately) in the late 1990s, there were definitely two distinct camps, especially for businesses that traditionally embraced one or the other. Like Yankees and Red Sox fans, each was critical of the other—often to the point of contempt. I never really understood the friction or animosity; it was all just baseball to me.

Incrementally, the two disciplines gravitated toward one another and merged into Lean Six Sigma. Today, you can hardly find a course on one discipline without the other incorporated into it. And this is how it should be. Lean and Six Sigma are both methods of realizing an opportunity, the means to solve a challenge. It is best to let the challenge drive the solution and not the other way around. To paraphrase Abraham Maslow, "If the only tool in your toolbox is a hammer, every problem looks like a nail."

Some Handy-to-Know Tools of the Trade

There is a plethora of tools in the Lean Six Sigma tool kit. Some of the more common ones that you should be familiar with include the following:

⇨ **Value-Stream Map (VSM).** Usually, the very first task in a kaizen event is to create a *value-stream map* of the existing *present state* of the process to be improved. The VSM of a process will detail all of the steps and actions taken in that process, including raw-material inputs, production steps, movements and wait states, and all feeder streams, through to conclusion. It is one of the primary tools used to identify opportunities for improvement and evaluate waste, and it is used as the baseline for determining improvements toward an optimized future state of the process. Sometimes, additional information is included, such as costs and even carbon footprint.

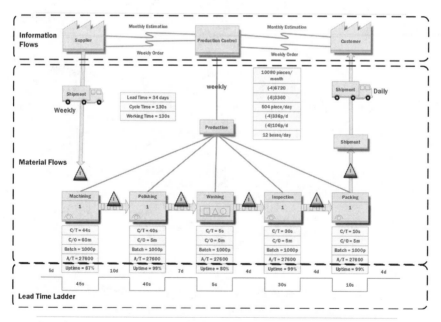

Figure 2.1. Example of a Value-Stream Map.

⇨ **5S.** The 5S methodology is used to bring order to the workplace and gets its name from five Japanese words describing its implementation: *seiri* ("sort"), *seiton* ("set in order"), *seiso* ("shine"), *seiketsu* ("standardize"), and *shitsuke* ("sustain"). A simple example of 5S would be cleaning your garage: You would organize the various materials in a meaningful manner, discard trash, clean off the filth, sweep the floor, and make the effort to keep it clean (the last part being the most difficult). Fine French restaurants have a similar practice, which they call *mise en place*, which translates to "putting [everything] in place."

⇨ **Cell Flow.** Sometimes called *continuous flow*, cell flow is the design of a work center or process in which there are no hesitations or unnecessary movements in the production process. Ideally, a production process will flow like water in a stream: never pausing, never waiting, but moving from one action to the next. The most common approach to implementing cell flow is to form the process in the shape of the letter *U*, where the inputs start at the top of the letter, are acted on, and end at the same place (e.g., raw materials moving from a warehouse though production and ending at the same warehouse as finished goods).

⇨ **Quick Changeover.** Sometimes referred to as SMED (for *Single-Minute Exchange of Die*), *quick changeover* is an approach used to minimize the downtime associated with the preparation and execution of a change in state. A simple example of this to which we can all relate is going through security at the airport. Before we reach the X-ray machine, we might prepare our laptop and fluids for easy access in separate bins; we might take off our belt, shoes, jewelry, watches, and jacket, all with the sole purpose of speeding up the process. Woe is the person who doesn't start this until it is their turn, since they will catch the ire of the other travelers.

⇨ **Root-Cause Analysis.** Referred to as the *5 Whys* in Lean, root-cause analysis is a method of determining the real reason something other than what was expected occurred. Usually, a person will see the end result of a process (a symptom), but its cause could be much more complicated than what seems apparent. In addition to determining the cause of a manufacturing defect, this system is also used in medicine, for treating the underlying disease and not the symptoms, and in the study of vehicle accidents, especially those involving aircraft.

⇨ **The Pareto Chart and the Histogram.** Six Sigma places an emphasis on the collection and analysis of data—statistics. Looking at tables of numbers is often very cumbersome. Instead, we use charts and graphs to represent this data pictorially to (hopefully) unlock the hidden meanings and significance of the underlying trends. Two of the most common graphs used in Six Sigma are the Pareto chart and the histogram.

o The *Pareto chart* is a combination of individual values shown as a bar graph in descending order from left to right and accumulated totals shown as a line graph. It is particularly useful in demonstrating the causes of various sources of defects and their impacts.

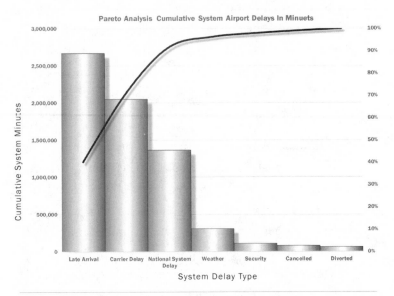

Figure 2.2. Example of a Pareto Chart.

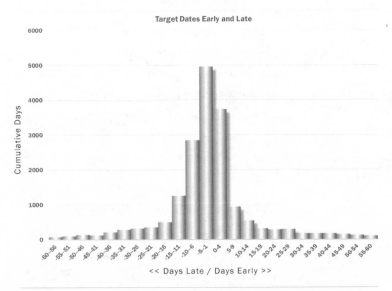

Figure 2.3. Example of a Histogram.

o A *histogram* shows the distribution of data and is used to estimate the probability of that distribution. It is especially useful in determining the expected results of a process and to illuminate the opportunities for improvement. Generally speaking, the tighter the grouping, the more predictable the model is, which is especially useful for demonstrating variable results (usually defects) in a process.

THE BENEFITS OF CONTINUOUS IMPROVEMENT

There are a great many ways companies can benefit from embracing Lean Six Sigma and its successful deployment. Although there are significant improvements in many key areas, I would like to focus on just a few.

⇨ **Lead-Time Reduction.** If we remove steps from the process, especially non-value-add steps like material movements and interim storage, the result will be increasingly closer to a continuous flow, and production time will be minimized. This means the time to fulfill orders will be reduced and the responsiveness to the client's shift in need can be quicker.

Years ago, I had custom replacement windows installed at my house. The lead time to delivery quoted by most companies was four to six weeks, and their prices were comparable. A couple of years later, I worked on a project with a manufacturer of custom windows. When I completed my study, I discovered the actual *value time*—the time and activity a customer would perceive as having a value to them and for which they were willing to pay— was less than an hour per window from start to finish. Yet it was taking them a minimum of three weeks to get an order out the door. That's three weeks of competitive advantage that could be gained through continuous improvement, not to mention the acceleration of the realization of revenue from delivering the sales faster.

⇨ **Work In Process Reduction.** It's no accident that reducing lead time also reduces Work In Process (WIP). By definition, WIP is the inventory and value-add activities that are accumulated by a product during the manufacturing process. If you significantly reduce the lead time, you reduce the value in WIP by a correlating amount. And where does WIP value go? It's cash in your pocket.

⇨ **More Efficient Use of Space.** With less inventory and WIP, you need less space for storage and staging areas. Add to this a reengineered production process to embrace cell flow, and you would be amazed at the amount of freed up real estate. I worked with one business that was contemplating building a 150,000-square-foot warehouse to store its inventory to make way for an expansion of its production lines. But a successful Lean initiative (primarily using value-stream mapping, 5S, and cell flow) freed enough real estate to expand their production line within their current space. This negated the need for a warehouse, eliminating the capital expenditure requirements of a new building and the ongoing cost of ownership.

⇨ **Increased Cash Flow.** All of these improvements will pre-cipitate into an increase in cash flow from operations and will improve the overall health and vitality of the company.

Any continuous improvement initiative will cost money, and to claim otherwise is naive. But these initiatives could be constructed to be self-funding from the immediate short-term results. The real impact is in the year-on-year benefits. If you take a million dollars out of your cost to deliver this year, it's also a million dollars you have taken out of your cost to deliver in each subsequent year. Add to those savings the additive savings from projects in subsequent years, and the amounts quickly inspire awe.

As Evertt Dirksen[12] famously said, "A billion here, a billion there, and pretty soon you're talking about real money."

But is continuous improvement as we know it today—the TPS, Lean and Six Sigma, even Theory of Constraints (ToC)—enough for a world that operates at the speed of thought? Is there a ceiling that sets limits on its potential? In fact, has the hype surrounding these methodologies, tools, and philosophies actually lived up to the reality? If not, why not?

CHAPTER 3

REALITY OR MYTH?

"The great enemy of the truth is very often not the lie,
deliberate, contrived, and dishonest, but the myth,
persistent, persuasive, and unrealistic."

—John F. Kennedy

It seems at every conference, symposium, or other gathering of thought leaders for higher learning where the topic is Lean Six Sigma, many of the attendees—and almost all of the speakers—glorify the supposedly unmatched performance of Japanese companies and their management techniques as enshrined in the most revered of holy scrolls, the TPS. And when followers of this scripture speak, they declare the virtues of all things Japanese and cast aside, as heretics, the nonbelievers.

However, when I attend similar gatherings at locations around the world where the audience is business leaders and the topic is business strategy and finance (e.g., events organized by the Association for Corporate Growth, symposia for Private Equity and finance, the various economic forums and congresses, and conferences on business strategy), there is rarely (if ever) any mention of Japanese companies nor reference to their styles of management.

This has always given me cause for pause. How can something that is supposedly an absolute truism and necessary for success in one circle be almost completely ignored in another—particularly when both circles purportedly share the same aspiration of improving business performance and accelerating success?

I know full well that taking a contrarian position will cast me as nonbeliever and draw the ire of those who hold the faith, especially those who are fanatic zealots. However, after careful consideration and investigation, I believe this reverence of Japan and Japanese companies is largely (perhaps entirely) undeserved and possibly even a myth. As they say, "sacred cows make the best hamburgers." And even if all the hyperbole about Japanese companies was ever true at some time in the past, it is certainly not true today and has not been true since at least the early 1990s. Furthermore, I would argue that any business that has drunk the Kool-Aid (or the *sake*) and is trying to emulate the way a Japanese business operates as a path to a better future for themselves is misguided. Their expected results are likely overestimated, and this will inevitably lead to disappointment.

This is not to say the tools and techniques of the TPS and Lean Six Sigma do not deliver positive results or otherwise drive value in an organization; they certainly do, as previously discussed, under the right circumstances and with pragmatically managed expectations. But today, awareness of these tools and techniques is now pervasive, even if they are implemented to a wide spectrum of completeness and achievement. By themselves, they are no longer a differentiator—nor do they offer the competitive advantage they once did. As such, they expose one of the limitations of the Japanese way of running a business.

Some might argue that it is because people have not been true believers or pure enough in its adaptation. But keep in mind that somewhere out there is also the world's last Communist true believer, plaintively insisting that real Communism never actually failed because it was never actually tried.

However, business people are data driven, so let's examine some data. For your consideration, we are going to examine several economic and business indicators from two time periods, 1982–1992 and 1992–2015.

MACRO VIEW: COMPARING COUNTRIES

During the period between 1982 and 1992, Japan was undeniably the envy of the world, with its economic prowess and productivity—the culmination of decades of evolving and quantifying the way Japanese businesses operated after World War II and as exemplified by the leadership of Toyota at that time. This was the period when Japanese companies were buying everything they could (including Rockefeller Center in Manhattan along with countless works of art).

It is during this period—the perceived assent of Japanese companies relative to companies in the United States at the time—when the envy of comparative performance and the reverence of the Japanese management methods began.

And not coincidentally, it is also the same period when the team of James Womack, Daniel Jones, and Daniel Roos at MIT wrote the book *The Machine that Changed the World* (1990), which put Japanese companies (specifically Toyota) and the

Japanese style of management and process execution on a pedestal. It also introduced the term *Lean Manufacturing* into the lexicon of business management.

But is this perception the reality? Does it hold true over time or just a vignette of time in history?

When we compare the Gross Domestic Product (GDP) of Japan and the United States (figure 3.1)[1] from 1982 to 1992, it is clear that the Japanese economy outperformed the economy of the United States. During this period, the Gross Domestic Product per capita (GDP per capita) of Japan grew an average of 4.03 percent—double the average GDP per capita growth of the United States of 2.05 percent (keeping in mind a 2.05 percent growth rate is a respectable pace for a large and mature economy).

Another interesting piece of data can be found by comparing Japan's GDP numbers in 1985 to those in 1986. In 1985,

Japan				United States		
Year	GDP per capita, current $US	GDP per capita, current PPP$	GDP per capita growth, %	Year	GDP per capita, current $US	GDP per capita growth, %
1981	10,218	9,655		1981	13,966	1.60%
1982	9,431	10,526	2.70%	1982	14,410	(2.80%)
1983	10,216	11,199	2.40%	1983	15,531	3.70%
1984	10,787	12,036	3.80%	1984	17,099	6.30%
1985	11,464	13,125	5.70%	1985	18,232	3.30%
1986	16,891	13,694	2.30%	1986	19,078	2.60%
1987	20,367	14,549	3.60%	1987	20,063	2.50%
1988	24,604	16,064	6.70%	1988	21,442	3.30%
1989	24,522	17,517	5.00%	1989	22,879	2.70%
1990	25,140	19,111	5.20%	1990	23,914	0.80%
1991	28,542	20,328	2.90%	1991	24,366	(1.40%)
Avg			4.03%			2.05%

Figure 3.1. Comparisons of Japan and the United States, Gross Domestic Product (GDP), GDP Per Capita (GDP-PC) and GDP-PC Purchasing Power Parity (GDP-PC/PPP) to US$ for the period 1981–1991.
Source: The World Bank and International Monetary Fund.

the GDP per capita was less than the Gross Domestic Product per capita based on Purchasing Power Parity (GDP per capita/ PPP).[2] But in 1986, the GDP per capita was far greater than the GDP per capita/PPP. The buying power enjoyed from 1982 to 1985 had evaporated. This tipping point—and it was a dramatic

Japan				United States		
Year	GDP per capita, current $US	GDP per capita, current PPP$	GDP per capita growth, %	Year.	GDP per capita, current $US	GDP per capita growth, %
1992	30,973	20,882	0.40%	1992	25,467	2.20%
1993	35,377	21,345	(0.20%)	1993	26,442	1.40%
1994	38,759	21,928	0.60%	1994	27,756	2.80%
1995	42,517	22,763	1.70%	1995	28,763	1.50%
1996	37,425	23,727	2.40%	1996	30,047	2.60%
1997	34,307	24,461	1.40%	1997	31,554	3.20%
1998	30,981	24,172	(2.20%)	1998	32,929	3.20%
1999	35,014	24,447	(0.40%)	1999	34,602	3.50%
2000	37,304	25,520	2.10%	2000	36,433	2.90%
2001	32,711	26,124	0.10%	2001	37,241	(0.10%)
2002	31,241	26,549	0.10%	2002	38,114	0.80%
2003	33,718	27,493	1.50%	2003	39,592	1.80%
2004	36,444	28,885	2.30%	2004	41,839	2.80%
2005	35,781	30,198	1.30%	2005	44,218	2.40%
2006	34,077	31,634	1.60%	2006	46,352	1.70%
2007	34,038	33,153	2.10%	2007	47,955	0.80%
2008	37,865	33,430	(1.10%)	2008	48,302	(1.20%)
2009	39,321	31,825	(5.50%)	2009	46,909	(3.60%)
2010	42,917	33,714	4.70%	2010	48,310	1.70%
2011	46,175	34,295	(0.30%)	2011	49,725	0.80%
2012	46,661	35,602	2.00%	2012	51,409	1.60%
2013	38,633	36,793	1.80%	2013	52,939	1.50%
2014	36,332	37,390	0.20%	2014	54,597	1.60%
2015	32,485	38,054	1.30%	2015	55,805	2.40%
Avg			0.75%			1.60%

Figure 3.2. Comparisons of Japan and the United States, Gross Domestic Product (GDP), GDP Per Capita (GDP-PC) and GDP-PC Purchasing Power Parity (GDP-PC/PPP) to US$ for the period 1992–2015.
Source: The World Bank and International Monetary Fund.

one—was an indicator that Japan's economy was being pushed over the edge.

Then, if we look at 1992–2015, the average growth of GDP per capita in Japan was only 0.75 percent (less than 20 percent of its previous growth rate), versus an average GDP per capita growth rate of 1.60 percent in the United States. Over this second period, which lasted twenty-three years, the average GDP per capita growth rate in the United States was more than twice Japan's. This period of time in Japan is commonly referred to as the *lost decade*—a period of severe economic malaise and underperformance as compared to peer economies, which has turned into two decades and is now going on three decades.

One would think, if Japanese companies outperformed companies in the United States as some would have you believe, the Japanese economy would also outperform the United States. But as these charts demonstrate, I do not believe it can be reasonably argued that Japan, and the industrial might of Japan by proxy, has outperformed the United States for some considerable amount of time. And, according to the International Monetary Fund forecasts, there is no indication of this trend changing anytime soon.

PEER GROUP: COMPARING JAPANESE AND AMERICAN COMPANIES

We must also keep in mind that the performance of an entire country may not represent the performance of companies within that country. So let's drill down a bit further and examine the performance of companies over similar periods.

I realize there are many ways of looking at the health of a company, and, as I mentioned earlier, cash flow from operations is certainly among those with more weight. But I believe the simplest, and arguably most accurate, way of comparing company performance is the value of their shares.

After all, share price is a forward-looking indicator. It is an arm's length reflection of how much value an investor perceives a company has. In evaluating the value, a shareholder will take into consideration all of the more objective financial aspects of the company including cash flow from operations, the common financial ratios used by analysts, return on capital, price earnings ratios as compared to industry peers, and so on. A shareholder will also factor into the value of a share innovation, quality, customer satisfaction, brand value, integrity, sustainability, politics, and other more subjective considerations. And lastly but most importantly, a shareholder will consider the short- and long-term vision of the future for the company as communicated by the leadership. Does the shareholder agree that the course chartered by the leadership is the best for the company? Will the pursuit of the vision result in an appropriate return on investment? Does the shareholder have confidence in the leadership team of the company to deliver on the vision as communicated? Indeed, the share price of a company over a period of time might not be the only indicator of company performance, but it is the weighted aggregate of all of the others. And this makes it the best indicator.

As such, a summative of values from a cross section of major companies within a country can be found in the major stock market indices of that country.

As with the previous comparisons made using Gross Domestic Product, we will compare the main stock market indices of

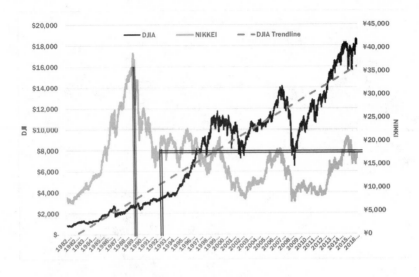

Figure 3.3. Historical values of the DJIA and the Nikkei.

the United States (DJIA) and Japan (Nikkei) as graphically represented in figure 3.3.

The Dow Jones Industrial Average (DJIA) vs. the Nikkei Average

Through 1982, the DJIA and the Nikkei tracked very close to one another, respective to each of their currencies, and growth was rather unremarkable, if there was any appreciable growth in the value of these indices at all. But in 1983, the rate in the increase in the value of the Nikkei versus the DJIA went almost vertical.

The Nikkei

From a value of approximately ¥7,500 in 1982, to a high of almost ¥40,000 on the eve of 1990, it was a heck of a run and fun while it lasted—an increase of over 500 percent in a span of nine years. The pace was relentless, with just a brief pause for the stock market crash of 1987. During this same period, the DJIA enjoyed an increase in value of approximately 100 percent, which is considered a very reasonable rate of return in its own right.

However, this dramatic acceleration in the increase of the value of the Nikkei had all of the obvious indications of being possessed by *irrational exuberance*.[3] The funny thing about financial bubbles is that people don't normally realize they are in one until it pops.

It was all downhill from there.

The fall from grace was swift and ruthless. Breaking through the ¥20,000 mark in 1992 on its way to ¥17,500 by late 1993, the Nikkei had lost almost 60 percent of its value.

The slope of the decline in the value of Japanese companies that comprise the Nikkei from 1990 through 1992 started by following the classic *V* shape[4] normally associated with a market under strain and represented by the expected sharp downstroke, as we see in the graph. But the Nikkei never experienced a recovery that produced a sharp upstroke in the graph to complete the classic *V*, as would be expected. Unlike the recessions endured by the United Stated and its free-market peers, there was never any recovery in the aggregate of companies that comprise the Nikkei.

Instead, over the next few years, the Nikkei experienced a few *dead-cat bounces*:[5] The index would rally to around ¥20,000 before falling back again. Then in 2000, the Nikkei began another dramatic slide in value, until it broke through ¥10,000 in 2001.

From then, there was a run-up in value until 2007 (along with its other G-7[6] peers), when the Nikkei closed in on ¥20,000 before falling back during the global financial crisis of

2007/2008. And from 2013, with the introduction of "Abenomics,"[7] the Nikkei made another run and reached ¥20,000 in 2015 before again sliding in 2016.

Certainly, these momentary recoveries in company value after the crash of the Nikkei from 1990–1992 were influenced by the macroeconomic economic stimulus policies of the Japanese government and coordinated with the Bank of Japan. But for all intents and purposes, the Nikkei—and the value of the companies that comprise the Nikkei—have been in a coma since 1992.

The DJIA

From 1982 to 1992 in the United States, we can clearly see that the growth in value of the companies of the DJIA (see figure 3.3) was steady, but rather unremarkable, especially when compared to the dramatic increase in value of those companies that comprise the Nikkei.

But in 1992, we can see the start of an accelerated and sustained upward trend where the value of the DJIA increased from approximately $2,500 to approximately $18,500 in 2016, an increase of over 700 percent—but over a twenty-four year period. The time period is important because it indicates a pace of growth that has been sustained over a considerable period of time and is not a bubble.

The two dips in the DJIA represent the recession of 2001 and the financial crisis of 2008. But on both occasions, the markets endured a sharp downstroke in valuation followed by a sharp upstroke: a classic V. The pain was felt, but recovery came quickly.

As is glaringly apparent in the graph, whereas the downstrokes endured by the Nikkei were as dramatic as in the DJIA, the upstrokes in the DJIA from 2000 onward were quicker and more dramatic than in the Nikkei. This resulted in step improvements in the value of the DJIA over the upstrokes in the Nikkei.

The bottom line is, at ¥20,000, the value of the companies of the Nikkei in mid-1992 is greater than the value today—twenty-five years later. And during almost all of that time, the value of the Nikkei was considerably less than ¥20,000. In fact, for a third of that time (seven years), at ¥10,000, the Nikkei was half the value it was during any of its run-ups between 1992 and 2016. Picture those numbers, sustained for as long as they have been (and still no end in sight) in any other developed, G-20 country. It seems remarkable.

And can you imagine the following speech from a CEO of an American company at an annual shareholders meeting? I can't.

"My fellow shareholders, I stand before you today to let you know your investment in our company is safe. And I guarantee your investment will be worth the same twenty-four years from now as it is worth today."

I certainly couldn't imagine the CEO of a company in the United States still being the CEO for too long after that speech. He or she would probably be fired before the sound of their voice faded from the room.

And I find it impossible to imagine how leaders in business might hold Japanese companies, and their leadership and approaches to management, in such high esteem when the results and numbers don't support it.

The Yen

Something else important to consider is the value of the Japanese Yen versus the US Dollar (see figure 3.4) and how these two variables (value of the yen versus the dollar and the value of the companies on the Nikkei) interplay with one another.

The value of the yen held reasonably steady against the dollar from 1982 to 1986, at approximately ¥240 to $1.00. But in 1986, the value of the yen abruptly rose against the dollar—a period that also coincides with the flip in the relative values of Per Capita GDP and Per Capita GDP adjusted for Purchase Price Parity as seen in figure 3.1—until it reached ¥140 to $1.00 in 1992 before continuing its rise to ¥80 to $1.00 in 1995.

Therefore, much of the run-up of the value of the companies of the Nikkei until 1985–1988 was not due to some prowess in company performance but, actually, a reflection of the amplification effect of an increase in the value of the yen from ¥250 to $1.00 to ¥130 to $1.00. Remember, the Nikkei is valued in yen, so the values of the companies didn't change as much as it was that the value of the yen that changed.

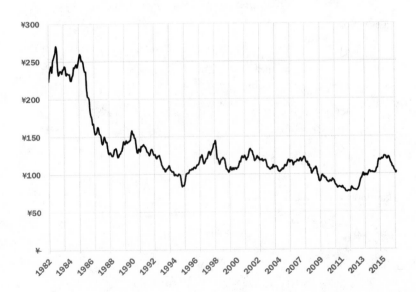

Figure 3.4. Value of the Japanese yen vs. the US dollar.

The Culture

In addition to the economic arguments of Japan and Japanese companies having superior performance to their Western peers, there is this notion that the culture of Japanese companies is more collegiate, open, and encourages engagement. However, a report from Ernst and Young[8] showed that full-time workers in Japan—whether employer, employee, or colleague—had the least amount of trust in the coworkers within their companies than any other country polled. In fact, of the Japanese workers polled, only an average of 21 percent expressed trust in the people in their companies. Compare this with 45 percent in the United States and 48 percent globally.

The lack of trust expressed by the Japanese was a *negative outlier* among all the countries polled *by a minimum factor of more than 50 percent.* And it certainly runs contraire to the expectations we would have after reading about the Japanese methods of management, with its emphasis on employee engagement, camaraderie, collaboration, and team building. What statement is this poll making with regards to the reality of the Japanese style of management?

There are four main takeaways:

⇨ The run-up of the Nikkei from all causes was relatively irrational and short-lived (eight years, 1982–1990), and the bursting of the bubble was equally swift.

⇨ The perceived run-up in value of the companies of the Nikkei was amplified as a result of the dramatic increase in the value of the yen to the dollar.

⇨ The value of the companies of the Nikkei is less today than it was twenty-five years ago. These are *not* companies in which I would want to invest or emulate.

⇨ The corporate culture in Japanese companies is not nearly as collegiate as some would have you believe. There are no choruses of "Kumbaya" being sung.

SPECIFIC EXAMPLE: THE SINGLE COMPANY

Thus far, we have taken a macro view of economics, comparing and contrasting the performance of Japan and the United States and also comparing and contrasting the aggregate performance of the companies within these countries as represented by the value of the Nikkei and the DJIA. And in each case, Japan and Japanese companies fared poorly.

But what about a single company? Can a single Japanese company be an outlier performer among its domestic peers? How does it compare to peers in other countries?

For your consideration—and since it is at the epicenter of the continuous improvement discussion—we will compare the stock price of Toyota Motor Corporation with Ford (see figure 3.5). The reason for my selecting Ford is that it is the only American manufacturer of automobiles that remained publicly traded for the entire period (Chrysler being purchased by Daimler-Benz and subsequently sold to Cerberus and eventually to Fiat, and GM declaring bankruptcy during the Financial Crisis of 2007–2008).

We can see, from 1982 to 1992, the value of a share in Toyota tracked very closely to Ford. Relative to one another and in US dollars, Toyota did not enjoy the dramatic rise in value that was reflected in the Nikkei, nor did it suffer the dramatic drop in value.

Figure 3.5. Share price of Ford vs share price of Toyota NYSE from January 1980 through March 2016. Toyota's actual share price is divided by 10 for scale.
Source: New York Stock Exchange.

In 1992, however, the value of a share of Ford started to increase at an accelerated rate as compared to Toyota and this pace quickened yet again in 1997. Ford enjoyed a share-value premium of 200 percent to 350 percent over Toyota for a period of four years, until the recession of 2001 brought the relative share-value of the shares of the two companies back closer to parity. Still, it wouldn't be until 2005 when the relative value of a share of Toyota would exceed the value of a share of Ford. And the relative values of the shares of the two companies since have tracked closely with one another, exchanging turns at the top spot several times.

Advocates of Toyota are always referring to the importance of long-term gains over the short term. And we can certainly see periods in these charts where each company exceeded the performance of the other from time to time on a short-term basis. But if we compare the relative value of the shares of Toyota and

Ford over the long term, it is apparent that Ford has consistently outperformed Toyota.

Can we say from this chart that Toyota was a better-managed company than Ford—a better-performing company than Ford—from 1982 to 2016? I don't see it, and the data doesn't support it.

ShareValue Aside, What about Execution?

Toyota has produced approximately ten million vehicles per year (including automobiles and trucks across all brands), plus or minus 5 percent, in every year between 2012 and 2015. But regardless, these have been very difficult years for Toyota and should challenge the claims to the effectiveness of the TPS to its core.

Information obtained from the Toyota website and the National Transportation Safety Board (NTSB) indicates, in each of the years from 2012 through 2015, Toyota *recalled a minimum* of 5.3 million vehicles, hitting a record recall of 8.4 million vehicles in 2015.

⇨ In 2012,[9] Toyota had 12 recalls affecting 5,300,000 vehicles.

⇨ In 2013,[10] Toyota had 15 recalls affecting 5,300,000 vehicles.

⇨ In 2014,[11] Toyota had 24 recalls affecting 6,000,000 vehicles.

⇨ In 2015,[12] Toyota had 27 recalls affecting 8,400,000 vehicles.

⇨ And 2016, at over 4,000,000 vehicle recalls, was not much better.[13]

This is a minimum recall rate of over 50 percent of annual production—and this does not include the unknown number of vehicles involved in "service bulletins," which are problems known to the company that require remedial action but do not warrant a formal recall. Here are some of the recall details:

⇨ In 2012, Toyota issued a recall for 7.4 million vehicles due to a problem with the power window mechanism posing a fire hazard.

⇨ On October 17, 2013, 803,000 vehicles were recalled because water from the air conditioning condenser unit housing could leak onto the airbag control module and cause a short circuit.

⇨ On August 7, 2013, 342,000 vehicles were recalled because screws that attach the seat belt pretensioner to the seat belt retractor within the seat belt assembly for the driver and front passenger could become loose over time due to repeatedly and forcefully closing the access door.

⇨ In 2014, just one of the many recalls Toyota issued that year was for problems involving airbag cables and rail seats, which affected 6.4 million vehicles.

⇨ In 2015, a recall issued to fix power window switches affected 6.5 million vehicles, and another recall involving defective airbags affected 1.4 million vehicles.

⇨ And in 2016, a few of the more significant recalls issued included 1.1 million vehicles with defective lap-belts, and another 337,000 vehicles were recalled because of defective rear suspension arms.

These are the kinds of numbers, and this is the kind of publicity, that should result in many sleepless nights for the leadership of Toyota and should give pause to the millions of disciples of the TPS and the principles of Lean. The assumptions of even the most fervent advocate of the TPS and Lean should be challenged to their core. To give some perspective, if the average burdened cost to Toyota of the recall was only $100 per unit (a modest assumption, to be sure), then that would put the *minimum annual cost of the recalls at $530 million and upward of $800 million for 2015.*

Certainly, with these outcomes, I would not want to emulate Toyota if I were a business leader (and I am) without a level of skepticism and some considerable due diligence. And I would be very distrustful and hesitant—even resistant—to embrace the approaches used by Toyota to improve the operations of my business blindly, based only on the past reputation of the TPS. After all, who wants to be known as *the company that makes defective products, but does so very efficiently?* This is hardly a path to sustainable viability or a rallying cry for converting customers into fans.

Of course, if we look at the nature of the recalls and their root causes, we find almost none of the recalls are the result of a defect in the manufacturing or assembly processes. I submit and agree the products were manufactured as prescribed and the steps involved in manufacturing did not cause defects resulting in the recalls. In fact, almost all of the recalls are the result of failures in the product or in production design and engineering.

Some people will point out that many of the defects were due to defective materials being delivered by vendors in Toyota's supply chain—as if this somehow absolves Toyota of the problem. The millions of vehicles recalled due to faulty airbags would be an example. But, to me, vendors in Toyota's supply chain (or anyone's supply chain) are merely extensions of the production process put in place for the convenience of Toyota. There should be no expected decrease in quality just because some other company actually manufactured the part. Besides, many vendors are also equity partners with Toyota. Where do you draw the line?

I am also sure there are many who will scream, "See! It's not the TPS or Lean that's not working at Toyota! There are no defects in the manufacturing process. They are doing just fine!"

I'm sorry to disappoint those people, but, in my opinion, *Toyota is not doing just fine.* In fact, there is a large part of the business that is operating at an entirely inadequate level of performance. And I will go even further and state that the general public does not recognize the nuance of who or what might be to blame the same way a zealot of the TPS does. All the general public sees—and rightfully so—is the output and results of the efforts of Toyota are defective.

It would be good for Toyota (and those who embrace TPS) to remember *customers are not buying the perfect manufacture of a car: they are buying a car.*

Another thing to keep in mind, but rarely mentioned, is that the ascent of Toyota (and the other Japanese automobile manufacturers) in the United States was largely the result of the Organization of Petroleum Exporting Countries (OPEC) Oil Embargo of 1973–1974.

This event caught American vehicle manufacturers flat-footed. Until then, Americans loved their big cars with big engines, and that is what the American manufacturers made. According to a report by the Economic Policy Institute (EPI) entitled "The Decline and Resurgence of the U.S. Auto Industry", [14] in 1974, General Motors, Ford, and Chrysler accounted for over

80 percent of the market share with Japanese manufacturers accounting for less than 10 percent.

I remember looking at some of the early four-cylinder engines made by the American automobile manufacturers during this time. They called them "in-line four-cylinders," but they looked like eight-cylinder engines cut down the middle lengthwise and were complete with a large flat wall where the "cut" would have been made. Engineering marvels they were not, and the quality was poor.

It took the American automobile manufacturers over a decade to learn how to build quality vehicles that were fuel efficient, and then only after creating partnerships with Japanese companies (such as the partnership between Ford and Mazda). And during this time, the Japanese automobile manufacturers were able to establish themselves in the United States.

So I would argue that the ascent of Japanese automobile manufacturers in the United States had as much to do with the geopolitical circumstances of time—being in the right place, at the right moment in history, with a product that proved attractive versus the incumbents—as it did with any particular management philosophy.

SYSTEM-WIDE INTEGRATION

I would like to clarify: I have no axe to grind against Toyota. I have owned Toyotas in the past and believe they are fine vehicles. I would even consider purchasing another.

What I am offering is perspective on trying to separate the hype from the reality when it comes to the TPS. In my opinion, the TPS is not delivering satisfactory results, even for Toyota. I only single out Toyota and the TPS because some overly enthusiastic advocates have a tendency to sell them both unreservedly as beacons to a corporate Valhalla and consume it without looking at the directions or reading the warning label—the disciples of the TPS who possess boundless hubris and display a great arrogance in their ignorance, looking down with contempt on those who question it.

There are many who would proclaim in defense of Toyota that Ford has had its fair share of defects and a similar number of recalls, and that is absolutely true. But neither Ford nor proponents of Ford and Ford's business operating system are holding themselves up as the standard-bearer of production or organizational performance prowess, as is the case with the advocates of the TPS and Lean.

The TPS was developed between 1948 and 1975, which makes it roughly forty to seventy years old, and Six Sigma is roughly thirty to forty years old. And although it might have been transformational back in the day, it is obvious from the experiences and results at Toyota that the TPS is in dire need of transformation to remain effective—even relevant—and to meet the needs of the twenty-first century organization. After all, even the TPS should be subject to kaizen.

You must always keep in mind and realize that the TPS (and Lean Six Sigma) are incomplete and imperfect—and one size does not fit all. They are not magic elixirs that you can swallow and make everything better. It takes work and lots of it. And the methodologies and tools as they currently exist and are employed are not enough, not nearly so. Just look at Toyota.

Leveraging TPS and Lean Six Sigma Across the Enterprise

Most TPS and Lean Six Sigma professionals think of the production line as what goes on inside the factory (see figure 3.6). They believe that if their intended output is created with minimal waste and at peak proficiency, they have accomplished their mission well. They might even consider the expansion of the TPS into any one of the other boxes. From this micro-level perspective—where the focus of the effort is on processes—that might be accurate.

However, if we examine the entire production line from a more macro- or systems-level perspective—marketing, through post-sales service, including all of the finance and supply- and value-chain points along the way—we can see the actual production process (any individual box in figure 3.6) is only a small part of the overall process of delivering a product to a consumer.

A basic tenet of the TPS and Lean is to rally resources when an opportunity for improvement is discovered, so it stands to reason that a defect discovered at any point along this production line should result in an alert and the dispatch of a kaizen team to resolve the defect before resuming production.

Certainly, the TPS and Lean Six Sigma have played a significant role in bringing companies to a higher level of performance over the past several decades, and those early adopters certainly realized rewards.

But today, most companies have recognized the benefits of these methodologies and have incorporated them as a cornerstone of their own continuous improvement programs, even if to varying degrees of completeness and success, including at Toyota. And, if everyone is doing it, it's no longer a differentiator, and it no longer drives the competitive advantage it once did.

Figure 3.6. Product support across business smokestacks.

The business that focuses on cutting waste over innovation and driving value to the customer—for which the customer is willing to pay a premium—is not at any particular advantage. Nor is the business that optimizes its processes but does not take the time to balance these processes so that they work harmoniously within the systems they comprise.

Instead, businesses that perform the following actions more quickly, efficiently, and effectively than their competitors have the advantage today:

⇨ Are innovative, creating demand and marketplaces

⇨ Thoroughly understand their capacity, capabilities, and weaknesses

⇨ Quickly recognize, anticipate—even seek—
an opportunity or threat

⇨ Rapidly formulate an effective response

⇨ Evaluate and make the go/no-go decision

⇨ Decisively deploy a response

⇨ React to the fluidity of engaging

The advantage now comes from balancing these processes so they work harmoniously within and across the systems of the enterprise. The differentiator is the speed, precision, decisiveness of decision-making (often from imperfect data), strategy execution, and operational excellence. And those companies that do not master these disciplines and skills—wherever they may be located—are punished by the markets.

As well they should be.

So how do we leverage the TPS and Lean Six Sigma to gain alignment and integration across the entire enterprise? We take it to the next level. We build upon what we know and grow it into a new way. We expand the toolsets of the TPS and Lean Six Sigma, even the name itself, so it involves, incorporates, and supports the entire company across all its aspects and endeavors. But how will this happen and by whom?

CHAPTER 4

THE STONE AGE DIDN'T END BECAUSE THEY RAN OUT OF STONES

"What we call the beginning is often the end.
And to make an end is to make a beginning.
The end is where we start from."

—T. S. Eliot

In business, not evolving—not seeking the new and fertile while retaining the old and sterile—means certain doom. For your business to remain viable over time, you must maintain a competitive advantage, to protect your existing customer base while always seeking expansion.

Take the story of Research in Motion Limited (RIM), which renamed itself Blackberry Limited in January of 2013. RIM's flagship products were their Blackberry mobile phones, and their primary differentiator was the ability to use the Blackberry Enterprise Server, a secure communication system whose encryption was close to impenetrable. This made the Blackberry the mobile phone of choice for government officials and employees, those in finance, contractors with the Department of Defense, and any other industries in which security was hypercritical.

Until January 2007, RIM and its Blackberry mobile devices enjoyed a nearly 50 percent market share in the United States. Then, the iPhone arrived on the market, followed by an explosion of competing smartphones, and Blackberry's market share dropped dramatically. With its commanding position of the marketplace, Blackberry had the opportunity to observe the threat of smartphones for what they were, formulate a meaningful response (a device and system redesign), and introduce that response. After all, Google did it by introducing Android, and they had no device and no experience before joining the fray. Instead, Blackberry did nothing; its leadership was satisfied with the status quo and failed to evolve. They falsely believed that their customers would stay because they offered a real keyboard and information security. When they did respond, it was too little too late. Eliminating this sort of feeble response is at the heart of operational excellence.

WHY DID THE STONE AGE END?

Most certainly, the Stone Age did not end because early humans exhausted the supply of stones. I am also certain the transition to the Bronze Age was more abrupt than incremental. Working with bronze for the first time would have undoubtedly been a thinking-outside-the-box moment.

Just imagine the scene: The master stoneworker in the tribe spent his entire life finding the appropriate stones and working them into some useful shape. What are the odds this person would have the imagination to take raw copper ore from a vein, heat it to melting, then add in tin before fashioning it into a tool? Perhaps a more likely scenario would be a cook roasting a brontosaurus burger over a fire surrounded by rocks. He notices one of the rocks has changed shape from the heat. When the fire cools, he sees that the melted rock retained its new shape but returned to the hardness of solid rock. He could then repeat the process on purpose, making the first tool for flipping brontosaurus burgers without burning his hand.

This was innovation. The artisan of a dying age is not usually the creator of its replacement. Each new age has been heralded in by an outsider—someone not directly involved in the industry of the previous age but, rather, an unattached free thinker.

Innovation is how all ages end.

Take the transition from sailing ship to steamer ship, for instance. Sailing ships have been used since ancient antiquity. Even the steam engine dates back to the first century AD but was a largely experimental device with few practical applications because of the inefficiencies inherent in early designs, the materials available for construction, and fuel. It was not until the second half of the 1700s when James Watt, a Scottish mechanical engineer, developed a commercially viable version of the steam engine.

Across the Atlantic, a clockmaker and engineer named John Fitch, who had no experience with shipbuilding or the sailing industry, became the first person to successfully integrate a steam engine to power a ship. Fitch's first steamships were not particularly innovative beyond the use of the steam engine for propulsion. They were simply sailing vessels with steam engines, but they evolved very quickly from that point.

By the mid-1800s, during the American Civil War, these wooden steamships began to give way to ones constructed, in part, of steel (called *ironclads*). And this innovation quickly paved the way to the engineering and scaling of shipbuilding to production of the great navies and ocean liners we see today.

Fitch was an outsider to the established industries of shipbuilding. And his innovation of integrating a steam engine into a ship was able to supplant the previous eons of accumulated wisdom of shipbuilding within a couple of generations.

This pattern of a paradigm shifting from the old to the new, where the new is ushered in by people detached from the old, is repeated time and again. More often than not, the new is created right under the noses of the old, and the old fail—or refuse—to see it, much to their detriment.

NOT A "KODAK MOMENT"

The Eastman Kodak Company was formed in 1889. Kodak grew into an industrial powerhouse and was added to the Dow Jones Industrial Average (DJIA) in 1930. If you ask the average person on the street what kind of company Kodak is, they will almost certainly tell you it's a photography company. But they would be completely wrong. Kodak is a chemical company. It's a chemical company servicing the photography industry, for sure, but a chemical company nonetheless.

At its peak, from 1975 through 1976, Kodak sold 90 percent of the film and 85 percent of the cameras used in America. As such, it stands to reason that Kodak also had enormous investments in the apparatus and infrastructure for developing film and creating prints, including the manufacture of all the chemicals used in these processes. Indeed, Kodak had billions of dollars in infrastructure and capital expenditure located around the world, all dedicated to the production of film and the development and printing of photographs, slides, and movies.

And it is at this peak that Kodak scientist Steven Sasson—an electrical engineer and not a chemist or a photographer—was hired by Kodak. His assignment was to take the *charged coupled device* (CCD), invented in 1969 at AT&T Bell Labs by Willard Boyle and George Smith, and to investigate whether there was any practical application in the photography business that Kodak could market. Within a couple of years, Sasson had invented the digital camera and was awarded a patent. Even though the device weighed eight pounds, had a resolution of 0.01 megapixels, and took twenty-three seconds to record its images, on a cassette tape, the invention was the genesis of digital photography. Kodak furthered the development of CCD technology for digital photography, and in the mid-1980s, scientists at Kodak invented the first CCD capable of capturing digital images with a resolution in excess of a million pixels and printing a five-by-seven photo in a quality that would satisfy the average consumer.

However, these new technologies—and the potential of the new markets that might be created through them—were not embraced by Kodak's leadership. In fact, they were repressed, because the chemicals that were their main product are not necessary in digital photography, and there was some doubt in the board members that digital photography was a valid threat. Besides, with billions upon billions invested in their chemical infrastructure, the prospects of a marketplace that did not leverage this investment were anathema to Kodak. As such, Kodak's leadership would have nothing to do with the development or promotion of digital photography—until it was too late.

Can you imagine the conversation at Kodak's board of directors when the scientist presented his invention and proclaimed it would transform the photography industry? All of their billions of dollars in chemical infrastructure would be rendered obsolete in short order and, along with it, the billions of dollars in sales of chemicals, chemical processing, and services. The board would have liked nothing more than to make this technology vanish, but the funny thing about inventions is that once something is invented, it cannot be uninvented. There is no going back.

In practicality, with Moore's law predicting that the ability of technology will double every two years, I can't see a path by which Kodak could have transformed itself from being a chemical company to a digital company quickly enough without eventually seeking the protection of the bankruptcy courts. Even a white knight acquirer would have only wanted to purchase the patents and new technology. Indeed, by inventing the bullet that would kill them, Kodak was faced with its own Kobayashi Maru[1]—the no-win scenario.

In 1994, Eastman Kodak spun off the part of the chemical business that did not work in the imaging industry, forming the Eastman Chemical Company.

Then, in 2004, Kodak was dropped from the DJIA, and it was dropped from the S&P 500 index in 2010. In 2012, Kodak filed for chapter 11 bankruptcy and began selling every asset and patent in its portfolio to satisfy its creditors. If only Kodak had given the outlier a second look. Sometimes outliers are anomalies, and sometimes they are an indication of things to come.

THE FINE LINE BETWEEN GENIUS AND INSANITY

Outliers are those who are not beholden to nostalgia or tradition but look at circumstances with fresh eyes and from a different perspective. For instance, many people believe consultants are somehow uniquely brilliant (at least, they are considered pretty smart people). However, the true power of the consultant comes from them being outliers to an organization. They don't know why anything might function or otherwise be set the way it is, and if they see something they don't understand, they question it.

A typical consulting conversation might go something like this:

Consultant:
"Why do you have this production line configured like that?"
Insider:
"That's the way it's always been, and it works very well."
Consultant:
"But, if you did this and that, you would increase yield by 15 percent and the reduction in cost and waste would be 22 percent. Does that make sense?"
Insider:
"Wow! That's so obvious! Why didn't we think of that?! You are brilliant!"

Consultants aren't brilliant; they just don't know any better.

Some of the most famous outliers include Albert Einstein, whose teachers thought he would never amount to much; Walt Disney, who was fired for lacking imagination and not being creative enough; and even The Beatles, who were rejected by Decca

Records because the insiders at the record company didn't like the band's sound and thought they had no future in the music business. In each case, these outliers were summarily dismissed by the inliers—those inside their respective industries who were in a position of authority and had the ability to pass judgment.

Evolution is the adaptation of what was into what is on its way to becoming what will be. And we must all evolve to survive, not to mention thrive. Organizations need the introduction of fresh perspectives and ideas to remain relevant and competitive in the marketplace. The challenge is for the leadership of an organization to seek and understand the outlier and to evaluate the true nature and scope of the opportunity or threat that the outlier brings to the organization (or marketplace) before deciding to embrace the innovation or not.

THE AGE OF LEAN SIX SIGMA

The reality is that the methodologies and tools of Lean Six Sigma are (intentionally or not) oriented toward improving processes, with a special emphasis on making these processes quite linear; reducing and even eliminating variants of a process is a primary objective. As generally practiced, it is not focused on systems, which involve a cross-section of business functions to support an outcome.

Improving processes throughout a business certainly has a positive impact on business performance. But there is a point at which the improvement of processes is no longer a competitive advantage, and that is when everyone has adopted the same approach. At this point, can anyone really claim Ford or Mercedes, for example, do a lesser job of embracing and deploying

Lean Six Sigma than Toyota does? Who is to say what business has an advantage over another in their method of improvement?

As an illustration of my point, consider two types of horse races that are very similar in nature; however, one emphasizes processes, and the other emphasizes systems. A sulky race involves one horse for each carriage, whereas a chariot race involves four horses for each carriage. See figure 4.1 below.

In racing sulkies, all of the efforts are concentrated on how to make one horse run the best it can, bearing in mind how it

Figure 4.1. A sulky race and a chariot race.

might perform better or worse based on conditions (short, long, mud, dry, inside, outside . . .). You can consider this a production process, with the conditions being production variants. In competition, the winner will be the one with the better-trained horse, running in the race for which they are best suited, who is feeling its best that day and has a masterful driver. And everyone in the race is similarly prepared.

In a chariot race, however, the efforts are parsed across four horses, each one with its own personality (what motivates it), its own strengths and weaknesses (running on the inside versus outside versus in the middle of the team), and its own different feelings from day to day. The training regimen for the horses is tailored to the individual, but as part of the whole: the processes within a system. The performance of one horse is influenced and balanced by the others. It is likely that the team with the best individual horses will not win if they do not work as a team—as a system. To win, all of the horses must work in harmony, and the driver must react in real time to the performance of each of the horses so the system maintains its harmony.

So, if we consider the evolution of business management systems (perhaps better called *business operating systems*) in the context of the chariot team and its driver, we can see, from Henry Ford and the automobile assembly line through the Toyota Productions System, Lean, and Six Sigma, the emphasis has been on increasing both the velocity of the throughput and the quality of the production process (see figure 4.2). Companies still experience delays and waste, and there are still issues with the quality of the end deliverables. There are still frictions and deficiencies, with the end result being the benefits and rewards realized as a result of optimized processes are diluted elsewhere in the enterprise.

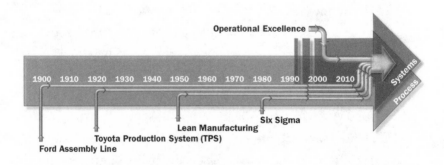

Figure 4.2. Timeline of business improvement paradigms.

But like the Stone Age, which did not end because they ran out of stones, the Age of the TPS, Lean Six Sigma, and Process Improvement will not end because all of the processes that can be optimized are optimized. And since we still use stones today—and lots of them—we can expect that these process and continuous improvement tools and techniques will always be a cornerstone of a business operating system. However, the real riches to be discovered are in taking the disciplines to the next level by optimizing systems—making the near countless individual processes that compose a system work in concert with one another and across the enterprise.

Whereas business improvement methodologies for the twentieth century company placed its emphasis on processes to gain a competitive advantage to much success, the twenty-first century company will need to go beyond processes and place its emphasis on optimized systems to remain competitive, even viable.

CHAPTER 5

SURVIVAL OF THE FITTEST

"It is not necessary to change.
Survival is not mandatory."

—W. Edwards Deming

Charles Darwin proposed that evolution occurs with the introduction of challenging or adverse circumstances to a population of a species. Only those who are able to adapt, either by natural selection or by action, survive. For instance, the shark evolved to be nature's eating machine. It must constantly swim, never sleeping, to keep water always flowing over its gills. If it ever stops swimming, it will suffocate. Without a state of rest, it needs to feed constantly. To ensure it is always able to eat, it continually generates rows upon rows of teeth, so when one is lost, another appears in its place.

Similarly, the history of humankind has been a never-ending series of advancements—sometimes evolutionary, sometimes revolutionary—and business follows the same pattern. As we discussed in the previous chapter, almost every occurrence of transformational progress has been initiated by outliers and almost never members of an established group maintaining the status quo. The time for the next leap of progress is when everyone has settled on some truth, some homogeny, and something comes along to disrupt that sameness with innovation.

In the early years of the Industrial Revolution, clock and scientific instrument manufacturers began relying on machine tools to create standardized components out of metal, which enabled them to create their mechanism in batches; before this, each apparatus was created individually by hand. Over the next two hundred years, the sophistication of the production lines and what was being produced on them became ever more complex.

When a transformational technology (or methodology) is first introduced, it is a game changer. At the beginning, both the technology and the know-how to deploy will almost always cost a premium over the old, but they also generate a premium in benefit and return. I refer to this as the *Innovation Value Premium* (IVP). As the technology becomes more pervasive with more and more people coming onboard, others will replicate the technology and create competition until the new technology becomes ubiquitous and commoditized. However, the know-how and expertise to implement the technology will remain at a premium for a time. This is because there is a lag between the introduction of the technology and the number of experts that know the technology at a level of proficiency: There are fewer masters of the tool than needed in the marketplace. However, even this know-how becomes commoditized as more and more people gain experience with the tool. And at this point, there is no IVP to be realized by either the creator of the tool or those with expertise. Everyone is back on a level playing field.

The reason for this is rather obvious: When everyone is the same, there is no differentiator except for price. And when price is the only differentiator, it is simply a race to the bottom. But with homogeny also comes complacency, which sets the conditions for the introduction of a disrupter. Someone or something will redefine what *is* into what *will be*.[1]

For instance, we've witnessed disruptions in transportation, with sailing vessels giving way to steam power giving way to diesel and even nuclear power. But perhaps the most significant transformation in transportation was the invention and introduction of the automobile. Unlike its sail and rail predecessors, the automobile lent itself to being mass-produced on an enormous scale because of the scale of the marketplace. No longer were automobiles built by engineers and artisans as one-offs. Vehicles could be manufactured in large volumes, leveraging the resulting economies of scale so the cost to own was affordable to the individual, average, middle-class consumer.

To ensure that your business performs at the top of its game—even remains in the game—you must also encourage disruption. You may be uncomfortable with the notion and with the proposals that might be conjured by your colleagues and employees, but a culture open to innovation is an absolute requirement. When considering and pursuing potentially disruptive opportunities, your leadership during strategy execution and the level of operational excellence that exists within your business—its ability to turn dreams into realities—will make all the difference between success and failure.

The same is true of continuous improvement methodologies, with Lean Six Sigma being the most widely embraced among them. Because their use has become pervasive in industry—even if there is a range of comprehensiveness and results—there is no longer the significant competitive advantage to an organization in deploying these methodologies and tools as there once was.

Today, manufacturing companies often focus on Lean Six Sigma process-improvement techniques, which is doing things right, but they may ignore, to their peril, the more important strategic alignment, which is doing the right things. The efforts place an emphasis on the optimization of processes within the business smokestacks but, unfortunately, usually far less frequently on the optimization of systems *across* the enterprise.

As such, the aim of continuous improvement methodologies has been to constantly drive additional value to the customer and to thereby retain a competitive advantage as the company pursues its strategies.

Yet problems persist. Customers continue to complain and file warranty charges. Recalls abound. Product reliability is not always up to expectations (e.g., toys that break after a few days of use). The cost of quality (waste and rework, in particular) seems to have a life of its own, and it is difficult to reduce to a sustainable level. Productivity, in many cases, has plateaued. Inventories stay obstinately higher than desired or expected. Overhead costs continue their upward spiral.

The question is *Why, after the introduction of all of these remarkable new methodologies, have many businesses failed to become high-performance organizations?* A large part of the problem resides in the fact that many—if not most—companies have smokestack organizations. Any tool or methodology begins—as does its use—as a solution to a specific problem. They improve an explicit action in a process that is often more or less linear. The tool and its impact are not often considered as a part of a system initially.

It's time for the next generation. Not (necessarily) the next generation of new technologies or methodologies, but a shift in thinking from linear to systems.

In order to reach the next level of organizational performance, rather than emphasizing the linear processes of the functional smokestacks of a business, we need to begin to emphasize cross-smokestack (horizontal) integration: We need to change from *process thinkers* to *systems thinkers*. This means we must have an awareness and appreciation (not a *command* or *granular knowledge*) of all of the assets available (and those not available) within an enterprise: What are they, where are they, what are their capabilities, what is beyond their capabilities, and what is their ability to engage? We also have to start looking at opportunities and threats from an enterprise-wide (macro) perspective, not just a myopic (micro) perspective.

Take a simplistic view of a company, one with three organizational units: operations, sales, and finance. This is a typical *smokestack organizational model*. Each functional unit acts independently of the others. Operations, for example, focuses on reducing throughput time, minimizing inventories, and improving quality. Sales focuses on adding more revenue every year, and finance focuses on keeping costs within their budgeted amounts while assuring sufficient operating capital to sustain the business. But there is a lack of alignment and an inadequate amount of collaboration among the smokestacks. Each is pursuing its own internal goals—its own Key Performance Indicators (KPIs)—and often without attention to overall company strategy. Each smokestack is inwardly oriented and not committed to business-wide, not to mention enterprise-wide, success.

The unfortunate result of this model is that company leaders all too often take their eyes off the ball and fumble, or they don't even see the ball at all. They are so focused on what they know—their individual smokestacks and the processes contained therein—that they fail to see how they are supposed to fit into the whole and to work as part of a greater system, the enterprise.

If business leaders had the ability and foresight to shift their perspective to *systems thinking*, they would be in far greater position to recognize opportunities and threats and would have an advantage in addressing these challenges. After all, the business horizon is only as reliable as its leader's ability to visualize the future.

For example, General Motors (GM) had ignition switch problems that the company hid from the public and the federal government for many years, and that resulted in a considerable number of deaths and countless injuries.

According to articles in Bloomberg, GM has paid $870 million to settle lawsuits for the deaths and injuries caused by the defect (with many cases still pending), $900 million to the Department of Justice to resolve a criminal investigation, and the cost of the recalls,[2] plus over $1 billion to repair or replace the defective ignition switches in vehicles still on the road.[3] In addition to these hard costs is the damage to GM's reputation and the risk of the buying public losing faith in the brand.

Compare this with how Tesla Motors reacted when faced with its own *Waterloo moment*.[4] A Tesla Model S erupted into flames while driving down the road. Instead of playing defense, Tesla went on the offense. The company immediately dispatched engineers to determine the cause of the fire. After discovering what had occurred (some road debris had punctured the batteries, resulting in the fire), the company had its product design engineers expeditiously create a remedy. The result was a triple underbody shield. Once it was available, the modification was immediately introduced into the production of new vehicles, and the company offered to retrofit all of the cars already on the road.

GM acted as a linear, process-optimized business operating within functional smokestacks, doing too little too late and without involving the whole enterprise. Tesla's responsive and decisive approach, on the other hand, retained the trust of the buying public. And Tesla's preemptive action rendered moot the eventual commentary from the federal government or actions from their customers. In fact, Tesla's actions won *fans*, which are even better than customers, because fans are willing to pay a premium. This is how a systems-thinking, high-performance organization conducts itself.

GM lost control of the narrative, whereas Tesla never did.

Systems thinking demands cross-functional management. Managers in all of the organizational components must emphasize the achievement of company strategy first and smokestack efficiency second. If business leaders have the foresight to shift their perspective to systems thinking, they will obtain not only the ability to anticipate problems and roadblocks but also the spur to devise innovative solutions, which, in turn, drives even more value to the customer.

This systems thinking is an integral part of achieving a constant *state of readiness*, and it's the ticket for companies to transform into a high-performance organization. As business continues to evolve, only the fittest will survive, and high-performance organizations are the fittest of the fit.

We know that a ceiling is being reached with the existing tools and techniques, and we have to stretch beyond. But what now? What can we do? What do we do? As they say, the devil you know is better than the devil you don't know.

For instance, consider the United States Congress. For a very long time, perhaps decades, the approval rating of the elected members of the House of Representatives has hovered in the high single digits or low teens—and the Senate has not fared much better. Yet, every election sees those running for reelection being elected, sometimes without opposition. How can that be?

If we want change, we have to take action. We have to be the change. We have to lead the change. Otherwise, everything stays the same. Are you good with that? Is your business good with that?

PART 2

LEADING CHANGE

"There is nothing more difficult to take in hand,
more perilous to conduct, or more uncertain
in its success, than to take the lead in the
introduction of a new order of things."

—Niccolo Machiavelli

I grew up in Endicott, New York. Its biggest claim to fame is that it's the birthplace of IBM. When I lived there growing up, a great many of the people in the area worked for IBM directly, including my father. Of those who did not work for IBM directly, most still indirectly depended on IBM for their livelihood. IBM's corporate motto back then was "Think." It was emblazoned on every piece of corporate tchotchke: pens, pencils, pads, pocket protectors. It was even cast in a concrete block that ran the perimeter of IBM's then corporate headquarters.

Indeed, growing up, I believed it was an elegant and bold corporate motto; I was a fan.

But after IBM moved its corporate offices to Armonk, New York, and its subsequent financial problems in the early 1990s, its employment footprint in the area (between Endicott and nearby Owego) shrank from over twenty thousand in the mid-1980s to approximately five hundred today. The impact of the employment base was significant and was a source of grave concern to the community. For decades after, there was a lot of thinking about what to do in response, but no action of substance was ever decided or materialized. I became concerned that "Think" was not powerful enough and became rather disenchanted with the motto. After all, nothing was really ever accomplished, actually completed, by thinking alone. Once you have thought all of the thoughts you can possibly think, it's time to do.

That is why my new favorite corporate motto is Nike's: "Just do it."

There are really two types of change.

The first category of change is evolutionary. I won't spend much time on evolutionary change, as these are usually step changes. Like watching grass grow or the progression of the seasons throughout the year. Evolutionary change is often so subtle and nuanced you might not even notice it's happening. Change is even happening to you right now, as you read this book. These changes are largely predictable, perhaps even expected, and there is no real preparation involved, just minor adjustments that have to be made.

The second category of change is revolutionary. These changes are dramatic either in scope or scale and almost always accompanied by compressed timelines. Here, preparation—or the lack thereof—can be the difference between surviving and perishing (with a near infinite number of possibilities in between), and almost certainly, you (or your company) will not be nearly the same afterward.

And within revolutionary change, the catalyst can be either internal or external.

Internal catalysts and the subsequent actions are largely under your control and implemented at a cadence you dictate. But since there is no real threat, revolutionary change originating internally normally lacks a sense of urgency. And the likelihood of the change stalling or stopping when it becomes difficult is significant.

External catalysts for change originate from outside your organization and can entail real peril. Whether the peril is subtle but building or obvious and swift, it can catch you completely unaware, and then it might be too late. There are two primary countermeasures when faced with an external catalyst for change: Increase your ability to recognize the threat early, and keep your company fit, nimble, and capable financially and organizationally. But it is not enough to be able to recognize a threat early, have a robust balance sheet, and have a nimble organization to overcome the threat and survive. These are just requisites that increase your chance for success.

Whether the outcome is success or failure will depend on your leadership, how knowledgeable you are of your company's capacity and capabilities, and how efficiently and effectively you and your team communicate with one another.

There are a lot of obstacles in the path of efficient and effective communication. Are the communications clear and understandable? How do we package our communications for delivery? Are we pulling together a team or are we conscripting? Is there clarity of purpose with the issues being faced? And we also need to understand why before we can prepare the who, what, when, where, or how.

CHAPTER 6

A CULTURE OF LEADERSHIP IS ESSENTIAL

"If your actions inspire others to dream more, learn
more, do more, and become more, you are a leader."

—John Quincy Adams

What it takes for any business-wide initiative to realize its
potential is leadership.

A leader is not a leader by rank, title, wealth, or lineage. A
leader is a leader because people are willing to follow them. To
paraphrase John Maxwell, if a leader looks behind and nobody
is following, he is not a leader. He's just someone out for a walk.

For example, the company may or may not be able to successfully reorient its employees under the existing management. This
success depends completely on the manager being respected by
the employees. Managers who are new to the team need to earn
the respect of those they lead. If the manager cannot gain and
retain the respect of their supposed followers, the manager must
be removed from their position. If the manager can be properly
coached, they can stay on with the company, but elsewhere.

For people to follow you through change, they need to understand where they're going. This means that an organization must know *why it exists* and *what its vision of the future is*—in the simplest terms (no MBA words)—so everyone in the enterprise can understand their individual role and expectations in the pursuit of that vision. Then the organization must *communicate effectively* so it gains alignment among its resources and assets to effectively engage in the pursuit of the strategies, because an enterprise does not change on its own; individuals change.

VISION

There are five main requirements for the success of any program, and this is certainly true when it comes to the development and deployment of an operational excellence program.

The first is *vision*. A vision is not nearby but rather something that exists beyond the horizon. It might not be well defined. Usually, the more bold and transformational the vision is, the less detail there will be.

You have to be able to paint a picture of this vision that is simple, elegant, and attractive. And the vision has to have a promise of being a much better place than what exists to overcome the complacency and fear of those you need to have onboard and follow. As such, a vision should never be about getting away from where you are, but about getting to where you want to be—for your company, for your team, and for yourself.

However, if enough individuals change, the enterprise is changed as a result. The emphasis must be placed on how we get those individuals to *want* to change, not just *need* to change. Everyone has needs, but nothing happens until the needs turn into wants.

Next, the organization should *establish a cadence* (think of everyone working together with a rhythm toward common goals), so all members of the organization can synchronize their efforts and reinforce one another. Their efforts must all balance and pull in the same direction. When this happens, the organization achieves a tempo that is appreciable and harmonious.

This harmony precipitates a level of *situational awareness*. All members of the organization are focused on the pursuit of the overall strategies and support of one another but are also aware of the chaos and unpredictability outside it. With a better understanding of the capacity and capability of the enterprise, a greater level of trust is established and the decision-making process and resulting responses will be accelerated. A tactical advantage comes with this speed and decisiveness. At this point in your journey toward operational excellence, your enterprise will achieve a state of readiness and will be on your way to becoming a high-performance organization.

A LEADER IS NOT BEHOLDEN TO NOSTALGIA

A company cannot have managers who live in the past—neither in their personal past glories nor in the past glories of the company. The proper managerial orientation toward the notion of time is to learn from the past, live in the present, and plan for the future.

A LEADER IS A HUMBLE SERVANT TO THOSE WHO FOLLOW

A company cannot have managers who are out for themselves; they must be focused on those under their charge. A manager knows to take the blame for failures and to give the credit to those he serves. In fact, you can easily tell a poor manager: They make no mistakes. There are only two possibilities for a mistake-free performance: Either the manager is not pushing themselves and their department, or they are passing the blame to someone else. Of course, if the company is intolerant of failure, the problem is rooted at the very top and must be changed there.

STRATEGY

The second requirement is *strategy*: the theory of the use of engagements to achieve an objective. In business, it is the use of engagements to earn new customers from creating innovative offerings or win customers from the competition.

In military terms—but the same is true with companies—*strategy* refers to the organization and deployment of the entirety of the organization's focus, resources, and capability in pursuit of its objectives with a perspective that is long term.

With a business, these strategies must be in support of, and dedicated to, the achievement of the company's vision. And since strategy consumes such a tremendous amount of energy and resources, it is important for a company to not pursue too many strategies simultaneously. They will compete with one another for resources, thus dividing the company and making it weak. It is far better to prioritize strategies, be selective in their pursuit, and concentrate the resources on their swift and successful attainment.

Remember, there can only be one "first, highest priority."

A LEADER IS PATIENT BUT PRESSING

A good leader must realize that companies do not change except for being guided to a change through effective leadership, which starts with building trust and confidence within the employees in their leadership. Therefore, the company that dedicates itself to true transformational change must be patient. For this process to begin, employee dispositions and attitudes must change so those employees are reinvigorated, trusting in, and supportive of, the company. This takes time. However, the company must press forward using constructive methods and must hold individuals accountable for their own progress and the achievement of their individual and collective objectives. The most obvious starting point for forming trust is to be empathetic to the circumstances, needs, and ambitions of the employee and to offer encouragement and support to that employee so they may enjoy personal growth within the company. Not only will a deep trust between employee and employer be built in this manner, but the employee will drive additional value to the company.

AGENTS OF CHANGE ARE NEVER HUGGED

Change is inevitable. Although people sometimes complain about their circumstance and clamor for change, they are very resistant to actual change. As a leader, you should expect trepidation and resistance to any truly transformational change. The magnitude and velocity of change—and whether that change is under our terms and conditions or we have those terms and conditions thrust upon us—are the only real variables.

Always keep in mind that those who embrace the idea of change are the minority within your organization and you will not easily find allies. You will be surrounded by those who wish to see you fail so they can continue on as they always have—even if their actions are passive. This is not intended to discourage you, but to prepare you for the challenge you are about to face.

TACTICS

The third necessity for program success is *tactics*, the use of resources in engagements.

The details of your tactics have two requirements: knowing where you are and knowing where you want to go. If I called you and asked you to give me directions to your house, your first question to me would be, "Where are you now?" Knowing where you are and where you want to be are the two precursors that must exist for tactics to be developed.

It is important to understand that plans are not static but dynamic. Sometimes, happenstance will get in the way, and we will have to adjust; sometimes, we will discover some things simply won't work, and we have to rethink; and sometimes, we will have to make the determination that the pursuit of the strategy is not worth the investment, that *the juice is not worth the squeeze.*

Therefore, we must remember two things about tactics:

First, they are never perfect. There is something that will always have been forgotten or ignored during the formulation of the plan, and there will always be something injected during its execution that will necessitate changes.

Second, they are never final. With near certainty, the strategy will be a moving target and will evolve after the initiation of the plan. Therefore, a proper plan will be elegant in its design—simple and efficient. It will also be flexible so it can react with agility to any changes without being so rigid it fractures.

DEFINE STRATEGY AND TACTICS

The very first action a leader must complete is to define the initiative and its purpose *for themselves*, so they possess a full understanding of what is going to be asked of others. What, precisely, is the nature of the initiative? How will we set about working toward these goals? What is needed of whom and when in order to achieve these goals? And most importantly, why are we doing all of this?

They should begin the development of the program by engaging as many of the stakeholders as is reasonable and appropriate in defining the parameters and desired outcomes of the initiative. I would caution against making the number of involved stakeholders too large, because it will make achieving a consensus elusive and will slow progress. However, it cannot be too small a group either, because people grow anxious in the face of the unknown. Besides, pride in ownership is a very powerful motivator—even more than monetary reward, which can be manipulated by management too easily and can actually breed distrust. You will have to work to find the right balance. But remember: Only God is perfect. To quote General George Patton, "A good plan violently executed now is better than a perfect plan executed next week." Success is a very simple thing, and the determining characteristics are confidence, speed, and audacity—none of which can ever be perfect, but they can be good.

Once the proper leadership skills are instilled, the strategy and tactics have been defined, and value-chain buy in is achieved: The roll-out of the operational excellence program can commence.

LOGISTICS

Fourth for program success is *logistics*, the use of supply chains in support of tactics.

Once you have developed your tactics, you can identify and quantify the resources necessary to support the plan. What human resources will you need? How many and what skills do they need to possess? Are there any materials or machinery required? How much time do you need to accomplish the plan? How much cash do you need?

Critically, once you have answered those questions, you can then calculate the total budget needed to support the strategy. It is important to compare this budget with the expected reward, because it is at this point you evaluate the Return on Investment (ROI) and make your go/no-go decision. You must also consider the amount of time it will take to achieve the plan. Are you able to execute in a timely enough manner to create (or maintain) a competitive advantage? If you are unable to justify the strategy in terms of budget or time to completion, you must change either your strategy or the plan, or even modify or abandon your vision.

Simply put, ideas will not be realized and plans will not be put into motion without the logistics necessary for their support. Therein lies a primary reason for the failure of many operational excellence programs: the lack of commitment on the part of the company to support the program. It is folly to expect a company to realize any improvement without allocating the necessary resources.

To ensure an optimal result, as a leader, you must do the following:

⇨ **Communicate.** All details of the initiative must be communicated clearly and concisely so there is no room for misinterpretation. You must also communicate the ongoing progress of the initiative. Be sure to recognize notable individual achievement. Communicate honestly and openly, and demand the same in return. Leave the political correctness, platitudes, and hyperbole for the propagandists—doing otherwise just muddies the message.

For instance, saying, "This needs to be done by . . . Can you do it?" is far clearer than asking, "If you are not too busy, can you do this for me when you get the chance?" The former is concise and demands a decision and commitment be made at the end, whereas the latter is ambiguous and will most likely lead to disappointment.

⇨ **Align.** Identify, allocate, and align all relevant resources so the mission is properly supported and the objectives are met. Do not ask people to do what they are ill prepared to accomplish, because the result will most often be failure.

⇨ **Commit.** Commit, and commit unreservedly. The initiative will be as great a success as can be achieved if the program has been planned well and is supported better: Contingencies have been identified, countermeasures are prepared, everyone executes as expected, and the job is properly done.

⇨ **Debrief.** The team should perform a review of what occurred and compare it with the original plan. They should identify exceptions and their consequences (negative and positive) and should communicate this new knowledge and experience to the rest of the business. More on the subject of debrief and debriefing in chapter 19.

⇨ **Adjust.** Make sure to take careful and timely consideration of the information generated during the debriefing so you can reflect on the experiences in a thoughtful and meaningful manner and contemplate recommendations for further improvements—all the while maintaining the momentum.

In the end, the philosophies, approaches, and methods contained in Lean Six Sigma, and all the other tools of continuous improvement, have proven effective in the pursuit of perfection. However, a tool is of lesser value without a motivated and skilled individual who selects it wisely and wields it with precision while working as part of an orchestrated team.

With a culture of leadership, the environment will be optimal for true transformational change, which will propel the organization forward to realize the potential of operational excellence or, for that matter, any initiative.

EXECUTION

Finally, we come to *execution*: the actual engagement of the pursuit of the strategies.

This is the moment of truth, but it takes guts—and lots of them. Once we begin, there is no going back; it is triumph or defeat. Certainly, we can stop, even retreat, but things will never be as they were before. This is the time when the burden of command weighs heavy on our shoulders, when we are confronted by all of our doubts and fears. And although we may be surrounded by people and by teammates, we feel the most alone.

We have to execute as a team, maintaining the highest level of communication. After you have designed, developed, and prepared and after you have considered all of your fears, consulted all of your advisors, and thought all the thoughts you can think, it's time to make your decision: execute, modify, or abandon your strategy. Without the vigorous prosecution of the plan, only mediocrity and failure will be found. If you have excellent leadership and followership with a high degree of communication, you have aligned your resources toward achieving the goal, those resources are sufficiently prepared and have the capability, and you have complete commitment throughout the organization, then the full realization of success will be the result.

(*Continued . . .*)

Keep in mind that, during execution, *the fog of war* will result in the introduction of variables (*injects*) for which you may or may not have planned. As Donald Rumsfeld famously said, "There are things that are known knowns . . . We also know there are known unknowns . . . But there are also the unknown unknowns." Be prepared accordingly.

We spend a lot of time and effort talking about leadership. There are countless books and workshops on leadership: how to become a good leader, what a good leader does and what they don't do, and so on. We evaluate the quality and caliber of leadership based upon the outputs of the leader, their results, what the leader has accomplished given the parameters of their objectives and the resources at their disposal. And perhaps these are good measurements of the effectiveness of a leader.

But being considered a good leader is really a reflection of the leader building good followers—a cadre of those who respect the leader and feel they are respected in return, that there is a level of mutual understanding, commitment, integrity, transparency, and trust—and how those followers engage when challenged. Do they hunker down, press forward, and get the job done? Or do they cut and run? Remember, most employees will not quit their company, but they will quit their leader.

So, if you truly want to get an idea of the caliber of the leader, look at the followers.

But an organization does not consist of a single leader and their followers. An organization consists of leaders who report to other leaders. Those on the lowest rung in the organization will be the leaders of those who come afterwards. And the leaders of these people will be the followers of those to whom they report, and so on up the corporate ladder to the CEO. But even the CEO is a follower of the board of directors and the customers for the company's offerings.

An organization consists of people who are simultaneously leaders and followers, and they must excel in both roles, creating an organization with a leadership culture. After all, for a company to become a high-performance organization, it needs to create high-performance teams built from high-performance individuals. The starting point is communication.

CHAPTER 7

REAL LEADERS NEVER SAY "BURNING PLATFORM"

"The more the panic grows, the more uplifting
the image of a man who refuses to bow to the terror."

—Ernst Junger

Those of us who are familiar with continuous improvement programs have undoubtedly heard references made to a "burning platform." We have come to understand this as a metaphor for a crisis situation, and, along with it, we have acquired the sense of urgency that is necessary to effectively react and overcome the crisis. If you Google the phrase *burning platform origin*, you get as many people claiming to be the originator of the phrase as you do postings attributing the origin to some anecdote involving—what else—a literal burning platform.

The most famous burning platform (and the most likely impetus for the phrase) was the Piper Alpha oil platform disaster, which occurred in the North Sea on July 6, 1988, after a fire on the platform became uncontrollable. The result was an explosion and fireball that engulfed the platform and killed 167 workers.

Whatever its origin, the burning platform has become nearly ubiquitous business jargon for a situation so dire and fraught with danger that people will focus all of their energy to overcome the threat so they can go back to feeling safe and secure again. Accordingly, a common belief and approach in organizations seeking change is this: For any major change within the organization to occur, a critical success factor is to find a catalyst that will motivate people at an emotional level to want to change the status quo. That this approach places an emphasis on the emotion of fear is important. By this line of reasoning, the people involved must believe that clinging to their current way is so perilous that it compels them into believing moving nearly anywhere is safer than staying where they are.

I do not believe this is an effective or sustainable approach or motivator.

Recently, I became engaged in a discussion in the Operational Excellence Group on LinkedIn that started with the following premise: "Convincing people to start an operational excellence initiative requires a compelling story. How do you convey the burning platform?"

Although I agree with the first part of the discussion—it is important to provide a compelling story—I do not believe you need to "convey the burning platform" to inspire people to change.

Interestingly, but not surprisingly, many of the comments in the discussion addressed the nuances of phraseology, definitions, and messaging. As a self-proclaimed wordsmith myself, I admittedly emphasized the importance of pragmatic, accurate, and open portrayal of the initiative—and its motivations and objectives—rather than injecting emotional hyperbole. You don't need to shout *Fire!* to get people to move.

One group of posters felt it was necessary to use fear and intimidation (much like a burning platform would conjure in one's mind) to compel people to get involved and change the way things are. The second faction (including me) believed people will change willingly if they understand the purpose and value of the initiative, how they are going to be successful, and what is in it for them. Only then will they willingly and actively engage.

Admittedly, the former path is easier for the leader to embark on than the latter, but just because something is easier doesn't make it better, or even right.

As the exchange evolved, it became apparent that very few of the people who felt the need to speak of the burning platform did, in fact, believe a do-or-die situation ever exists. They were merely leveraging the rhetoric to compel people to follow. Truly propagandists at heart, maybe these folks should work in politics. But as a leader, you have to know and always keep in mind that if your followers catch you lying or exaggerating, they won't be your followers anymore.

Besides, why does everything need to instill panic? How much of this frenzy and accompanying stress are self-induced? Are the emotional and physical states involved sustainable, or is burnout inevitable? Is there anything that isn't a "burning platform"? Is there really any difference between the drama on Facebook and what we often conjure in the organization? And to what useful or healthy end to the company?

I refuse to subscribe to this mentality. Instead of seeing the situation as a crisis, we need to somehow see through the rhetoric and simply recognize the need to change and the work that needs to be done. Why not just call it that, a "need to change," and then rally around that? I can't reconcile that a burning platform must exist as a prerequisite for change, as if change cannot occur without the threat of dire, life-threatening consequences. I refuse to buy into this as a requirement for a continuous improvement initiative to be successful.

Let's look at the metaphor a little closer. What would you actually do on a "burning platform"?

You find yourself on an oil platform in the middle of the sea. All around you is a raging inferno with saturating heat hot enough to melt steel. You know you have to beat the flames and get the situation under control immediately or face your demise. That is, unless you can find another way to save yourself. After all, it's not your platform. Are you going to stay amid the flames and try to save it? I bet not.

In the dire situation that is the "burning platform," I can assure you that each and every member of the firefighting team is going to divide their dedication between accomplishing the mission and self-preservation. And when the decision has to be made between the two, self-preservation will always win.

Weak leaders—those who are immature in their role and who have nothing in their tool kit—use fear and intimidation as a substitute for reason. I use the term *weak* because fear and intimidation are far easier methods for encouraging action than is reason. The goal of using fear and intimidation is to excite the emotions of the leader's close followers, to excite their minions into a state of frenzy so they feel compelled to fight some enemy. Sometimes the enemy is real, even if it is somewhat exaggerated, and sometimes it is fictitious, but the reaction of the minions serves the ambitions of their leader, not the enterprise.

However, to use reason requires that the leader understand the situation at hand: what has to be done, why it has to be done, what it will take to accomplish the mission in real terms, and what all the stakeholders have to gain and to lose. And the leader must communicate this information effectively to their team.

PRESERVING OPERATIONAL EXCELLENCE

I was asked to conduct a workshop, deliver a keynote, and chair a three-day conference on manufacturing process excellence in Munich, Germany. Although it was a lot to ask of me, the lineup of speakers and content was pretty strong, and I was looking forward to gaining knowledge as much as I was to sharing mine.

During the conference, I met the director of operational excellence of a publicly traded company in Europe, who was also a speaker. He was a bright and passionate individual, for sure, and we promised to have a follow-up conversation in a month's time.

When it came time for the follow-up call, this much-learned and passionate individual told me he had lost his job. I was rather shocked and asked what had happened. He told me the company had killed the entire operational excellence program to "cut costs."

And so it goes.

Believe it or not, I see this more often than you might imagine—operational excellence programs being cut or killed to save costs, continuous improvement programs ceasing to be continuous, Lean Six Sigma programs being starved of oxygen. Corporate leadership places incredible (read: *impossible*) demands on the improvement teams to accomplish grand goals with little or no support, and, incredibly, the improvement team leadership accepts these demands under such conditions.

(*Continued . . .*)

In cases like this, I don't place responsibility for the misalignment of program objective expectations and the ability to deliver that on the corporate leadership, however. I am more inclined to place responsibility for the pending doom on the leadership of the improvement teams for not understanding what is being asked of them and what they truly need to accomplish the task. In essence, they are setting themselves up for failure—being held accountable and responsible but without authority—before they even start.

Professionals who work in actual extreme circumstances (such as military personnel and firefighters) spend an extraordinary amount of time being educated on the latest tools and techniques, training on their use, and practicing to hone their skills and proficiencies. In most cases, these professionals will spend in excess of 90 percent of their time preparing before being called on to use their skills. When they are called upon to use these skills, the situations are truly a matter of life and death.

I can safely say there is no company that devotes such time to training their continuous improvement resources. In fact, the reverse is true: They use their skills 90 percent of the time and train 10 percent. But there is a reason for this: The good people in continuous improvement (almost always smart and capable) are busy applying their skills almost constantly and not sporadically, and they never actually have to face a dire, life-or-death situation such as having to fight a burning platform.

Several years ago, I worked with a company delivering a workshop on operational excellence. Over the course of the few days I was there, I watched the management as they tried to manage situations (none of which could be considered an emergency).

They would respond to one "crisis" and, before it was resolved, another appeared. As if on cue, they would abandon the first crisis to engage the second, repeating this pattern of behavior as the third crisis hit, then the fourth crisis, and so on. In the end, none of the crises were resolved, and both the management and their teams were exhausted from the great energies they'd spent.

It is reminiscent of watching young children playing football. There is general disorder on the field until the ball moves—then chaos ensues. The children never stay in their assigned positions; rather, they all chase the ball. Then there is a pause, or a change in possession or direction, and whatever was happening stops when they all move as one into a dense huddle. Nobody scored. And how could you tell if they did? All that is created are bruised egos and scraped knees. Fun times.

If everything is a "burning platform," then nothing is. We become numb.

It is unwise, unfair, and just plain wrong to believe—even for an instant—that your operational excellence team can operate at "fire-fighting" levels all the time and for the foreseeable future. People, like machinery, experience wear and tear and need maintenance. If you try to maintain a high level of intensity in engagement at all times, you are setting them, and your program, up for failure. And if you make the mistake of portraying your company in a permanent state of crisis and you expect your people to engage accordingly, they will help as able, but they will also update their LinkedIn profiles and depart at the first convenient (for them) moment.

In life-threatening situations, it's freeze, fight, or flight.

If you believe your team will fight for you, you are wrong. But your team might fight *with* you. Well, maybe—if they believe in you and in the cause. Just like "The Boy Who Cried Wolf," such a mental and emotional state only serves to dilute the alignment necessary to succeed. And if there is a never-ending series of "burning platforms," people become numb and dismissive.

This is an example of our general tendency toward hyperbole, like the overuse of the words *Nazi* and *Holocaust* or comparing people to Hitler. They are used so often, in such inappropriate contexts, that the true horror of the original atrocities and evil is minimized. To give an example closer to our current context, the European debt crisis has been going on for so many years I have lost count. When does the "crisis" stop being a crisis and just become the new norm?

I believe people work better and with greater enthusiasm *toward* something than they do to *avoid* something. A good leader will know how to get their team aligned to working toward the achievement of a strategy. If the leader cannot achieve alignment, there is something wrong with the strategy, the message, or the leader.

Start with clarity and openness. In my world, I say what I think, and I do as I say. People ask straight questions, and I give them straight answers, and I expect the same when the roles are reversed: good, honest, open, direct, concise dialog.

I don't seem to have issues with motivating people to pursue the mission objectives. I make sure that those objectives are crystal clear and that the team has the necessary support. Each member of the team has the opportunity to acknowledge and accept ownership of their responsibilities or to voice concern.

What's the mission? You have to train your team for the mission and then execute the mission. And you need—

⇨ The right people in the right positions

⇨ The preparedness that consistent and intense training brings

⇨ The commitment of the company in support of the team

⇨ Alignment of resources toward the company's strategies

When it's time to go, we press on in a professional, confident, and businesslike manner—keep calm and carry on. No artificially induced drama is necessary.

Ultimately, if a leader feels they need to instill the fear, drama, or anxiety of a burning platform to get their people motivated to work toward a goal, they probably have the wrong people on the team and changes should be made—starting with the leader.

CHAPTER 8

THE NEED FOR SIX HONEST SERVING MEN

"Question everything."
—Maria Mitchell

"Why?"
—Me

From time to time, I enjoy a good read of one of the classics. There are so many basic life lessons that transcend the ages that can be gleaned from the tales of literary greats such as Dickens, Thoreau, Twain, Hemingway, Homer, and so on—far too many to list here.

I am not a big fan of today's "popcorn literature" that is being taught in schools. It's flavorful for a moment but possesses no substance; it has no real staying power. I have read many of these books, and they come up lacking. In my opinion, they pander to a video game mentality and are focused on delivering instant gratification and messaging, leaving nothing to the imagination.

So I recently picked up a copy of Rudyard Kipling's *Just So*

Stories. It's a book of (very) short stories. One of them is entitled "The Elephant's Child," and at the conclusion, I came across the poem "Six Honest Serving Men," which pays homage to the five Ws (and one H)—a formula for getting the full story.

> *I keep six honest serving-men*
> *(They taught me all I knew);*
> *Their names are What and Why and When*
> *And How and Where and Who.*
> *I send them over land and sea,*
> *I send them east and west;*
> *But after they have worked for me,*
> *I give them all a rest.*
>
> *I let them rest from nine 'til five,*
> *For I am busy then,*
> *As well as breakfast, lunch, and tea,*
> *For they are hungry men.*
> *But different folk have different views.*
> *I know a person small—*
> *She keeps ten million serving-men,*
> *Who get no rest at all!*
>
> *She sends 'em abroad on her own affairs,*
> *From the second she opens her eyes—*
> *One million Hows, two million Wheres,*
> *And seven million Whys!*

I have even seen references to these six honest serving men (usually called the *six wise men*) in various science and technology texts, including on operational excellence and Lean Six

Sigma. However, I have to admit I never really queried the significance or origin much further. So I was rather struck when I read this passage of Kipling's and it caused me to ponder it further.

Even Kipling's statement that he "let[s] them rest from nine 'til five/For I am busy then" goes to the Lean Six Sigma mantra of *Plan, Do, Check,* and *Act* in that he consults with his six honest serving men when he is not working. In other words, when he is not "doing." The time for consulting with these six honest men, the time to ask questions, is when you are planning, checking, and adjusting.

After some contemplation, and I am quite certain I am not the originator of this observation, I have formed the opinion that one of the honest serving men is not quite like the others. His name is Why.

All of the others—Who, What, When, Where, and How— are forensic and factual by their very nature. They are observable and quite specifically identifiable. They can be defined or otherwise determined, and they're objective. However, Why is largely, if not entirely, subjective.

So I think about these six honest serving men and how they are leveraged in an operational excellence initiative and exercise. We spend a lot of time examining and evaluating the specific values for the following types of questions for a given process:

⇨ What are the movements of materials, resources, and information?

⇨ How much time does it take?

⇨ When is the product to be purchased, produced, or delivered?

⇨ How much do the activities cost?

⇨ Who is doing the work, and who is responsible
   for the outcome?

⇨ Where is this activity taking place?

If we gather and assemble the above information, we can establish a fairly complete (if not absolute) value-stream map and can demonstrate with a degree of precision and clarity what the present state of a process is. We can also clearly define what our ideal future state might be and create a plan to migrate from the present state to the future state.

But what about Why?

⇨ Why is it done that way in the first place?

⇨ Why do we want to improve this over something else?

⇨ Why do we need someone from corporate or consultants?

⇨ Why do we have to be in these stupid meetings?

Why is Why so often overlooked or otherwise given such short shrift?

It's because Why is an art more than it is a science. Why is deduced or derived and is often largely intangible. It implies nostalgia, culture, reasoning, and opinion. Why often cannot be easily measured, defined, identified, or even agreed on. Its essence lies mostly in the subjective areas of an evaluation and, as such, is the subject of much argument and debate—activities that are healthy and necessary. Take the following list as an illustration of the relevant questions for a project:

⇨ Who is that person? We need to identify someone—done.

⇨ What is that sound? We can discover the source—done.

⇨ Where is that tool? Here, we locate the item—done.

⇨ When will it next occur? This is easy enough
to determine—done.

⇨ How will that happen? Here, we'd define the implementation path—done.

But Why is different:

⇨ Why do we (or don't we) look at a new way of doing this?
Ummm . . .

When I speak to people at conferences or talk to them about the books they have read, they seem to always gravitate toward the frameworks and the tools and the approaches. They want to understand how it is all done and what makes it all work. But they seem to skim over the Why except in the most elementary terms. Why do we have a continuous improvement program? To cut costs, to reduce inventory, to improve quality, and so on. Each of these is a noble endeavor and of some benefit to some-one, but each is also shallow or single dimensional. However, none of these reasons seemed to be organized in concert with the others, lacking a holistic approach. They do not leverage into one another to become a force-multiplier in pursuit of a greater, unified, goal for the benefit of the enterprise—the entire value-chain, as a whole.

Perhaps evaluating the first five serving men—Who, What, When, Where, and How—is to seek knowledge, to know the details of a process. But evaluating Why leads to understanding, which is deeper than knowledge.

You might ask, "Why is this important?" Good question; I see you are learning.

To know Why is to know the complete story in context. From this position, fully informed decisions can be made with clarity, and decisions should only be made from a position of understanding.

The decisions you make as the leader of an organization will be implemented and made a reality by others—or maybe not. If not, it is most likely because you failed to communicate effectively and because they don't have an understanding of what they are doing and why they are doing it. They don't know what is expected of them, and they don't know what success means. They are untethered. This lack of understanding, the lack of knowing the answers to Why, is the root cause[1] of most failed initiatives (whether they are operational excellence initiatives or others). To communicate effectively, you have to make them understand Why. *Just because* is not enough reason for someone to understand, believe, and follow.

However, if you do effectively communicate, the understanding of the objective and the means will cause those responsible for the pursuit to align and engage. Simply put, in order for those you lead to follow, they have to understand the purpose, the methods, and the goals of your path. For them to perform at their very best, they have to believe and have confidence in it. They have to know Why.

This is why Why is so difficult and also why Why is so important.

And maybe—just maybe—this is the reason Kipling writes, "She sends . . . One million Hows, two million Wheres, *and seven million Whys!*"

But once you know and understand the Why—and you know the How, Who, What, When, and Where—then what? Understanding is not accomplishing. What's next?

CHAPTER 9

DECISIONS, DECISIONS . . .

"A good decision cannot guarantee a good
outcome. All real decisions are made under
uncertainty. A decision is therefore a bet, and
evaluating it as good or not must depend on the
stakes and the odds, not on the outcome."

—Ward Edwards

Every decision we make is based on an analysis of the risk versus the reward. Most entail little or no risk, so the emphasis is placed on the reward. The decision is often between a selection of multiple rewards, and we prioritize our decision based on which decision will deliver the greatest reward with the minimal risk.

We don't spend a lot of time collecting and analyzing data to make most daily decisions. We have years of experience and have become experts in our daily routine, which results in a high degree of confidence in their outcome. So why do we obsess so much over data at work? After all, we are experienced experts at that too, aren't we?

DECISION-MAKING MODELS

All decision-making starts with recognizing that an opportunity or threat exists.

Most decisions are simple binary choices, a selection between two paths: yes or no, on or off. For instance, *Would you like some coffee? Would you like cream in your coffee?* and *Would you like sugar in your coffee?* only have two possible answers. But decisions get more complex when an *or* is introduced—for example, *Would you like coffee, tea, or something else?* This response entails a near-infinite number of variables and permutations, even if considering only the number of possible teas.

When decisions involve a group of people, who usually have different perspectives, priorities, and self-interests, the decision-making process can become overwhelming and can quickly spiral out of control. Therefore, it is imperative that the leader of the group maintains order but not be dictatorial. They should remember that a leader leads; that is what they do. Given the complexity of decision-making, people have created frameworks and models to guide the process to fit various circumstances and conditions and to predict the paths and ultimate outcomes.

There are many decision-making models and many of them are quite complex, but remember: Complexity kills. The more complex something is, the more difficult it is to manage and the more likely it is to become counterproductive and corrupt. Integrity, quality, and speed are the order of the day, so I am going to compare and contrast the three models[1] I believe meet these requirements the best after briefly introducing each.

OODA Loop: Accelerated Decision-Making

John Richard Boyd,[2] a colonel in the United States Air Force, is credited with developing a decision-making model for gaining the advantage during aerial combat based on an iterative four-stage process: Observe, Orient, Decide, and Act. This is the OODA loop (see figure 9.1). The premise and strength behind the OODA loop is the assumption that time is the dominant factor in engagement and decisions need to be made from imperfect data. The pilot who can engage the OODA loop in the shortest amount of time will have the advantage and will likely be victorious, because the opposition will be caught responding to circumstances that have already changed. A critical key to the OODA loop's success as a decision-making method is the loop itself, which acts to guide and refine the decisions in a series of continuously improving outcomes.

The OODA loop's simplicity and elegance in design and its effectiveness in use make it a popular decision-making method. It is especially well suited for decisions based on imperfect data. This is a key accelerant in the decision-making process and is especially advantageous during strategy execution.

In any engagement, speed is an advantage: speed in identifying an opportunity or threat, speed in formulating an action plan, speed in executing the action plan, speed in reacting to the changing dynamics during the execution phase, and speed in deciding to disengage when you are at an irrecoverable disadvantage (and knowing when that is). Paralysis by analysis will almost certainly precipitate a less than stellar result or even doom. Therefore, the key to success in an engagement will be you and your company's execution of the OODA loop quicker than the opposition or, in the case of business, the competition.

And this will require an aggressive regimen of learning, practice, and application of the necessary skills—beyond those of your competitor—which will tilt the odds of success considerably in your favor. To maintain this edge, continual evaluation and revision of our strategies and tactics are crucial as technologies, conditions, capabilities, and circumstances evolve.

Let's examine the stages of the OODA loop in greater detail.

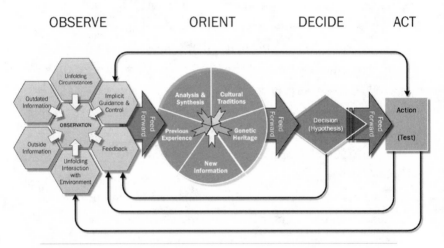

Figure 9.1. Colonel John Boyd's OODA loop.

Stage 1: Observe

The loop begins with observation. You must focus on external parameters and quickly filter what is important from what is not. This is your data collection stage. At this point, all of your senses should be heightened as you seek and absorb and evaluate all manner and forms of data. The more data you can collect, the more accurate your insight will be and the faster it can be absorbed and evaluated. Ask yourself the following questions:

⇨ How might this primordial soup of data affect me?

⇨ What's happening that directly affects me?

⇨ What's happening that indirectly affects me?

⇨ What's happening that may have lingering effects later?

⇨ What circumstances are developing?

⇨ What are the present conditions?

PARALYSIS BY ANALYSIS: WHEN DO YOU HAVE ENOUGH DATA?

Nothing creates confidence better than a fact-based argument, and the more facts to base it on, the better. But how much data needs to be collected? How many times have we seen decisions put off indefinitely as one study after another is commissioned to investigate a subject? We eventually begin to confuse *study with progress* and never reach a go/no-go decision.

Recently, there was a discussion in the Operational Excellence Group on LinkedIn promoting the rule of 200. I had never heard of the rule before, but I guess rules can be made (or at least promoted) by nearly everyone. The article was mainly about hiring people and collecting as much data on the candidate as possible before hiring, but it extrapolated the premise to all decision-making. It spoke of the need to collect at least 200 data samples before making a decision. But it left me wondering, *Why 200? Why not 2,000? Or 20?*

We make decisions when our confidence exceeds our trepidation. The more familiar we are with the subject, the variables, and the resources at

(*Continued . . .*)

our disposal and their capability, the more likely we are to actually make a decision. The purpose of collecting data is to build that confidence within yourself and your team to the point where fear is overcome. Then it is time to make the decision. Besides, how much data needs to be collected and analyzed before an outcome can be guaranteed?

Stage 2: Orient

Orienting is taking what you observe and formulating an approach. You analyze the data collected in the *Observe* stage and focus on your business's internal condition and capabilities to assess your current reality. This is how you interpret a situation in advance of making a decision. Boyd recognized five main influences in transforming data into information:

⇨ Cultural traditions

⇨ Genetic heritage

⇨ The ability to analyze and synthesize

⇨ Previous experience

⇨ New information coming in

The objective here is to increase the velocity and effectiveness of your movement through each successive trip around the OODA loop to arrive at a decision. This process is iterative; as you observe additional information, you will need to evaluate the impact with a balance of speed and accuracy and update your orientation accordingly.

MORE ON CONSIDERING CULTURAL TRADITIONS AND GENETIC HERITAGE

In this age of political correctness, it's necessary to expand on these two aspects of Orient so as to avoid offense. Having traveled the world, I have had the privilege to work in a variety of countries, each with their own nostalgia and unique circumstances. What I find fascinating is that the challenges people and companies face are the same everywhere, but the way they develop and deploy a response to those challenges is based largely on what they have learned from growing up with their family, friends, community, and in school. This is not to say they and their approach are better or worse, just different. If you work with them often enough, the way they think becomes predictable.

But homogeny has its drawbacks. If everyone is thinking the same way and from the same perspective, the opportunities for innovation diminish.

This is one of the reasons I believe companies in the States have an advantage. Their decision-makers come from all over the world and their backgrounds are more varied than in other countries. This means that there are many perspectives and approaches to a challenge that are introduced for discussion. Diversity in your team is a strength and an advantage.

Stage 3: Decide

Next, you must determine a course of action. Always keep in mind that, even if you have all the data in the world, decisions do not guarantee success; they're just best guesses. Success or failure will be based on your capabilities, your experience, and the quality of your observations, orientations, and actions. Decisions are rather dynamic in nature and should be considered fluid works in progress. For every trip around the OODA loop, new data will be transformed into new information, driving new suggestions, creating opportunities to modify your decisions and to drive subsequent actions. Remember that a decision does not require you go with either plan A or plan B; discontinuing the determination is also a valid decision.

Stage 4: Act

The final stage in your trip around the OODA loop will be to execute your decision. Then, you immediately cycle back to the Observe stage after you evaluate the outcome. Making a decision and taking action will have an impact on the data you have observed, which drives the information you've created and influences the decisions you have made. Therefore, the loop perpetuates until the opportunity is fully resolved by either completion or disengagement.

The OODA loop is not like a checklist; rather, it's a smooth, continuous, and dynamic process with an emphasis on training, experience, and wisdom to determine an action. The objective is to move through each stage as quickly as possible while maintaining a high degree of quality—quicker and better than your opponent. Considering this, it should be obvious that to take the time to map out each step and create a sort of standard operating procedure would slow down your progression through the OODA loop. But be cautious when emphasizing speed. Generally speaking, speed results from less data being collected and analyzed, so the information on which decisions are based is less reliable. The key to repeated success is to learn to balance the amount of information required against the speed necessary to maintain an advantage and the consequences of a poor decision.

The objective and strategic advantage of the OODA loop is the increase in velocity of decisions. It also increases speed in subsequent OODA cycles, as new data is collected and new information is formed. If the OODA cycles are performed quickly enough, you can command the tempo and direction of the engagement, force your competition to react to you instead of you reacting to them, and give yourself the clear advantage.

The macro-level decisions that are made quickly from imperfect data by employing the OODA loop precipitate ever-smaller tasks and subtasks—each with their own desired outcomes but all in alignment with and in support of the top-level strategy. As the granularity of the tasks increases, the variants and variables will decrease. The result will be an increase in the volume of data that can be collected and analyzed.

THE OODA LOOP AND HOSHIN KANRI

Hoshin Kanri is a strategy deployment framework contained in the Lean Six Sigma tool kit. Once a corporate strategy is decided on, it is intended to facilitate the creation of a strategy execution roadmap—and communicate and align those involved in the strategy execution to the corporate strategy. Its steps are to (1) create a strategic plan, (2) develop the tactics, (3) take action, and (4) review and adjust.

Hoshin is Japanese for "methodology for setting a strategic direction," and Kanri is Japanese for "administration" or "management." On the surface, Hoshin Kanri looks very similar to the OODA loop in all regards, except that it dives deeper into detailing the implementation

(*Continued . . .*)

plan up front and managing the execution phase to preestablished metrics more intensely.

But where OODA loops depend on shorter decision cycles, quicker engagement, and more simple and concise steps as the engagement unfolds—and thus is suitable where the opportunity time is short and the data incomplete—Hoshin Kanri details the granular aspects of strategy execution and relies on top-down consensus and the careful establishment of KPIs for progress management. It lends itself to the execution of a strategy that has had much more time to develop and is based on the collection and analysis of far more data than would normally be available when using the OODA loop.

THE OODA LOOP AND AGILE

Agile is a method of project development that relies upon smaller, iterative steps than on a master project plan. It assumes that the final outcome is not known in absolute terms at the beginning but will be discovered through the completion of a series of activities that will incrementally progress the development to its conclusion.

In essence, Agile is making decisions from imperfect data with the expectation that the outcomes desired will be achieved as they become more defined with each iteration.

The OODA loop was introduced in the 1950s, and Agile was introduced in the early 2000s. But each favors speed and being nimble over complexity and brawn.

PDCA: Institute a Framework for Action

The PDCA cycle (for *Plan–Do–Check–Act*, aka the *Deming cycle*)[3] represents the four stages you must complete to move from a problem faced to problem solved (see figure 9.2). PDCA is at the heart of the TPS and Lean.

Stage 1: Plan

You must first clearly identify the opportunity, develop the strategy, and evaluate the expected end state of the intended action. Once this is complete, you must develop the tactics for achieving the strategy, including identifying any logistics required for the support of the effort, such as time, money, materials, and talent. The output of the *Plan* phase is a defined end state and a detailed roadmap and bill-of-resources for the engagement and pursuit of the strategy.

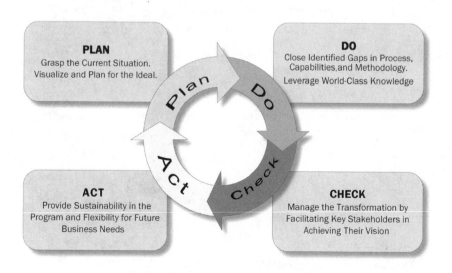

Figure 9.2. Deming Cycle Diagram; Plan, Do, Check, Act (PDCA).

Stage 2: Do

The second stage is *Do*—the actual execution of the plan formulated in the first stage. It is often advantageous to test the plan as an experiment, under controlled conditions, to ensure the expected outcomes are realized and to minimize the risk if they are not. This is especially important if the full implementation of the plan is expected to be very disruptive or otherwise entails a high degree of risk.

Stage 3: Check

In the *Check* stage, you evaluate the results of the plan's implementation to determine your level of success and note any lessons learned from its execution that can be adapted to each subsequent iteration of the plan's execution. Some points to consider include how closely the execution phase adhered to the plan; whether the desired outcome was achieved; what worked and what didn't; and what some of the unexpected injects were, how they were addressed, and what impact they had on the rollout and in the outcome. What would you do differently next time?

Stage 4: Act

The *Act* stage is the last step in the execution of the PDCA cycle before going back to the beginning with an updated thesis. It's when the decision to adopt (to rollout change on a larger scale), adapt (revise), or to abandon the plan is made. If the decision is to adopt or adapt the plan, it is important to standardize, document, and train employees in the new way. Replicating this process on same (or similar) business functions throughout the enterprise can result in a multitude of benefits. In essence, your company is identifying its own best practices.

You will notice the PDCA cycle and the OODA loop appear

to be quite similar. The main difference is that more emphasis is placed on detailed data collection, analysis, and planning using PDCA, whereas the OODA loop emphasizes speed, which is the result of training and experience. Your team will consist of people who have a mix of knowledge, experience, wisdom, confidence, dispositions, strengths, and weaknesses—all to differing capacity and capabilities and in a variety of disciplines. Some will need more convincing before they decide, and some will need less. Accordingly, some will gravitate toward OODA and some will gravitate toward PDCA. Speed and accuracy; it's a good mix.

DMAIC: Create a Structure for Evaluating Success

You will eventually gather enough data for statistical analysis; this is where Six Sigma comes in. The Six Sigma approach is usually represented by the following steps: *Define, Measure, Analyze, Improve, Control* (DMAIC; see figure 9.3).

Figure 9.3. Define, Measure, Analyze, Improve, Control (DMAIC).

Stage 1: Define
The first step is to define the project charter. This is accomplished by creating a high-level view of the process and then drilling into the process to understand the needs (inputs) of the process and its desired results (outputs).

Stage 2: Measure
Next, you must measure the current process and its performance. Decide what data is required to support the hypothesis and resultant decision. Then, determine what data is available, including its source and any determination of its quality and completeness.

Stage 3: Analyze
In the third stage, you analyze the current state of the process and document the findings. Through analysis—both statistical and qualitative—begin to formulate propositions of how to best realize the desired outcome.

Stage 4: Improve
After the analysis is performed, the next step is to improve the performance of the process by selecting an approach based on the analysis, keeping in mind simplicity and elegance are far superior to complexity. Remember, deciding not to act is a valid act itself.

Stage 5: Control
Finally, you must control the improvement process by documenting the present state, the rollout plan, and the expected and actual future states. If the approach is to be replicated, it is important to standardize and update all related documentation associated with the system and its processes; a control plan must be effected to observe ongoing performance.

Because one of the primary foundations of DMAIC is an emphasis on measuring and analyzing—more so than in PDCA and certainly more than in OODA—and its tool kit includes many approaches for crunching data to unlock the wisdom the data might contain, it is best suited for opportunities that have a lot of data.

The Relative Strengths of OODA, PDCA, and DMAIC

If operational excellence is when an organization reaches a state of readiness to quickly engage opportunities in a meaningful, efficient, and effective manner, it stands to reason that no single inception-to-completion engagement framework will adequately satisfy all of the requirements and nuances involved in pursuing these opportunities under all circumstances.

Certainly, there will be many advocates of one framework over another who will make the argument that each framework can be applied to all instances, and perhaps, in absolute terms, this argument might have some validity. But the primary consideration should be which framework is the best to leverage, given the nature of the challenge. A successful outcome—in terms of agility, velocity, quality, efficiency, and effectiveness—will be the result of using the proper framework for the nature of the particular opportunity at hand.

The OODA loop's strength is in its ability to draw on training, experience, and observation to rapidly synthesize an action from an incomplete data set but with the highest probability for success. Because the emphasis is on speed, the framework does not require all potential variables to be evaluated. The heart of the OODA loop is rapidity and agility under complex and often mysterious conditions. It allows numerous adjustments in real time, continually addressing unpredictable events that surface during execution.

The PDCA cycle's strength over the OODA loop is its granular analytical nature. Because the PDCA cycle involves a hypothesis, the collection and analysis of data, and the testing of the hypothesis before a commitment to a full rollout of a decision, the speed and effort involved from inception to completion are far greater than in the OODA loop. However, the more structured (less gut instinct and more cerebral analysis) framework in the PDCA cycle allows for scalability of the team.

DMAIC's strength is control—specifically, control over the process of change. This control is established by the collection of data and a heavy reliance on the statistical analysis of this data in formulating hypotheses, carrying out decisions, and measuring effectiveness. Because of this reliance on data, the amount collected is normally far more voluminous than required in the PDCA cycle or the OODA loop. It therefore stands to reason that DMAIC is less suitable for evaluating entire systems and more suitable for evaluating the processes within the system, especially less-chaotic processes without variants. The rather obvious weakness of DMAIC is its inability to easily be applied to processes that involve decision points (variants).

Visualize taking a trip in an automobile. You decide on a destination (using OODA to make the one-off decision), you take a series of turns (using PDCA to manage, refine, and replicate managed events), and you monitor the performance of the engine (using DMAIC to evaluate the millions of actions involved in evaluating mph, rpms, mpg, and so forth).

OODA loops are primarily appropriate for strategic decision-making when speed is important and you are using all

Chart Comparing OODA, PDCA, and DMAIC

OODA Strategic Decision-Making Strategic	PDCA System-Level Change Tactical	DMAIC Process-Level Change Logistical
Observe Unfolding circumstances Implicit guidance and control Outside information Unfolding interaction	**Plan** Identify opportunity Determine future state Assess present state Create plan Identify resources Create budget Decide go/no-go	**Define** Identify opportunity
Orient Culture and traditions Genetic heritage Previous experience New information Analysis and synthesis		**Measure** Select quality standards Define performance standards Validate measurement system
Decide Identify opportunity Go/no-go		**Analyze** Establish capability Define objectives Identify variants and sources
Act Execute plan	**Do** Execute plan Collect data	**Implove** Determine potential causes Evaluate variable relationships Establish operational tolerance
	Check Evaluate results Make updates	**Control** Validate measurement system Determine process capabilities Implement process control
	Act Update plan based on results Replicate and roll out	

available analytical data, supplemented by natural capability and experience, with the caveat of incomplete data. The PDCA cycle is most suitable for change management and optimization at the system level, where a system-wide evaluation, complete with variants, is the expectation. And DMAIC is most appropriate for effecting optimizations and standardizations at the process level, where there is a volume of data with a minimum of variants. Presented this way, it is easy to appreciate how each of these frameworks can be leveraged to great effect in a complementary, rather than competing, manner.

HOW IT ALL WORKS TOGETHER

Strategic elements are associated primarily with policy goals and are oriented toward external, real-time circumstances—the natural purview of the OODA loop. Because there will never be enough data to make the perfect decision, it must be synthesized using incomplete data. Circumstances beyond the control of the enterprise (perhaps even beyond predictability) will cause changes to the environment in which the enterprise operates, necessitating a rapid response.

The tactical elements involve planning (concepts, approach, and methods). This is ideal for the PDCA cycle. This tactical level will leverage the methodologies and tools necessary to evaluate and resolve opportunities and threats, including many of the common approaches associated with Lean to keep the PDCA cycle rolling, such as kaizen events, value-stream mapping, control charts, and root-cause analysis.

The logistical elements involve significant amounts of transactional information associated with business process activities (data) and the relationships between and among them. This is perfect for DMAIC. This logistical level will rely heavily on the techniques (such as the design of experiments and statistical process control) and tools used to analyze the data. You then use charts and graphs, such as Pareto and scatter charts and histograms, so that data can be interpreted by people.

Accordingly, the OODA loop is the most capable approach to ensure the enterprise is nimble and responsive to navigate the enterprise through the complex, enigmatic, and nonlinear business environment. The PDCA cycle creates the structure through which the strategies of the business might be realized and might allow for scalability. And DMAIC optimizes the individual business processes for efficiency and effectiveness.

If we look at the executive leadership of the enterprise, generally speaking, the CEO is responsible for strategy, the COO is responsible for tactics and logistics, and the CFO is responsible for maintaining the financial health (even viability) of the enterprise as an entity. This tight group (and select second-level individuals) would constitute the leadership team who would exercise the OODA loop before spinning off the action items to others to be governed by the PDCA cycle and DMAIC, as appropriate, using all of the various tools and techniques available so they can compress the time to deliver and ensure alignment across the strategic, tactical, and logistical levels (see figure 9.4).

Accelerated Strategy Execution: Case Studies

Using OODA, PDCA, and DMAIC together should be the norm in the operation of your business, rather than the exception. Your level of success will depend on how proficiently you execute the OODA in the C-suite and PDCA and DMAIC

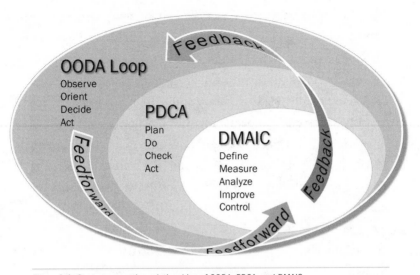

Figure 9.4. Strategy execution relationships of OODA, PDCA, and DMAIC.

during the execution phases. Not many businesses execute all approaches to a level that would be consistent with a high-performance organization.

Execution proficiency, the rapidity with which a company executes OODA, is heavily influenced by the culture of the country in which the company's world headquarters is located. Companies located in countries that have a culture of punishing failure are more likely to be reserved in the rapidity of their decision-making. The company culture (e.g., are they accustomed to making quick decisions from imperfect data?) also affects proficiency.

The usual disconnect can be found between strategy formulation in the C-suite and strategy execution, which occurs in operations across the enterprise. The challenge is ensuring constant alignment with the ever-evolving strategies of the company. This is the performance gap where the opportunities for excellence exist.

THE CASE OF FACEBOOK AND INSTAGRAM

The acquisition of Instagram by Facebook in April of 2012 is an example of accelerated strategy execution. The value of the deal was significant—$1 billion in a combination of cash ($300 million) and shares in Facebook (valued at $700 million at the time of the announcement). But the timing of the deal and the speed of the decision to do the deal were striking; they were both somewhat controversial when they were first reported.

→ **OODA.** The timing of the deal was controversial because Facebook was in the process of launching its Initial Public Offering (IPO). Such a significant deal, without the burden of the more strict oversight that comes with being a publicly traded company, was bold indeed. But it was obvious that Mark Zuckerberg, cofounder and CEO of Facebook, believed there was no perfect time to do a deal; when it's time, it's time. Zuckerberg's decision to purchase Instagram and Instagram's Kevin Systrom's decision to sell to Facebook occurred in one day. The round figure and the fact that the deal was financed mostly in stock rather than cash demonstrates the macro-level nature of the discussions.

→ **PDCA.** But making the decision was just the very beginning of the deal-making process. What came next was the harder work of due diligence. This is when the deal facilitators get involved to ensure what each company looks like prima facie matches reality. And since the deal relied so heavily on the value of Facebook shares, the due diligence had to be bidirectional, with equal intensity. All of these tasks are projects. They have objectives. They require resources. And they will take time to complete (but the less time, the better). Within each of these

(Continued . . .)

projects, there are systems that have to be evaluated for efficiency and opportunities to eliminate waste, but there is no real statistical analysis to be performed. What was most important was the speed with which these systems could be integrated into the combined company. The participants had to define their desired outcomes and determine a course of action (Plan). They had to execute the plan to accomplish the necessary tasks (Do). They had to test and validate that their approach achieved the desired outcome (Check). Finally, they had to establish these end states as the new standards (Act).

→ **DMAIC.** There were, however, many aspects of the business that were highly transactional and would best lend themselves to statistical analysis for further evaluation. Such aspects focused on Instagram's user base and included its growth rate, engagement, geographical penetration, demographic analysis, relationship networks, and all the many other ways the users engaged the environment. Afterward, they were able to model how users might engage in the merged environment (including what redundant features might be removed or combined) and explored opportunities for revenue based on touch points of user engagement (high volume, low cost).

In September of 2012, the deal was complete. The only substantive change from the initial deal to its completion was the value of shares in Facebook, which had dropped significantly, making the deal worth about $736 million instead of $1 billion.

The End of the Beginning

Making a decision is not realizing success; it is only the end of the beginning. Success is realized in the act of engaging the decision and realizing the objective. As such, success is entirely dependent on those responsible for the pursuit of the decision rather than the decision itself.

The Marine Corp speaks to the *seventy percent solution*: If you have a plan with a seventy percent chance of success, execute the plan with great vigor. There is no perfect plan or perfect time. Let's face it, decisions are imperfect and always will be. The best that can be expected is that our decisions are sound.

The best decisions are not made in a vacuum. So if you are going to be successful in your decision-making, it is imperative to surround yourself with the wisest people you can, those whose experience and expertise is relevant and whom you can trust to be open and honest with you. Of course, this means you need to be capable of hearing the truth, even if you don't like what you hear. And you need to do your part by offering the best support, training, and outfitting possible, so when the call comes, your team is able to succeed.

And remember, it is easy to be seduced by data. It gives but asks nothing in return. If examined in its most pure form, data never tells the complete story. There is always some nuance, some circumstance, something beyond the obvious, something subjective, that is necessary to complete the story. How can performances by two actors reading the same lines have such different impacts? How can a team that is statistically superior to another lose? Why is one production run on a line by one team superior (or inferior) to the production run on the same line by another team? Why are Sherpas all from Nepal? Or the best stock-car racers from the southern states? Or so many professional baseball players from the Dominican Republic or Cuba?

CHAPTER 10

CULTURE AND CUSTOMS MATTER

"No man ever looks at the world with pristine eyes.
He sees it edited by a definite set of customs and
institutions and ways of thinking."

—Ruth Benedict

My father, who was a manager at IBM, once shared some wisdom with me: "If it were not for the 'people problems,' management would be easy." In the world of management and management consulting, truer words were never spoken. This is the challenge with most consulting engagements, especially when the words *transformational change* are uttered.

From my experience, the primary reasons for such challenges and conflicts with respect to people working together effectively and harmoniously are twofold—namely, empathy and cultural differences.

EMPATHY

Empathy is the capacity to understand or vicariously experience the circumstances of others. As a general rule,[1] men want to fix problems, whereas women oftentimes just want to express their thoughts and feelings without the need to have something fixed. Men tend to live in a black-and-white world and are more likely to think linearly and simply, whereas women tend to think in a more nuanced fashion, with many shades of gray—certainly more than fifty.

Deborah Tannen, an American academic and professor of linguistics at Georgetown University in Washington, DC, and author of *You Just Don't Understand*, believes men and women differ in the focus of, or driving force behind, their communication. According to Tannen, men communicate to achieve social status and to avoid failure, whereas women communicate to achieve a personal connection and to avoid being socially isolated. She wrote, "Men want to report; women want rapport."

CULTURAL DIFFERENCES

People come from different backgrounds and circumstances, have had different life experiences, and have different lifestyles and priorities; enormous differences can stand between cooperation and progress. The challenge is to set a course that works within your organization's culture and aligns with your goals.

In a nutshell, American businesses are an impetuous lot—not spending nearly as much time on making decisions and taking action as their European or Asian counterparts. European and Asian businesses, on the other hand, tend to be ultraconservative, spending an inordinate amount of time (to an American) studying and analyzing virtually everything, from every angle, until progress seems to move at a glacial pace.

Over the past several years, I formed three companies in the United States, all *Limited Liability Companies* (LLC), and three in the European Union—one in United Kingdom, a *Limited Company* (Ltd); one in Germany, a *Gesellschaft mit beschränkter Haftung* (GmbH); and one in Poland, a *Spółka z ograniczoną odpowiedzialnością* (Sp. z o. o.).

Each type of company, regardless of the country or designation, achieves the same end: the creation of a legal entity that is allowed to conduct business and where the limit of the owner's liability is the amount invested in the entity. This effectively shields the owner's personal assets outside the business in all but the most extreme circumstances of criminal fraud. But in reality, there are a great many loopholes for the European Union (EU) companies that allow breaches of this supposed firewall, placing the owner's assets at risk.

Besides the differences in ownership risk, the American LLCs each took just a few hours to create, including obtaining of all required federal and state tax numbers. The UK Limited Company took almost a week to create (not bad, but not great). However, the German and Polish companies each took nearly three months to create, and the Polish company was a "shelf company," which was intended to speed the process. In addition, the German GmbH requires €25,000 in equity be deposited in a bank account and acts like a bond—not to be spent or invested in anything in case of a liquidation event.

In the EU, the formation of a company is followed by an ongoing river of red tape, forms, regulations, and other formalities, all of which serve to distract a business from its purpose—to do business. But to the EU's credit, there are slow-moving efforts to reduce the bureaucracy, and to the EU's benefit, the United States has quicker-moving efforts to increase bureaucracy.

When I mention this to a German businessman, he insists, "The German Entity type must be far superior to the American." Sorry to say, this simply is untrue. Just because something requires much more effort does not mean the results must be better.

But even more paralyzing and stifling in Europe is the thought of making a mistake, not to mention outright failure, in business decision-making. For instance, I met with an executive responsible for operational excellence at a large German multinational. During this meeting, I talked about the critical need for a debrief—a necessary exercise in self- and mutual analysis and a critique where opportunities for improvement can come to light and where team confidence is built.

His response was alarming, and I will never forget it. He said, "A German in a German company will never admit they made a mistake."

Hmmm. . . .

Contrast this with the nearly cavalier approach to business decision-making in the States. Certainly, there is contemplation before a decision is made, but leaders don't dwell on the negative possibilities as much as they focus on the positive.

For instance, how many times has Facebook, under Mark Zuckerberg, made a mistake in privacy policy? And almost always, his response has been, "Oops. I don't understand the issue, but I hear what you are saying and will take corrective action. My bad." Afterward, he moves on and doesn't give it a second thought.

Europeans have a long history of tribalism and violence, which occurred as one tribe fought another over resources or some grievance or disagreement. Because of this, the populous and their inhabitants clustered together to provide a common defense, often within walled cities. In such communities, the success or failure depended on each of the inhabitants following strict rules of cohabitation or else placing their very existence at risk. This nostalgia and resultant individual and societal behavior eventually became an inherent part of the culture.

Those who made the decision to leave Europe, destined to eventually become Americans, were "defective" to this social order. Having left the security of their European enclaves, they had to practice self-reliance for their very survival. This heightened awareness of personal risk, and lack of a support network became a core tenet of their new culture. Without supporting infrastructure and social network, making mistakes and experiencing failure became routine and how these failings were overcome was a source of romantic storytelling and even pride. Even the most iconic of American symbols is the cowboy—all alone, with just his horse, living off the land and relying on his wits. This image plays out today in the form of entrepreneurs (ironically, a word of French origin) and the guy riding his "hog" (Harley-Davidson motorcycle) on the open road.

Ultimately, the difference in how failure is perceived between an American and a European manifests in the decision to start a business and how a business is run afterward.

In America, if you own a business and it fails, it's almost considered a rite of passage. A person whose business has failed is usually considered wiser, more mature, and better capable to recognize risk factors in the future. This is a driving entrepreneurial force, perhaps even a requisite, in Silicon Valley with its many fast-moving tech start-ups.

Consider the case of General Motors (GM), whose entry and exit through the bankruptcy courts took just one month (entering into bankruptcy in June of 2009 and emerging in July of 2009). Afterward, and within fourteen months, GM then became a publicly traded company again, all seemingly forgiven.

Compare that with what might be expected in Europe.

The Economist published a great article entitled "European Entrepreneurs: Les Misérables" in June of 2012. It detailed the challenges European start-ups have, from initial funding to labor laws to second- and third-level funding.

But what struck me most was the incredible risk of failure an entrepreneur must accept. This risk goes far beyond capital loss. The risk is an enduring punishment of being considered a failure, unfit morally or intellectually of ever being in a position of responsibility again.

According to the article, "Many aspiring entrepreneurs simply leave. There are about 50,000 Germans in Silicon Valley and an estimated 500 start-ups in the San Francisco Bay area with French founders. One of the things they find there is a freedom to fail."

For instance, in France, if your business fails, it can take up to nine years to start anew. At six years, Germany is not much better. And in every case, a person might even be barred of starting a business again—for life. It is a small wonder entrepreneurs in Europe, whose ambitions are grand, are reluctant to start businesses. It also explains why many immigrate to the States, where the access to capital is easier, the personal risk is so much less, and the rewards can be a magnitude greater.

My family and I moved to Germany from Upstate New York several years ago. Although we had been visiting friends and family there for years, and we thought we had it all sorted out, we didn't. In speaking with a new German acquaintance, I mentioned the difficulties we were experiencing in getting many things done. I made the comment, "I guess we didn't think things through enough."

His response was, "Typical American."

Cultural differences can be overcome and progress can be made, provided we all take a moment to try to understand why people do the things they do, what is important to them, their history, and common ground to build a new future. We have to understand that the pleasures and pains of past generations, and even our own personal past, define who we are.

Given that these differences exist and they always will, how do we learn to see and appreciate the perspective of others—their opinions and ideas? How do we persuade those who hold an opinion or idea different than ours to embrace (or at least tolerate) ours? Or, how do we learn to be open enough to accept those of others? Is there an opportunity for empathy, understanding, and compromise? Or do we dig in?

CHAPTER 11

THE ART OF PERSUASION

"It is better to debate a question without settling it
than to settle a question without debating it."

—Joseph Joubert

For change in a company to occur, you need to effect change in
the people within the company. You need to get them to abandon what *is* for what *will be*. And to accomplish this mighty
task, you need to be a skillful communicator, especially in the
art of debate.

Undoubtedly, debate is hazardous duty. A primary expectation should be that it seldom ends in agreement. Rather, debate
forms the framework for a vigorous examination of the question
at hand. We enter into a debate thinking that we will offer them
facts to prove we are correct and that, logically, they will embrace
the same conclusions we have determined. But we all know this
is not how it works. When is the last time someone changed
your mind? I am not referring to the last time someone helped
you to form a belief but when they actually caused you to abandon your belief and embrace theirs.

Debating should not be confused with quarrelling, which is when the logic and pragmatism of the debate is eroded by the introduction of emotion (think Spock versus McCoy in *Star Trek*) until it ultimately degenerates to a shouting match, and perhaps fisticuffs—to the point of abandoning the Marquess of Queensberry Rules.[1]

But a proper debate needn't involve shouting, fistfights, or imposing your will on someone. A good debate shouldn't involve a heightened emotional state at all. Such confrontation is rarely beneficial to anyone and almost always leads to personal attacks. If you win, you are the bully, and if you lose, you have been bullied. As a general rule, a good debate is healthy. Quarrelling is not, and this gives us the primary rule of debate:

RULE 1: WHOEVER LOSES THEIR TEMPER OR MAKES IT PERSONAL FIRST LOSES

Never, ever, forget this rule. Always keep your temper, but don't cause your debate partner to lose theirs either. And never, ever—under any circumstances—make the argument personal. In either case, you will lose the argument, cause damage to your personal and professional reputation, and perhaps forever lose the respect of a colleague or even a friendship.

This is rule 1 because it's more important than the others, but none of the other rules really rank as more or less important. They are all equally important, so they are listed without numbers.

BE PREPARED

Not only is this the motto of the Boy Scouts of America, but it is also critical for a successful debate. Make sure you are prepared. Whatever you do, never engage in a surprise debate. Doing so will mean you're operating in a state of conflict, and you are likely to lose. The first thing that needs to be done for a good debate is to agree to a time and place for having it (often the debate before the debate).

Then, begin preparing for the debate. Make sure you know what you want to get out of the engagement. How do you know if you have won? Do you want the other person to understand your point of view, or do you want to convince them to do something and realize some tangible result? Ensure you know the essential points you want to make, organize your thoughts, and look for critical weaknesses in theirs and how you might respond. Research the facts; nothing will kill your position quicker than inaccurate information.

KNOW WHEN TO DISENGAGE

If the debate becomes emotional, have the inner discipline to call a time-out. If you don't disengage, the debate will enter a death spiral, degenerate into a quarrel, and nothing good will come of it; in fact, considerable damage to the relationship might occur. Always attack the issues and arguments, never one another, and remember rule 1.

LISTEN INTENTLY AND RESPECTFULLY

I often tell people, "God gave you two ears and one mouth. There-fore, you should listen twice as much as you talk." When people feel strongly about something, it's important to hear them out.

Listen very carefully to what the other person is saying and how they are saying it. What is the tone and inflection of their voice? Is this an argument where there is no opportunity for compromise? Is there some hint of doubt or other weakness where the grounds for compromise might be found? Are they saying what they mean to say, or are they shielding their true thoughts?

Respectful listening requires recognizing their feelings. Whatever you do, don't tell the other person how they should feel. Be empathetic. Save sharing your point of view until the other person is satisfied you appreciate their perspective, even if you don't quite get it.

LEARN HOW TO EXCEL AT DELIVERING AN ARGUMENT

What is your end goal? Will what you are about to say (con-tent and structure) and your manner of saying it (tone and body language) help you progress toward that end goal? If not, reconstruct or strip it out of the debate. Make your argu-ments clear and concise—less is more. Use easily understood language, and don't rush the delivery. Be very deliberate and clear. Stay away from absolutes such as *never* and *always*, and keep pronouns (e.g., *it*, *them*, *he*, *she*, *they*) to a minimum to diminish confusion.

If at all possible, anticipate the arguments that might be presented by the other side and present your position first. Not only will this steal the wind from their sails, but it will ensure you maintain control of the narrative. But be very careful and selective; do too much of this, and you will come across as arrogant and aloof. Keep it simple and clear.

Remember, the goal is not to beat the other person into accepting your position but to gain their respect and appreciation for your position (and vice versa) so a common path forward can be crafted. What type of arguments will your opponent have empathy for and find convincing? Which ones will be the "third-rail" and just incur needless, counter-productive emotion? Focus on the former and avoid the latter.

Don't be defensive. Defending *yourself* injects emotion into the debate and risks escalating the intensity of the fight (remember rule 1). Defending *your arguments* with facts is appropriate if done in a noncombative manner. An effective approach is curiosity: Ask for additional information, points of reference, details, and examples. Meet and challenge with curiosity, and you open the door for understanding, which can lead to compromise and resolution.

And, finally, always speak softly but confidently. The louder someone speaks (or, worse, shouts), the less likely they are to be heard. So don't speak in a hostile tone even if your opposition does (again, remember rule 1). Keeping it civil, even if only one of the parties is doing so, makes it possible to focus on the issues instead of reacting to the rhetoric.

BE VIGILANT AGAINST RUSES AND OTHER DISTRACTIONS

Often referred to as *logical fallacies*, if your opponent is ill prepared or they realize their arguments are weak and they are losing the debate, they might attempt to deflect or otherwise alter the course of the discussion by changing topics in hopes of baiting you and steering you sideways. So always be alert for diversion tactics such as personal attacks, concealed questions, and false choices.

A LIST OF LOGICAL FALLACIES

→ The *loaded question* is a variation of the psychological game "Now I got you, you son-of-a-bitch" and is an easy trap to set and a difficult one to avoid. Its simplicity is its beauty, and, once tripped, it is very difficult to work out of. It tends to spiral, because each attempt at defending can actually precipitate a series of other loaded questions.

→ The *straw man* argument is a common form of counterargument based on a false representation of the opponent's argument. Although it is usually not effective on the person delivering the original argument, it could be very effective on an ignorant or inadequately informed audience.

→ The *slippery slope* is also a common form of counterargument. It holds that, if some action were to occur, it would become a primary reason for some undesirable later action, with the natural conclusion being that the original action should not occur.

→ **The *false cause*** is most often used to relate two points whose relationship is either weak or totally nonexistent. When this fallacy is played, some event first occurred, then some second event occurred, and the person making the argument will claim the second event occurred as a result of the first.

→ **The *gambler's fallacy*** derives its name from games of chance. Its false premise is that past results will influence a future event even though the two are entirely unrelated.

→ ***Ad hominem*** is probably the weakest form of argument, because it attacks an individual and not the facts. It will most certainly mean the person who made the personal attack will lose the argument and the debate, even if their argument is otherwise correct. The individual who made the personal attack loses credibility, which reduces the value of even their credible arguments.

→ ***Tu quoque*** attempts to deflect an argument by claiming the opposition's argument is hypocritical. For instance, a parent might have learned a lesson by doing something stupid in the past and will try to coach their child to not do the same thing. But the child might counter, "Why can't I do it? You did!"

→ **The *bandwagon*** is a difficult argument to overcome. Its power is in the mass of people who believe one thing while fewer believe in something else, even if the smaller group has facts and science on their side. Usually, the facts win, but only over time.

(Continued . . .)

→ **Special pleading** is often used by those of privilege or elitists and involves claiming an allowance or exception without basis for the exception.

→ An **appeal to authority** is a superficial yet pervasive persuasion technique we often see in commercials and advertisements, especially in social media. It assumes a speaker is an authority on some topic, so whatever they say must be true.

→ An **appeal to emotion** is an attempt to partner with the opponent in an effort to get them to agree with your argument or ambition, to emotionally connect with them to gain their support rather than actually convincing them.

→ **Burden of proof** is a passive-aggressive counterargument in which the onus is placed on the attacker by the defender to win the argument by proving the defender wrong. In most cases, the defender knows their position is strong because there is a lack of solid proof to discredit the argument.

→ **Arguing from fallacy**, also called *arguing from ignorance*, is a form of argument that plays what can't be proved (or adequately proved to the opponent) as proof that the opposite is true. A classic argument from fallacy is "You cannot prove God exists, therefore God does not exist."

→ **Personal incredulity** plays on one's ego: You don't believe something is true simply because you "can't believe" it to be true. It's often merely a denial of something shocking, but it can also be a form of passive-aggressiveness if used to maintain the status quo.

→ **Ambiguity** is a smokescreen argument used when you don't want to commit, but you also don't want to concede the point.

→ **Composition or division** extrapolates the analysis of a subset and applies the findings to the entirety of the set.

→ **Black-or-white** (or the *false choice*) is most often used by propagandists and those who want to cause divisions and leverage extreme (and often unrelated) views.

→ **Begging the question** is a circular form of argument where the justification or proof of the validity of the argument is included in its premise. It is a rather incoherent argument and is falsely strong because it is circular. To counter, you can't attack the premise or the proof; rather, you have to attack the circular structure.

→ **The *Anecdotal argument*** is an extreme form of composition or division that is based on either personal experience or an isolated (perhaps even extreme or unproved) example.

→ **An *appeal to nature*** is an argument that is based on the false pretense that everything in nature is good and inherently acceptable. And furthermore, if something is not from nature, it must be not good or acceptable.

→ **The *Texas sharpshooter*** proposes that an outlier vignette of data is somehow proof positive of the argument's validity. But as Mark Twain famously said, "There are lies, damned lies, and statistics."

(*Continued . . .*)

→ **No true Scotsman** is more of a follow-on argument. It is used to quantify a previous argument and gets its name from an anecdote. The purpose of this argument is to cast doubt on the purity of the nature of the rebuttal.

→ A **genetic argument** judges and dismisses something based on the origin of a person or product. The rather obvious coun- terargument to the genetic argument is to cite enough excep- tions that it is discredited.

→ **Middle ground** is a form of argument that seeks a compromise and is usually invoked by the party with the weaker position. Although compromise is almost always a reasonable goal, it is not always appropriate, attainable, or practical. For instance, a half-truth is still a lie.

THE ENDGAME

If you wish to win the debate, make sure to engage in the debate for which you prepared; guard against topic drift and false argu- ments. Remember, the objective of the debate is not to beat the other person into submitting to your beliefs (they never will) but to gain a mutual respect and craft a way forward together. In fact, a successful conclusion of the debate might be one in which everyone goes away neither completely satisfied nor completely dissatisfied.

If a debate is going nowhere, it's time to change perspective or to get creative. Are there ways of increasing the pressure on the opponent so they adjust their position? Is a compromise possible?

Points of agreement can almost always be found in specific aspects of a conflict. Finding and leveraging this commonality is an important start to forging a solution. Don't be afraid to pause the debate, but only as a tactic for progress—not delay.

The fighting ends when the cooperation starts. Asking for ideas or another possibility encourages collaboration. The careful contemplation of alternatives demonstrates respect. And suggesting alternatives of your own demonstrates you are also willing to compromise. So don't be afraid to make concessions; perhaps you should even be the first to do so. Even the smallest of concessions can cause an opponent to consider concessions of their own. These small initial compromises build trust and will most likely lead to larger ones on both sides. And the compromise doesn't necessarily mean you're always meeting each other exactly halfway; each side should feel that there is balance. In the end, it's not about keeping score; it's about engineering a workable outcome.

CHANGING A BELIEF IS NEAR IMPOSSIBLE

I was in Monterrey, Mexico, a couple of years ago to give a keynote address at an Industrial Congress where the subject was about culture change. The evening before I delivered my keynote, the United States National Soccer Team had beat the Mexican National Soccer Team. And there was, in black and white, the undisputed fact that the team from the United States was superior to the team from Mexico. Yet, as if to illuminate the point in its most stark reality, I was unable to convince anybody in the audience the team from the United States was, in fact, the better team.

MAINTAIN CIVILITY, PRESERVE RELATIONSHIPS

Maintaining civility is the key to success. Even if you don't reach commonality (this time), there will be enough mutual respect built that your next debate is not soured before it begins. Remember, each of us has to move forward, to live to debate another day.

If your desired result is to win at all costs—to aggravate, embarrass, and humiliate your opponent—you might win the battle, but you will lose the war. Remember, your and your opponent's paths will cross again (maybe even later the same day). Each of you has your own personal and professional networks, and theirs may conspire against you if they see you as a bully. You will regret your aggressions eventually, perhaps sooner rather than later. So at the end of the debate—win, lose, or draw—make peace.

Debates and the individual arguments within them—and, for that matter, discussions and conversations in general—should be about having the ability and willingness to see things through the eyes of another, to be empathetic, and to jointly build on the common ground so we might successfully chase our individual and collective aspirations. This means the "game" of debating is always more important than any individual outcome.

Of course, sometimes we don't want to debate. We would rather avoid the conflict. But avoidance does not make the challenge evaporate. In fact, avoiding a debate can actually make the challenge more acute by not engaging in a meaningful manner early on and allowing time for the conflict to escalate. And when the deferred debate is finally engaged, it often involves emotion, because the threat associated with the challenge has been allowed to grow.

In a community, it is not enough to know that you are the expert or leader and to expect others to follow. You have to *convince* them that you are an expert or a leader. This is usually accomplished by building a case for your decisions and by being able to articulate your case so others accept it.

In the end, one of the single most important endeavors you will undertake in your efforts to progress a company from its present state to its future state will be to engage the people and get them to embrace your vision, and this will require mastery of the skills of debate and argument. Although not a guarantee, gaining the support of others will increase your likelihood of success. You will certainly fail without it. Therefore, it's imperative to have a crystal-clear understanding of what needs to be done by whom and why and to be able to articulate your ideas in a succinct and persuasive manner so others will decide to share your vision, become aligned to the vision, and work with you to realize that vision.

Just remember, after there is a conflict, you cannot go back to the way it was before. Your new starting position is where you ended up after the conflict. So, embrace the conflict; there is no need to dread it. Conflict is a normal state of being and is healthy if engaged properly. The differences you have with others are occasions to learn. And the conflict and debate will often illuminate opportunities for change and personal growth.

PART 3

PREPARING FOR CHANGE

"Do the difficult things while they are easy and do the great things while they are small. A journey of a thousand miles must begin with a single step."

—Lao Tzu

Change and what it truly means to change causes a large mix of emotions in people. To those wanting change, it evokes feelings of excitement and enthusiasm, only to be followed by frustration when the change is met with mighty resistance. And to those not wanting change, it evokes feelings of anxiety and fear, only to be followed by frustration when the change causes disruption and results in resistance.

I am reminded of an anecdote. A man and woman get married. The man hopes she will never change and the woman believes she can change him. They both end up disappointed.

Who we are is the cumulative result of our past: the influence of our upbringing, the people around us, our cultures and traditions, and our experiences. In the abstract, all of these elements conspire to shape us into becoming who we are, as we are, today. Though we might be uncomfortable at times and are often faced with having to endure mighty struggles, we are loathe to change, even if we recognize the possibility might improve our circumstances.

The same is true of companies.

Any specific company exists as it does today as a direct result of its history, traced right down to its moment of being founded. And what the company will be in the future depends heavily on its history. It is a solid line with little variation, just step evolutionary changes—unless . . .

Unless the change is not evolutionary but revolutionary, caused by the introduction of some external happening that challenges the company to its very core and for its very survival. Every company will face this Waterloo moment at least once, and, should it survive, then it will face another one someday.

How organized and ready the company is to see the challenge early—and its level of preparedness to engage—will determine its future.

CHAPTER 12

ASSESSMENTS: THE RALLY POINT OF THE JOURNEY

"Your present circumstances don't determine where
you can go; they merely determine where you start."

—Nido Qubein

So, you are thinking about embarking—or, more than likely, *reembarking*—on an operational excellence journey at your company. But where do you start? At the beginning, of course. You have to take that first, lonely step.

But what has to happen before you take that first step?

Preparing for your operational excellence journey starts with defining your destination (your vision, your future state), but equally important is understanding where you are (your present state). You can't start your journey without knowing the starting point and ending point, which need to be defined up front.

Then, you need preparation—and lots of it: How are you going to get there? What's the plan? What are the waypoints so we can measure progress against the plan? This is going to be a long journey, not a day trip. What talents, skills, provisions, assets, and amounts of cash and time might you need on the journey, and when are you going to need it?

Do you think Edmund Hillary woke up one morning, decided he was going to be the first person to scale Mount Everest, and by the end of the afternoon, he was on top of the world? Of course not. You need to know both where you are and where your destination is so you can connect the two with a path. After all, if you don't know where you are, a map won't help you. Then, you need to know the strategy of your climb and what provisions to take, and you may even need a Sherpa—your personal Tenzing Norgay.

Having a vision of your destination, knowing where you are, having organized what is necessary to get you from where you are to where you want to be, and having the capability to be successful should all be determined and validated before you take that first step.

Assuming a defined strategy for the operational excellence journey exists—and this is no small assumption, since most companies I have visited have not done a good enough job of crystalizing their objectives and detailing what success will look like—the process of planning for the journey starts with an assessment. In its most simple form, an assessment is an evaluation of the present state of something. In school, students are assessed as to their position and the progress of their education by a series of tests that evaluate their knowledge of a subject and their readiness to proceed with the material. In an operational excellence assessment, this evaluation determines where an organization is with respect to its intended destination and its state of readiness to progress forward.

Companies can initiate an operational excellence assessment in one of three ways: internally (a self-assessment), externally, or a hybrid approach.

INTERNAL SELF-ASSESSMENT

An internal assessment is performed by using resources owned by the organization, perhaps through obtaining and leveraging external assessment tools (some of which are available for free or at low cost). Internal assessments are most successfully executed by companies with a mature and successful operational excellence program, with an assessment methodology defined and performed by seasoned and available internal expert resources who have the ability to be—and can be—completely candid.

An example of a successful self-assessment and operational excellence program can be found at United Technologies Corporation (UTC) and their Achieving Competitive Excellence (ACE) program, which is billed as UTC's *operating system*. A core belief of ACE is every employee, from the highest position to the lowest, is involved in the efforts to improve the company and with the shared goals of eliminating waste and delighting customers. As such, UTC is in a continual cycle of assessing, planning, acting, and evaluating. I had the opportunity to personally visit the UTC Sikorsky facility in Mielec, Poland (before UTC sold Sikorsky to Lockheed Martin). This is where the "generic version" of the Black Hawk helicopter is manufactured—the version of the helicopter without all the cool secret gadgetry the ones for the United States Armed Forces have. I left very impressed by their assessment process, their implementation of ACE, and the results the program generated.

A benefit of an internal assessment is that it is highly customizable and specific to the company creating the assessment. The company can identify a desired outcome from the effort, target specific areas to assess, and determine the assessment criterion.

However, the integrity of a self-assessment can be compromised, and the results skewed, by politics and self-interest: "If

I don't like the results, I can just make the numbers work." In addition, a company that does a self-assessment often does not have the opportunity to benefit from the fresh eyes of an outsider (unless the now-internal experts have been hired fairly recently from the outside).

EXTERNAL ASSESSMENT

An external assessment is performed with resources external to the organization. Almost always, the company that hires out an assessment in its entirety is facing considerable challenges and has lost its faith in its internal capabilities on the basis of the past performance of the operational excellence team, the company, or both.

Private equity and turnaround firms, which take an ownership interest in distressed companies, will believe (rightfully or wrongly) the company is in distress—or believe the company isn't doing as well as it can—because of an inability of the present resources to perform. Because of this lack of confidence, they will usually seek external resources for an assessment.

Even if the lack of confidence in the existing resources is well founded, during challenging times, employees become increasingly anxious about their future and might not be willing participants in an improvement initiative because they fear it might mean losing their jobs through redundancy or critical performance reviews. Introducing trusted outsiders whose allegiance is aligned with ownership and who have no personal ties that might stand in the way of analyzing and effecting the change needed might accelerate improvements at the magnitude necessary for the company to overcome its challenges more quickly.

But the risk is that minimal leveraging of existing knowledge of the business, or the lessons learned from the past by those who have worked there, might return results that are less than what might have been achieved if existing knowledge were more actively sought or engaged.

Keep in mind, you should not hire consulting firms merely for engaging improvement projects unless your challenge can benefit from fresh eyes or perspective, you have a short-term need for a talent or skill that is not needed long term in your company, or the need is short term and its urgency warrants and justifies an acceleration that staff augmentation can provide. Otherwise, you risk losing the consultants' knowledge and wisdom after the engagement is complete.

Also, you have to be wary of turning over the keys to the kingdom to a consulting firm. Always remember and never forget: It's *your* company, it's *your* project, and it's *your* responsibility—nobody else's.

HYBRID ASSESSMENT

A hybrid assessment is performed by the organization's internal resources in conjunction with external resources. It can yield optimal results by leveraging the best of both approaches while mitigating the risks of each approach. Accordingly, a hybrid assessment is the route most companies take, especially when they are new to operational excellence and are not in a turnaround or distressed situation.

Many companies that do not have a mature and successful operational excellence program seek to expedite their journey by engaging outside consulting resources specializing in operational excellence program development. Here, engaging outside resources can accelerate the development and deployment of the operational excellence program and minimize missteps, which are often fatal to an operational excellence program if they happen at the beginning. There are many such firms (including my firm, XONITEK), but you should realize sustainable success depends on building internal capacity and capability.

In a hybrid assessment, the company gets the benefit of fresh eyes and, at the same time, leverages the knowledge and capacity of the people who worked the processes (usually for a considerable amount of time).

However, there is a potential for friction between the internal and external resources, which needs to be guarded against. To mitigate this risk requires the establishment of a partnership, and this begins with the building of trust between the insiders and outsiders and alignment of all toward the shared goals.

To help get started, many small to midsize manufacturing companies will leverage government-sponsored programs for improving their competitiveness. Through such programs, they can obtain services from program resources at a discount from market value (or as a source of funding for a company to hire a consulting firm of their choosing). In the United States, this mission is often accomplished by the National Institute of Standards and Technology's Manufacturing Extension Partnership (or NIST-MEP), which will, as a function of its value proposition, perform assessments in conjunction with the existing company staff.

In addition to partnering with consulting firms and leveraging government programs, many universities also have their own programs for conducting assessments (usually in conjunction with government programs). A quick Internet search will probably return a result that is suitable for almost any company, almost anywhere.

For many reasons—from valid (market advantage) to less valid (ego)—many companies will seek recognition in the form of being awarded some "prize" for their operational excellence efforts. Some believe they will be able to leverage this recognition to gain respect among their peers and also demonstrate to customers and vendors that they take their improvement programs seriously. I have even had some companies ask me for guidance on how they might win a prize. But winning a prize should not be the goal of an operational excellence program; rather, winning a prize should be a by-product of a successfully implemented program. And a prize is not a guarantee the company will be considered a viable long-term partner. For instance, consider the case of Delphi Corporation: Although Delphi was a serial recipient of the prestigious Shingo Prize[1] during the years 1999 to 2007, Delphi declared bankruptcy in 2005. Other companies had similar fates. I will let you draw your own conclusions.

In the end, it is important to remember an operational excellence assessment is only the starting point from where the journey is about to begin. To be successful, a company also needs to know where it is going (the future state), how it is going to get there (strategy and tactics), and what it needs for the journey (logistics). And, of course, an operational excellence assessment is not worth doing at all unless you are dedicated to embarking on the journey.

But once you have defined where you want to be, and know from where you are beginning, how and where do you start the transformation? Do you go "big-bang" and try to convert what is to what will be all at once like some nuclear event? Or do you move at a glacial pace, so slow that movement cannot be seen with the naked eye? Do you start where there is the most resistance thinking, if it works here it will work everywhere? Or do you start where your ideas are most well received?

CHAPTER 13

GUERILLA TRANSFORMATION: CHANGE AN INSURGENCY INTO A MOVEMENT

---

*"The only way you survive is you
continuously transform into something else.
It's this idea of continuous transformation
that makes you an innovation company."*

—Ginni Rometty

I was meeting with the CEO of a client company to discuss the status of the various projects we were working on. After a spell, we decided to take a break and went for a walk around the sprawling corporate campus. I could tell he was frustrated about something, but I was not quite sure what it might be. We reached a bluff overlooking the campus and sat on a bench, admiring the view.

He turned and looked at me and blurted out, "The problem I have is that I am surrounded by the lazy and the uninspired."

I looked at him, puzzled, and responded, "Is that your policy?"

He looked at me, equally puzzled, and asked, "What do you mean?"

"Is it your personal policy to hire the lazy and the uninspired?"

"Absolutely not!" He seemed shocked that I would consider that.

"Perhaps it's the policy of your human resources department?" I pressed.

"No way!" he exclaimed. "We look for and hire only the best and the brightest we can find, wherever they may be! We recruit and hire the top in their class from university! We hire the stars away from our competitors!"

So I asked, "If you hire only the best and the brightest, how is it you are left surrounded by the lazy and uninspired?"

He looked rather bewildered and said, "I don't know."

I said, "Although you start with the best and the brightest, you—and your corporate culture—beat them into being the lazy and uninspired. There is really no other plausible reason. Can you think of one?"

He just squinted and didn't say a word.

It seemed like hours passed, but after only five minutes or so of sitting there in silence, he got up and said it was time to go back to work.

An employee comes to work for a company like a child; they are filled with wonder and excitement. The new employee needs structure, nurturing, and support to grow to the best of their abilities. The employee looks to management for these key ingredients for growth, and it is the responsibility of management to supply this support if there is any reasonable expectation the employee will grow to benefit the company in a meaningful way and to the fullest of their potential.

Above all else, employees need to be respected and valued.

But in most cases, employees are given wholly inadequate support and guidance from the very first day they are hired, so their inspiration immediately begins to erode.

Most new employees will sit through a class soon after being hired and conducted by human resources on the *do*s and *don't*s as well as the *how-tos* of the company. During this exercise, the employee has a passing thought that he is a cog in a process, and he leaves the class with a seed of apathy planted.

The employee then arrives at their designated department and is introduced to the manager, who makes it a point to introduce the new employee to colleagues and show them around. Then the manager proceeds to assign a "mentor" from the department to bring the "new kid" up to speed. With some luck, the mentor is capable. But normally, the mentor just shows the new employee the ways of the department, perhaps the various shortcuts in the systems, and ways of keeping out of trouble. The seed of apathy is watered.

Add to this a couple of high-priority projects that require the forfeit of a couple of weekends and holidays, only to have the project scrapped without explanation or recognition of the efforts made. The employee's transformation from eager engagement to indifference is almost complete. The apathy grows strong.

And the coup de grace: Tell the employee they have to make some considerable improvement in some aspect of the business, but they will get no additional resources or budget and have to work it into their schedule with no overtime. You've just asked them to accomplish an impossible, and possibly arbitrary, task without support. If they fail, it will be a black mark on their record. The apathy is fully grown.

The once-inspired new hire has been properly and completely beaten into a cog.

And so it goes . . .

If you wonder about the validity of this, contemplate the jobs you have had, even the one you have now: What were your feelings about your new position when you were newly hired? How about a few years later? How about when you left?

GAME THEORY AND THE NASH EQUILIBRIUM

Each of us belongs to a community or network. In fact, each of us belongs to a great many different communities or networks, with each network being defined by some kernel at its core. These kernels may be physical, ideological, geographical, genetic, religious, or one of countless other characteristics. In each case, the members of the kernel possess a set of values and beliefs unique to that kernel, which serves to attract and unify the network.

As such, the individual members of a network have a shared commitment and affinity to the beliefs and values that define the kernel and will behave in a manner that is highly predictable. Since all the members of the network share common beliefs—and no member of the network can gain an advantage by changing their beliefs or challenging the beliefs of others in the network—the integrity of the network is perpetually preserved and will continue on as it always has. In reality, disturbing the predictability rarely crosses the minds of the network members. This existing state establishes and perpetuates a Nash Equilibrium.[1]

As the network grows and matures, the dedication to the

kernel persists and coagulates and the beliefs shared by the members of the network become more entrenched and increasingly unimpeachable, until they become inseparable and indistinguishable from the members of the network. These beliefs are, in fact, requisite in defining the growing network and establishing its culture.

The equilibrium will face threats over time, both non-credible and credible.

Non-credible threats will challenge the equilibrium but will not have the ability to overcome it. Credible threats are those that possess destructive power (although not necessarily invoked) to defeat or otherwise overcome the equilibrium. In either case, the stronger and more real the threat, the more powerful the defensive response will be.

As the network increases in size, factions will naturally come to exist within the network. These factions localize and standardize the core beliefs of the kernel to maintain the overall equilibrium but permit some variants in order to increase the number and strength of the overall members of the network. These non-credible threats to the entire network result in evolutionary step changes and help to maintain the overall stability and health of the equilibrium.

Such variants differ in their degrees of coexistence and cooperation. They can even directly compete and conflict with one another, but they always rally together when an external threat to the community as a whole manifests itself. For example, take the nearly unprecedented political unity in the United States after the 9/11 attacks; only the attack on Pearl Harbor precipitated greater national unity. However, just as naturally, each faction reverted to the previous state once the threat had subsided. The Nash Equilibrium is therefore maintained.

The same holds true in a business. A corporate culture—usually born of the company's founder and largely perpetuated over time—will be pervasive and will remain unimpeachable. The Nash Equilibrium will ensure the status quo is maintained, because there is no real motivation to change. That is, unless an external threat disrupts the equilibrium.

NON-CREDIBLE DISRUPTERS: SOCIAL MEDIA

Let's reflect on our personal networks, perhaps our networks on social media, and how a disrupter might be engineered and introduced. Regardless of our position on any given issue—social, economic, or political—we have connections in our network who take opposing views. And I am certain, regardless of how eloquent and complete an argument you make is and regardless of how solid the facts might be, your connection cannot be persuaded from their opinion. As such, I would argue all of the participants behave in a manner consistent with there being a Nash Equilibrium.

If I examine any individual and know the networks to which they belong, I can predict with confidence, if not with certainty, how each will react to any presented circumstance. Without motivation to change, they will react as they usually do.

CREDIBLE EXTERNAL DISRUPTERS

Each network, each company, has its own threats. Most are non-credible and fail to disrupt the Nash Equilibrium. But some are significant enough to represent a potential catastrophe for the network should they go unrecognized and unaddressed.

Like a tsunami in the deep ocean, one can hardly detect the threat at all. A person sitting in a rowboat in the middle of the ocean would not notice as the wave and its destructive energy passed beneath. However, the destructive power of the wave increases as the wave approaches land and its energy is compacted. At this point, it is too late to do anything except endure and recover.

Such is the challenge with business. When the threats are known and distant, the amount of energy and effort to prepare, react, and repair is miniscule compared with what is required after waiting too long. Unfortunately, human behavior being what it is, we have a tendency to discount or dismiss distant threats—kick the can down the road or hope that the threat won't actually materialize—no matter how tragic being caught ill prepared might be.

Take the sad case of General Motors as an example of a tsunami and the destruction it unleashes if you wait too long. During the 1950s and 1960s, General Motors commanded the automotive marketplace. At its peak in the 1960s, it had an almost 50 percent market share in the States. Compare this to the share of all imports in the 1960s that enjoyed a market share of less than 10 percent. But in each and every year and in each and every decade following the 1960s, GM's market share slipped while the market share of imports surged. Until, by the 2010s, GM's market share was less than 20 percent and imports were at 50 percent.

Everyone knew GM was in trouble for decades, the tsunami on its way. Not only was their market share slipping, but their per-unit cost was rising, the quality of their production was plummeting, and they had too many brands, which resulted in their competing with themselves. And this drove the per-unit revenue down even further. They were a company in increasingly desperate trouble. Everyone saw it, and everyone knew what had to be done—yet nobody did anything.

In 2007, the global economic meltdown hit and unleashed its destructive power. This event forced GM into bankruptcy in June 2009. One month later, they emerged from bankruptcy, the company reborn. During the process, the leadership was swept out, the company and value chain was restructured, and GM was forgiven of most its past sins, shed of most of its bad habits, and cured of many of its cancers.

Indeed, the changes that should have occurred incrementally and with little pain over decades at the hands of the leadership at GM were devised and deployed in a single month because of a tremendously powerful external disrupter and the facilitation of the federal bankruptcy courts.

So why do people and the companies they run wait too long to change? How might we be able to engineer and introduce this sort of disrupter internally?

CREDIBLE INTERNAL DISRUPTERS

A business and its culture will not change without a credible disrupter. And a credible external disrupter thrust on a business will necessarily be traumatic, perhaps fatal, in its form and response. It is best avoided. In the face of such peril, might a business under threat be able to engineer and introduce a credible disrupter from within the business?

Unfortunately, the Nash Equilibrium asserts that this is impossible. A credible disrupter cannot be found and grown from within the business.

However, if the leadership of the business is wise and acts early enough, a credible external disrupter can possibly be identified and introduced into the business—in effect engineering a credible internal disrupter. As such, the likelihood of the business perpetuating increases, most likely in a dramatically different form, but under terms and conditions that would be more favorable than the alternative.

Such credible external disrupters turned credible internal disrupters might take the form of a new C-level executive, the merger of two businesses, the introduction of new financial partners, the hiring of consultants or other subject-matter experts from outside the company, and so on.

Take IBM, for example. Thomas Watson founded and grew the company largely along the lines of his vision and created an unimpeachable corporate culture. This served the company well, until the internally grown leadership was faced with external threats for which they were ill prepared and untrained. These threats resulted in the near collapse of the company in the early 1990s, which was averted when Lou Gerstner, an outsider to IBM and former CEO of RJR Nabisco, was called on to turn the fortunes of the company around.

Gerstner spent a considerable amount of time examining the present state of IBM, its various business units, offerings, and structure. He had the leadership make pitches about their value propositions and how they functioned. Then, he percolated this information to formulate a strategy for IBM's future and a path to get there.

The many reforms and restructuring introduced by Gerstner

were possible only because he had no past at IBM; the fact that he had previously made Oreos and had no history in the technology industry at all was a strategic and tactical advantage. He was able to evaluate the many problems at IBM objectively, pragmatically, and without emotion. His outsider status gave him the opportunity to redefine and then realign the entire company. But, most importantly, he had the freedom and authority to put new strategies into place without being beholden to the past.

The key to successful change on the most favorable terms is to purposefully design, engineer, and introduce the disrupter. Start with a small cadre of specifically selected participants to create the beginnings of an insurgency. Then methodically, continuously, and deliberately convert and add additional members so that the process of transformational change begins to gain momentum. In effect, you must get members to *defect* from their old culture and adopt the new culture. You must be able to target the disrupter (to be most effective) and to modulate the speed at which the disruption occurs, so control is maintained and adequate support provided. The insurgency will become unstable if control is not maintained, and it will atrophy to its previous state if not supported.

A WORD ON WORDS

People don't like change; we know that. But people are more inclined to accept a new way if there is a sense of ownership—that it's theirs, it belongs to them, and not to anybody else.

For your consideration, instead of using a bunch of Japanese words to describe a tool or approach, why not create a counterpart name that is in your native language. In this case, I will pick English. This will help to increase a sense of ownership and reduce the level of intimidation that many might feel and help to overcome the barriers of resistance.

As an example, would you be surprised to know that Ford, under Henry Ford, developed a parallel to 5S long before 5S came to be? It was called CAN-DO, which stood for Cleaning up, Arranging, Neatness, Discipline, and Ongoing Improvements.

Ford's CAN-DO	Lean's 5S	Japanese
Cleaning up	Sort	Seiri
Arranging	Set in order	Seiton
Neatness	Shine	Seiso
Discipline	Standardize	Seiketsu
Ongoing Improvement	Sustain	Shitsuke

So we can see the "anglicization" of Japanese terms; we somehow were able to find a synonym in English that started with an S. (Never mind the fact there is no letter S in the Japanese language because they use symbols instead of letters.) We can also see the use of anglicized terms corresponding to waste, such as *unevenness* (*mura*), *overburden* (*muri*) and so on. So, why not extend it to kaizen and the rest?

After all, we are trying to effect improvements, not teach a foreign language. Clarity in communication is important.

So if I wanted to effect true transformational change in my network and did not have infinite resources (as would surely be the case in a business situation), I would want to engineer and introduce a disrupter so it resulted in the greatest number of people defecting from their native state to my desired state of being.

However, engineering and introducing disrupters is not without its risks. Their deployment may be improperly engineered, oversold, or introduced too widely or too quickly, to name just a few.

We have all heard of leaders stating grand plans and initiatives, only to fail on the delivery and to cause themselves discredit. This overselling of the disrupter is readily observed in politics, in the many promises made on the campaign trail and then quickly broken after the election.

The risk in introducing a disrupter too widely or too quickly is to introduce a grand plan with great fanfare and get the network engaged, but then not be able to support the effort and momentum. The project then stalls, and the defectors lose faith, becoming even more resistant than they were before.

It is best to communicate the nature and form of the transformational change to take place in the business and to selectively target your starting point and path of expansion. In a network, the more connections a person has, the more inclined they are to share the core beliefs of the network and the more credibility they will have to facilitate change.

Unfortunately, most operational excellence initiatives are deployed logistically rather than strategically. There is an emphasis on tools and frameworks over a more holistic approach. The operational excellence teams consist of a small cadre of enthusiastic and talented individuals who are given very few resources or very little authority to successfully execute their mission. In most cases, they are set up for failure, which I'll define as having responsibility and accountability but no authority.

These operational excellence professionals are forced to act like scrappy hot dog vendors on the streets of New York City—going from department to department (their customers), trying to sell their operational excellence hot dogs. The customer has no real incentive to purchase (they often get no funding from corporate), and the hot dog is seen mostly as a cost rather than a value. We can all hear the conversation, "Would you like some 5S on your Kaizen?" they might ask. "Maybe some VSM and DMAIC in a Pareto wrapper?"

It is a wise hot dog vendor who knows his customer and how to sell his hot dogs. He knows the customer would enjoy a nice tasty hot dog, but the customer doesn't want to know what goes in it, and he especially doesn't want to see it made. Sell the satisfaction, not the hot dog.

The disrupter must be properly engineered and targeted; otherwise, the gains will be marginal, if any are realized at all. A properly engineered disrupter will appeal to the target's sensibilities and seduce them into defecting, because it is truly in the target's best interest to address the WIIFM (What's In It For Me) question.

When engineering a disrupter, it is critically important to ensure the motivation to defect is seductive enough to the target to instill a sense of desire, to make defection a want. The best way to do this is to ensure the KPIs (Key Performance Indicators) are properly defined so they facilitate the correct alignment of the target. To get someone to change, you can't focus on the whole group; you have to focus on the individual, because, in the end, communities (or companies) don't change. Change starts at the individual level. And if you get enough individual people to change, the community (or company) changes from within.

Change agents have a difficult path. It's even harder to

properly engineer, deploy, and manage a strategic disrupter. But it's far better to introduce your own disrupter and to effect the changes necessary to keep your business relevant than it is to react to someone else's disrupter, thrust on you from outside. What it will take is instilling a desire in others to move from one reality to another.

CHAPTER 14

CHANGING A WANT TO A NEED

"Don't give people what they want,
give them what they need."

—Joss Whedon

Everyone has needs, and everyone has wants. What is the difference between a need and a want?

A need is something we cannot live without. We need air, we need water, we need nourishment, and we need shelter. Without these things, we would surely perish. We might also need love and attention and a sense of belonging, a connection with others, to maintain a healthy mental state.

In business, we need customers—and happy customers at that. We need customers who will return time and again. We need employees working to satisfy those customers. We also need reliable suppliers, who share our ambitions and deliver quality products and services to help us satisfy our customers. Finally, we need cash and cash flow, which is the fuel for the economic engine that is our business.

A *want*, on the other hand, is something we would like to

have, for which we might even have a great desire, but it is not necessary. We can live without it, at least for the present. On a personal level, we might want many material things, such as a car, a widescreen television, a dog, even to purchase this book. (Well, maybe the last should come under *need*.)

A want in business can take many forms. The real trick is determining the difference between a need and a want. Most of the investments I see made in businesses when there is a Private Equity partner involved are definitely in the *need* camp: well thought out and frugal but effective. But many of the investments I see in family-owned businesses and publicly traded companies often serve the image the leadership wants to convey. For instance, transportation might be a need, but the new corporate jet might be just a want. In business, the difference between need and want is often a matter of scale and form.

When does a want become a need? Is that even possible?

LESSONS FROM MY FATHER

When I was thirteen years old, in 1975, I asked my father for a raise in my allowance from fifty cents per week to seventy-five cents per week. He was a manager at IBM at the time and told me to write a paper stating why I deserved the raise. So I wrote a two-page paper on how expensive everything was and how fifty cents didn't pay for the things I wanted to buy.

We reviewed the paper together. And afterward, he told me he was going to deny my request for a raise. I was very upset and asked him why.

He told me, "You told me why you need it, but not why you deserve it."

That just pissed me off.

So, the next day, I got off the school bus a few stops earlier, at Nanticoke Gardens (which was a nursery and greenhouse), went up to Donald Ferguson who owned it, and told him I wanted a job. He asked what I could do—and I told him I would do whatever needed to be done. He hired me for $1.85 per hour, and I would work every day after school for three hours and on Saturdays.

I was thirteen years old and making fifty dollars a week.

And my brother, Christopher, was now doing my chores.

When we are children, we might want that first job for some extra spending money, but we don't need that job because our parents take care of all of our needs. But when we grow up and are on our own, we need that job for our basic survival.

Is there a want that might become a need in business? Certainly, we might want more customers, but if the customers we have are sustaining the business, new customers might only be a want. But what if we lose those key customers? Instantly, that want becomes a need. The same holds true for the supply chain. If you have a primary supplier that is wiped out by a tsunami, your wanting to have a reliable back-up supplier has turned into a need.

More challenging still, sometimes we have to create a want before we can convert it to a need. My father did a fine job creating a want in me for working and earning a living long before it became a need. Similarly, as employers and leaders, we have to create a want in our people to always seek improvement in operations and performance before there is a need.

But how do we do this?

DIFFERENT STATES OF ENGAGEMENT

I have met many people in business who have held various leadership roles over the years—from shift leaders to department heads, business unit executives to C-suite executives. Almost all of them have pride and passion for their roles within their companies, even if there is sometimes a lack of passion (not to mention affection) for the company itself. The one thing they all have in common is that their ways are not easily changed once they are set.

If you consider your own career, you will see this is more often true than not. Take your present place of employment, for example, and think about the first few days or weeks there. During this time, if someone told you something is done a certain way, you would ask questions to clarify, but you probably didn't overtly challenge them (unless, of course, that was your job). Over the coming months—perhaps years—you accepted the way things were done as the way they should be done.

Then, one day, a *change agent* calls into question the very core of how everything is done. How do you feel? How do you react? How do veterans and new hires react differently?

For the change agent to be successful, they have to identify and quantify the opportunity for improvement. They have to develop a plan to get to the new way. And they have to convince those used to the old way to willingly convert. The success or failure of the change agent's ideas depends on the clarity of their plan and the disposition of the people who will be affected by the changes.

So the main challenge all change agents share is understanding the circumstances and conditions under which they must operate. They must help both employees and leadership align themselves toward the strategies of the company and motivate them to embrace the coming change. Some of those facing the change will require the change agent to be empathetic, and some will require them to be persuasive. Therefore, one of the most important tasks a change agent needs to undertake is to assess the psychological state of those who will be required to change. We can group the psychological states into three categories.

Consensus State

In the consensus state, the parties share the same aspirations or beliefs. The challenge here is to make sure both parties understand the needs of, and are empathetic to, the other. Once this is accomplished, the development and deployment of a plan to go forward occurs fairly simply.

Conflict State

In the conflict state, the two parties hold divergent aspirations or beliefs. The challenge here (and it is a considerable challenge) is to persuade one or both of the parties to change their aspirations or beliefs—perhaps even abandon them—to become aligned with the other. However, it is very rare that one party will truly abandon their beliefs. More than likely, they will surrender their will to the other party and take on the role of a contributing resource. Perhaps, over time, they will increase their acceptance and graduate to becoming a resource who helps develop plans for engagement.

Inert State

In the inert state, the aspirations of the parties are neither shared nor divergent. Neither party has any appreciable degree of passion in the subject and will go along with whatever comes, unless and until some line is crossed challenging their understanding or beliefs. Then the state will change to either the consensus state or the conflict state.

Frameworks for change might be able to guide and measure progress toward change—and your leadership will be essential in shepherding your company through any major change. It's herding cats; no wonder being a successful change agent is a difficult, sometimes thankless job. *Change agents are not loved.*

Where to Start the Launch Phase

> "Do what you can, with what you got,
> from where you are."
>
> —Theodore Roosevelt

We all look at the world from one perspective: our own. The perspectives we hold are born out of the circumstances of our upbringing and further developed by experience. As such, one would expect the perspective of those with more varied experiences to be wider than those with more limited experiences.

And so it is true for professionals dedicated to operational excellence. Those who are exposed to operational excellence through some methodology tend to see opportunities for improvement from the perspective of that methodology. I find it especially intriguing that an advocate-turned-zealot of a certain methodology will argue theirs is the best for effecting improvements and the others are obviously inferior, regardless of whether it is true or not. Restricting your approach to a single methodology brings inherent limitations and sometimes peril.

My experience has been that the fatal flaw of most operational excellence programs, and the reason they fail to deliver their potential, is that leadership tends to marginalize the people in the process, regardless of what might be written in the operational excellence charter to the contrary. Instead of gaining the trust and engagement of those who will be directly affected by the improvement initiatives, the operational excellence team usually arrives under time pressures. After all, one of the primary KPIs on which they are measured is the number of projects they complete. So the operational excellence team will focus on the mission without connecting with, or involving except on the periphery, the people actually working the process. And when the project is complete, they immediately move to the next assignment without performing a thorough debriefing. The end result is that the operational excellence team is never fully embraced by those they are trying to help, because they never bother to connect on a personal level. Neither is the operational excellence team fully respected by senior management, because without this connection, they fail to deliver. And what's worse is that the operational excellence team has not left behind their wisdom or taken the opportunity to build capabilities or capacity.

So what can be done—what must be done—in order to optimize an operational excellence program, to maximize the net results, and to bring them more in line with expectation? The answer lies in operational excellence itself. First, we have to honestly and thoroughly answer two questions.

First, what is important to the company? And second, what is important to the people who work for the company? In essence, we have to answer the WIIFM question—*What's In It For Me?* This is not what you *think* is in it for someone else, but what is actually in it for that person—from their perspective.

PERSPECTIVES IN LIBERATION

A few years ago, I was planning my annual trip to Southern Africa to visit my offices there and to do some brainstorming with the staff and partners. One of my friends in the States, an avowed feminist, wanted to go with me so she could conduct workshops with some of the local women and help "liberate" them. Being a sensitive and avowed feminist myself (it's true; ask anyone who knows me), I suggested, instead of conducting workshops, she should build some wells in the villages as a convenient source of water.

She was aghast, but not entirely surprised at the callousness and perceived lack of empathy in my suggestion. "How can building a well liberate women?" She wanted to help these supposedly repressed women in Southern Africa, and the best way to do that (in her mind) was to conduct workshops to demonstrate a better way.

I informed her the women in the rural villages of Southern Africa can spend up to five hours a day fetching water (oftentimes even more), walking miles each way, every day, to the nearest (somewhat) potable water source. I further explained the easiest way to liberate a woman (or anyone, for that matter) is to give them time—especially a significant amount of free time—every day of the week. This had not dawned on my friend, but she understood.

What might be of interest to the company includes customer satisfaction, increased quality, decreased costs, reduced lead time, increased EBITDA, and a reduction in carrying costs. And some examples of what might be of interest to the employee include pride in ownership (of their job or process), recognition for effort, job security, safety, career advancement opportunities, compensation rewards, a change in performance measurement from input to output, a company-sponsored day-care program, and health benefits.

Next, we have to discover the intersection between what is important to the company and what is important to the people who work for the company. If an honest and objective assessment is performed, this intersection of interests will yield opportunities for improvement where the alignment of company and employee are most natural. Start your operational excellence program there.

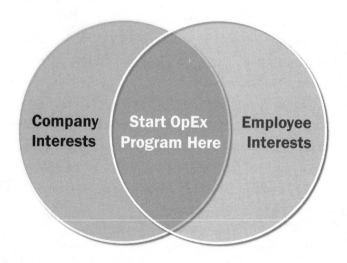

Figure 14.1. Venn Diagram showing where to start a program at the project-level.

The reason we want to start the program at the intersection of company and employee interests is that our first objective at the beginning is to win over the employee to the new way. The best way to do this is to teach them the skills and demonstrate how their personal lives will benefit from them. In this way, they will become a believer in the new way and will become advocates. Then, when asked to work on something that is more important to the company and less important to them, they will be inclined to want to help because they believe.

However, you can't just say, "Today we start our operational excellence program. All aboard!" and assume your program will be a success. To achieve the true potential of the effort, you have to be determined to transform your continuous improvement program into an operational excellence program. You must go from making reactive improvements to spotting needs before they become problems and institute a more comprehensive, enterprise-wide approach to making synergetic, integrated, and proactive improvements. In essence, a culture of transformational improvement must be built across the entire organization.

But transformation across an organization is difficult. How do we parse the time necessary to complete the tasks that are our primary responsibility and ensure a proper level of integration with colleagues across the smokestacks in our business? If we are meeting, we are not doing. Perhaps we need a facilitator of our communications—and not just an email system that transmits the text, but one that can also deliver the context and be an advocate.

CHAPTER 15

STEWARDSHIP

"A leader must be a good listener. He must be willing
to take counsel. He must show a genuine concern
and love for those under his stewardship."

—James E. Faust

As a long-time member of the Institute of Industrial and Systems Engineers (IISE) and being on the Advisory Board of its Industry Advisory Board (IAB), as well as being on the Advisory Board of Binghamton University's System Science and Industrial Engineering (SSIE) Department, I have been intimately exposed to the materials related to continuous improvement and Lean Six Sigma, from the latest research to the tried-and-tested application. Yet, although enthusiastically advocated by everyone in the discipline, the results fail to achieve the promise time and again. This gap between the promise and the reality puzzled me a great deal, and I decided to investigate the reasons for such poor results, as well as the increasingly poor reputation and expectations associated with operational excellence initiatives.

During this endeavor, I examined the curriculum offered and the materials used—from both academia and industry sources around the world—in teaching various disciplines associated with continuous improvement in general and Lean Six Sigma in particular. I also examined websites and articles written by practitioners and consultancies and discussed the experiences of many companies who pursued a path of operational excellence.

All of the materials discussed the benefits of embarking on such programs in great detail. They all created a compelling picture of what the world can be if only we embrace the disciplines of Lean Six Sigma as the critical baseline component of any operational excellence program. Almost all of the material referred to the forensics of the disciplines—a focus on *how*, including the tools of the trade and the methods of leveraging and deploying them. One book emphasized 5S, another focused on value-stream mapping, another was based on kanban and another on kaizen, and so on. Every book I read made some reference to the (now alleged) miracles performed at Toyota and advocated replicating them in any industry, in any business, anywhere. And most of the content also addressed Kipling's remaining Six Honest Serving Men: What, When, Where, and Who. Unfortunately, in practice, people give less attention to Why. As a result, they lose sight of their target and their reason for doing any of this at all.

Certainly, all of this knowledge and instruction is necessary, well, and good. I would support any argument that it is important to know how to properly use the tools in your toolbox, which one to grab under any given circumstance, how to wield it, and where to do so for maximum effectiveness. I would also support the vision of what could be achieved by doing so.

However, the one thing I noticed in almost all of this

material—very subtle in nature, but with a profound and devastating impact on the results—was the consistent reference to the singular. There were many mentions of *you*, *me*, and *I*, but far fewer references to *we*, *us*, *them*, or *they*. And they almost never mentioned *the team*. It is almost as if any results that might be achieved in an operational excellence program are solely the consequence of an individual's efforts and not that of coordination among many, much less involving an entire company. The use of the passive voice was extensive—*then this is done, followed by that, to achieve the goal*—as if operational excellence could magically happen without human involvement. If leadership, program management, and communication skills are mentioned at all, they are usually given short shrift and tucked toward the back of the book.

When I look at a traditional organization from an operational excellence perspective, I see four major roles people fulfill in the effort. These are not necessarily positions or titles, but the responsibilities they have and functions they perform. Except for the unindoctrinated (who have not yet had the opportunity to become involved in the operational excellence initiative), each is a distinct and necessary member of an overall operational excellence team, but their deliberate *integration* is required for success.

I see these roles as the following:

THE LEADERSHIP

The *leadership's* role in the organization is to be the visionaries; their sights are set beyond the horizon. Their primary responsibility is to build a vision for the organization and to communicate the vision to all who are either directly or indirectly involved.

We must distinguish between the leadership *position* held by an individual (which might be more of a management role) and actual *leadership*, the role of creating the vision; they may—but do not necessarily—coincide. Being oriented and focused on the future state of the business, the leader should (by definition and by necessity) remain focused on defining and refining goals to be most effective and should not be distracted by the details that are in the realm of tactics or logistics unless truly necessary.

THE PRACTITIONER

The *practitioner's* role in the organization is more tactical, oriented toward implementing the strategies. To be successful in this role, they must have firsthand knowledge of the vision set by the leadership, and their responsibility is primarily to define, deploy, and lead the specific actions necessary to realize the strategic vision of the leadership. It is important for the practitioner to remain focused on plan development and deployment to be most effective in this role and to not get dragged into the actual execution, except for offering the critical support of mentor and facilitator as appropriate. To do otherwise will diminish the practitioner's potential as a force multiplier.

THE INDOCTRINATED

The *indoctrinated's* role in the organization is more logistical, with an orientation toward deployment. This person is either new to the doctrines and various tools of operational excellence or a seasoned veteran who is more comfortable and better at doing the work than managing others. The indoctrinated will also know the vision for the organization set forth by the leadership (but probably to a considerably lesser detail than the practitioner does). Their responsibility is to be the resource who will actually do the bulk of the analysis and effort in effecting the change.

THE UNINDOCTRINATED

The *unindoctrinated* are on the outside. They don't really know the vision from the leadership (who may not be working to drive the message down so deep in the organization, though they should), and they don't possess the skill sets of the indoctrinated—either because they are very new to the organization or because the decision (passive or active) has been made to not convey the skill sets to them.

A SHIP AT SEA

In the context of roles and responsibilities of the people from across the spectrum of an operational excellence program, consider a ship at sea:

→ The *captain* of the ship is the leader, the visionary of the future state who is responsible for getting the ship and all aboard safely to its destination.

→ The *petty officers* on the ship are the practitioners, the tacticians who are responsible for various ship functions and its systems, such as engineering, navigation, galley, and communications.

(Continued...)

→ The *crew* are the indoctrinated, the logistical support personnel who are responsible for carrying out the duties of the ship functions at a more granular, process level.

→ The *passengers* are the unindoctrinated; they're just along for the ride. Once at sea, they might be taught the basics of survival (e.g., life jackets and life boats), but that is about it.

However, the ship's *steward* is the strategist and performs a critical role. He is charged with hearing, understanding, and acknowledging the orders and intent of the captain, communicating them though the entire ship and ensuring they are carried out. He must make sure that the entire vessel is aligned with, and capable of, achieving the captain's objectives. The steward also has the responsibility of communicating the needs of the ship to the captain so that he might understand the capabilities of the ship and consider the entirety of the circumstances, in context, as they might affect the achievement of his objectives and he may need to consider countermeasures as appropriate.

Perhaps this is why the materials written about leadership do not dive deeper into the details of the tools and techniques of operational excellence and why the materials written about the tools and techniques of operational excellence do not adequately address the importance of effective leadership and the required skill sets: The materials are written by leadership for leadership, or by practitioners for practitioners, or as textbooks for the newly indoctrinated, for the same audience as the role held by the author.

A lack of cohesion is the natural result of all participants focusing on executing their own responsibilities within their business smokestack, rather than performing in a collaborative team environment. This results in a program whose efforts come in fits and spurts, whose results are unsurprisingly inconsistent, and whose future outcomes are difficult—if not impossible—to predict. Since funding and support follows success and success varies so widely, the actual results are destined to fail to meet expectations, and this will lead to an assessment that the program is unsuccessful.

In my opinion, a prime reason why operational excellence initiatives fail to realize their full potential is, in a word, *stewardship*—or the lack thereof. This should be the goal of operational excellence program directors: to be stewards of the company's operational excellence program.

To be a steward, you must have something entrusted to your care, and you must hold dear the trust and responsibly that goes along with it. A steward needs to be empathetic but pressing to the needs of all those involved but also Socratic in their engagement. As a steward, you are mentor, coach, and facilitator. You are master of communication and diplomacy; you nurture, support, and protect rather than command. You are a critical member of the community for which you are responsible—a community that depends on you as much as you depend on it in order for everyone to be successful. Stewardship is the strategic function that bridges the vision of the future state, through the tactical, to the logistical, and back again.

Remember, the role of steward is not necessarily a position (however, it could be) but, rather, a role taken on by qualified people in the organization. I am certainly not endorsing an additional layer of management; personally, I believe most organizations have far too many layers as it is. That is why I advocate assigning this as an additional role to an existing position within a hierarchy.

In the navy, a ship's steward is also responsible for assessing risk and being the advocate of the petty officers, crew, and passengers, ensuring their needs are properly communicated for evaluation and action, the appropriate resources are allocated, and the entire crew is prepared and committed to achieving the objectives. The steward is the trusted advisor who helps the captain change the strategy if it is determined—through communication with the crew and evaluation—the strategy is unachievable or fraught with undue risk under the present circumstances. As such, it could be argued the steward is the most important role on the ship, because the steward ensures that everyone is working toward a goal that is crystal clear, that everyone has what is required for them to successfully fulfill their responsibilities and objectives, and that the expectations are managed throughout the ship.

To be successful, the intent of the vision, the assessments of opportunity and risk, the determination of needs, the recommendations to the leadership, and the evaluation of the crew's capabilities should all be conveyed in an environment of intimacy and unreserved trust. Because the steward is trusted, all communication being passed through, or originating from, the steward should be unbiased. This is not to say that the steward does not form opinions and offer recommendations. They absolutely do. It's just that the facts are conveyed in an unfiltered manner without spin. The results associated with defining and deploying the role of steward in an operational excellence initiative—or any initiative, for that matter—are going to be the difference between success and failure. If such trust does not exist, the steward is no longer the steward.

With the steward in place, the following benefits will result:

⇨ Goals are established with continual management of expectations set on an ongoing, closed-loop basis. Because goals are modulated from the realities communicated bidirectionally, there should be a dramatic reduction in failed objectives. The dreams may not always be realized, but the expectations will be clear and actionable.

⇨ Support resources are properly identified and allocated. The team has an advocate who will assess the needs required to successfully carry out the objectives and who will communicate these needs to the leadership.

⇨ The roles of all crew members will be clear, and their value add will increase in a far quicker, predictable, and measurable manner. They will also increase their positive impact across the organization, because the priorities and manner of implementation will be communicated, shared, and coordinated.

As argued here, addressing the need for stewardship and teaching stewardship skills are critical to the success of any operational excellence initiative. Stewardship establishes the necessary precursor environment through which the full achievement of the benefits of any such program is possible and through which the maximum potential reward associated with leveraging the tools and methods of operational excellence can be realized consistently.

Teaching these stewardship skills should be integral to the curriculum and materials and not an elective or afterthought. As an individual member of the community—regardless of the role they fulfill—the steward will ensure that everyone is working as a team. And working as a team makes all the difference.

The challenge now is how to engineer and construct a structured program that builds awareness, capacity, and capability across the enterprise such that the inputs are the result of a pull (demand) and not a push. This will ensure all resources are introduced into the program to achieve uniform knowledge and alignment to the requirements of the organization. Without this result, there really is no opportunity to accurately establish the expectations of the program for the organization and certainly no opportunity to properly prepare an environment in which stewardship can be an effective conduit for change.

CHAPTER 16

WHAT IS THE BEST TRAINING FOR YOUR TEAM?

"On the mountains of truth you can never climb
in vain: Either you will reach a point higher up
today, or you will be training your powers so that
you will be able to climb higher tomorrow."

—Friedrich Nietzsche

As operational excellence practitioners, it is natural (even a passion) to always seek ways to improve ourselves and the value we drive to our colleagues and the companies for which we work. During our quest for this personal and professional development, we sometimes know precisely which skill sets we wish to improve and where we need to concentrate our efforts, and we sometimes seek, instead, to satisfy our curiosity in some subject matter.

Once we determine our focus, we need to decide what level of knowledge and competency we wish to possess at the conclusion of our training, and, most important, we need to ensure that the method we select for obtaining the knowledge and competency will yield those expected results. Therefore, during this evaluation process, we must always remember the following corollary: The level of effort required is directly proportional to the depth of the knowledge and competency acquired.

We must also evaluate the comparative value of the efforts and their results, with *comparative value* being defined as the investment requirements associated with gaining the knowledge versus the benefit to you and your company.

When considering investment requirements, it's inadequate to just calculate the direct costs associated with acquiring the knowledge, such as curriculum costs, tuition, delegate fees, travel, room and board, and materials and supplies. We must also consider all of the indirect costs, such as the time away from the job, the development and maintenance of internal curriculum, and the delivery medium and infrastructure.

I grade comparative value on a three-tier scale:

⇨ A **low value** indicates elementary content. The participant should expect to learn the terminology used, the value derived from proper use of the content, and perhaps some basic applications.

⇨ A **moderate value** is for reasonable content. At this level, the participant should expect to learn how to plan the use of the content, when to deploy it, and how to manage its implementation.

⇨ A **high value** indicates robust content. At this highest level, the participant should expect to learn how to define objectives in the discipline and should be able to communicate how these objectives will be realized.

In addition to comparative value, we must also keep in mind the credibility of the origin of the content: the curriculum. What are the credentials of the instructor? Do they have the proper experience and success in the field, and can they stand as a sufficiently qualified authority on the subject? Especially when it comes to certifications in Lean Six Sigma for the individual student, my advice is *caveat emptor*, Latin for "Let the buyer beware." There are a lot of "certification mills" out there that will offer a "certification" for little cash and little effort. Don't be duped into engaging one.

For instance, I was speaking with a recent university graduate who wished for me to review her Curriculum Vitae (CV). I noted she had earned her Six Sigma Green Belt Certification at the university, so I asked for the details of her Green Belt project. To my surprise, neither she nor anyone in the class had worked on a Green Belt project—or any project. All that was required of her to earn her Green Belt was she had to sit through a week-long class and pass a test. My advice to her was to change her CV to state she received Green Belt training.

Unlike the legal profession with the Bar Association, there is no universally recognized governing body for certifications in the disciplines of Lean Six Sigma or any other dimension of operational excellence nor is there a recognized standard for curriculum or other metrics. And, unfortunately, there are many people out there who just want to pad their resumes and who feel any certification is better than no certification. I have witnessed firsthand some students and workshop attendees who don't even show up for class but receive their certification at the end of the semester simply because they paid for it. Because of this, hiring managers should also remember *caveat emptor* during the interview and vetting process to ensure the candidate is properly credentialed from a reputable source and has the proper level of practical experience the position requires. Make sure the certification is worth the paper on which it is printed.

There are a great many reputable organizations where an individual might become Lean Six Sigma certified, including the Institute of Industrial and Systems Engineers (IISE), Villanova University (USA), and the University of Michigan (USA). Of special note and worthy of inquiry is a new joint program offered by an alliance of the American Society for Quality (ASQ), the Society for Manufacturing Excellence (SME), the Association for Manufacturing Excellence (AME), and the Shingo Prize. And then there is the Operational Excellence Enterprise Readiness Certification Program, offered by the Operational Excellence Society,[1] whose objective is to establish performance programs within and across an enterprise, with a focus on optimized systems and not just processes or trained individuals, such that the end result is that the enterprise as a whole becomes a high-performance organization.

And there are many companies who have their own robust internal programs, such as General Electric, Motorola, and UTC (to name just a few).

A simple way to qualify the quality of a certification is simply to listen to how the person announces their certification: Do they seem embarrassed? For instance, I would become immediately suspicious if someone were to simply say to me, "I am a Black Belt" as opposed to "I am a GE Black Belt." Leaving out the origin of a certification indicates the candidate's lack of confidence in its credibility. In any case, I am going to ask them about their projects and practical experience in great detail to determine the true level of knowledge, since the application of knowledge is where the value is realized.

The following is a list of various approaches for corporate training and education, the approximate per-participant investment requirements for each, their pros and cons, and the comparative value that should be expected by the company.

WEBINARS

Whether live or prerecorded, learning by watching a webinar is the least costly and most convenient method of learning, but what you will learn is greatly limited. As such, a webinar is a great way of gaining exposure to a topic (or a refresher course for updates to knowledge), but you should not expect to become proficient in any topic. Would you trust your surgery or the filing of your taxes to someone who learned only by attending a webinar? An additional risk of webinars is that (since they are so inexpensive to produce) those who charge the attendees might not be credible or capable instructors. And if the webinar is free, I can almost guarantee you they are merely infomercials—sales pitches disguised as learning experiences in most cases.

Expected investment requirements: Free or up to $250, plus minimal soft costs

Expected duration: Thirty minutes to half-week

Pros: Low cost, short duration, convenient

Cons: Don't expect to learn too much

Comparative value: Low

SEMINARS AND CONFERENCES

Attending seminars and conferences is a good way to dive deeper into a subject in a more collegiate setting. One of the most significant benefits of attending a seminar or conference, and one that should not be dismissed, is the ability to interface with peers one-on-one. This interaction and the exchange of practical experience will enable the participant to better understand the material as it is applied in context, will help to build invaluable interpersonal and communication skills, and will expand the participant's professional network to facilitate problem-solving in the future.

However, as with webinars, you should expect to be listening to sales pitches if the event is free. (Think along the lines of a pitch for time-shares.)

Expected investment requirements: $1,000–$5,000, including considerable soft costs associated mostly with travel expenses and time lost

Expected duration: 1–5 days

Pros: A deeper dive into subject matter, usually from several perspectives, and the ability to network with peers to compare experiences and learn, build relationships, and improve your social IQ

Cons: Requires considerable time and cost to attend; there is risk the speakers will be paying

to deliver the content and you are actually sitting in an infomercial

Comparative value: Low to low moderate

ON-THE-JOB TRAINING

Assuming the on-the-job-training program is well developed and structured (which is not always a safe assumption), the successful trainee should have an understanding of the tools and skill sets necessary to satisfactorily perform their duties. However, this training will be limited to the performance of tasks and processes as they directly relate to the job to be performed and not much more. Although this has definite value to the trainee and their practical functions within the company, it would be misguided to expect the trainee to learn, understand, and apply the theory behind it.

Expected investment requirements: $2,500–$15,000, mostly internal soft costs

Expected Duration: Half a week to one month, depending on complexity

Pros: Rapid ramp up to get you generating value for the company

(Continued...)

> **Cons:** Usually very vertical content; you learn the job but not the context, the how and not the why.
>
> **Comparative value:** Low moderate to moderate

CLASSROOM TRAINING

Learning by attending a formal class (even if delivered via webcast) will result in the trainee receiving a much broader and deeper understanding of a subject. Since there is much more heavy lifting involved in producing a classroom-delivered curriculum, there is almost always an investment requirement on the part of the trainee and the risk of non-credible instructors greatly diminishes. Even so, you will want to ensure that the organization (whether it is a university, an institute, a learning company, or another entity) has a track record for success and clearly details the level of effort and the expected takeaway for the trainee.

> **Expected investment requirements:** $5,000–$20,000, including internal soft costs
>
> **Expected duration:** 1–12 weeks
>
> **Pros:** Focused content delivery and ability to work with outsiders

> **Cons: Subject matter not taught in the context of the employer**
>
> **Comparative value: Low moderate to high moderate**

INTEGRATED LEARNING

Sometimes referred to as *blended learning*, an integrated learning program melds several content delivery methods, including webinars, self-directed study, classroom training, and one-on-one mentoring and coaching. Teaching the theory on the subject is delivered classroom style—with supplemental self-study on additional structured materials. And the trainee gains experience and wisdom by leveraging the theoretical content into a practical application with the support of a knowledgeable coach who is assigned to the trainee.

> **Expected investment requirements: $5,000–$20,000, including internal soft costs**
>
> **Expected duration: 4–16 weeks**
>
> **Pros: A combination of general education and practical experience applied at your place of employment, with greater scheduling flexibility and delivered at a pace more compatible with the demands of the trainee's work responsibilities**

(Continued...)

> **Cons: Considerable commitment on the part of the trainee and the employer to complete**
>
> **Comparative value: Moderate to high moderate**

COMPANY-SPECIFIC EDUCATION PROGRAMS

Best-in-class companies do not follow the best-practices documents created by consulting companies and analysts; they create their own. They realize the published best practices should be considered guidance as they are always in the past tense—what is documented as best at one time has evolved since then. If the company were to actually achieve the practices identified as best, it would mean the company is years behind the industry leaders.

Best-in-class companies create their own education programs by teaching the known tools and methodologies as they are applied in the context of the company, within the company. These programs start with the company acquiring (*not creating*) a robust base curriculum. They then merge this acquired curriculum with the company-specific materials associated with on-the-job training and deploy on the learning delivery platforms associated with integrated learning.

If properly and fully developed, this approach and the resultant program will yield the highest comparative value for a company by enabling the company to identify what actually needs improving and to go about improving it. Then, the company can identify, quantify, and capture their own best practices and make this content part of the curriculum to be replicated across the enterprise as appropriate.

Expected investment requirements: $10,000–$40,000, including soft costs

Expected duration: 10–32 weeks

Pros: The program should be self-funding. Since each trainee must satisfactorily complete a project that has been approved by the company, the benefits realized should more than offset any investments made. Over time, the curriculum becomes more company specific, acting as a force multiplier by capturing best practices and accelerating their replication across the enterprise.

Cons: This method requires a significant amount of effort; the program trainees need to be properly vetted to ensure they can complete the program and will remain with the company so the investment is recouped.

Comparative value: High moderate to high

VARIANT: DEFICIT-BASED LEARNING

A possible variant to integrated learning or company-specific education programs might be to consider the appropriateness of deficit-based learning.

Most people who are to be involved in a continuous improvement or operational excellence program will have gained certain knowledge and experience from their involvement in previous initiatives, whether those were in your organization, in a previous position, or from other learning opportunities. As a result, they might actually become disengaged in the new program due to the boredom of having to endure redundant training: *Why do I have to learn this? I already have been trained on this material.* You should instead leverage preexisting knowledge, either to immediately recruit the employee to a team or to have them train others.

To minimize redundant training and to take advantage of expertise, it is advantageous to assess the trainee for their preexisting knowledge (theoretical) and ability (practical) and to compare that with the minimum expectations of the proposed instruction. As with all other dimensions and variables in the program, the organization needs to establish minimum levels of knowledge based on their needs. They should then be able to score the assessment against these established minimums. Therefore, flexibility is built into this assessment to suit the specific requirements of your company. The trainee can then be educated only in the areas they need improvement in.

It is important that the assessments are not simple tests based on true/false or multiple-choice questions. Rather, the assessments should be a combination of basic information coupled with an evaluation of the trainee's ability to think critically and apply their knowledge. Accordingly, there should be a written portion in which the trainee is presented with a situation and they must explain, in a narrative essay, their approach to the situation, the results they would expect, and any considerations that might need to be deliberated. A further practical assessment, wherein the trainee is presented with an actual situation that exists in the company, might also be incorporated.

Expected investment requirements: $10,000– $40,000, including soft costs. Any investment savings here would be marginal as compared with the company-specific integrated learning program.

Expected duration: 4–22 weeks. The real benefit of this approach is that the student will pass through the course more quickly (4-22 weeks as opposed to 10-32 weeks) and therefore the benefit to the company would be realized sooner than by learning using the company-specific integrated learning program.

Pros: The employee completes the program more quickly, which results in less indirect time spent learning (and being taught), and the company benefits from the employee's capabilities more quickly; the employee maintains a higher level of engagement; it enhances the training experience and keeps the employee motivated for the program by concentrating learning efforts on what is unknown rather than reviewing what is already known; it minimizes the effort (and investment) required to train the employee.

Cons: The company needs to determine the acceptable level of proficiency for each of the capabilities

(Continued . . .)

being taught and be able to measure the existing proficiency of the employee against these metrics; this is something the company may not know, and it will cost time and treasure to develop. Deficit-based learning should only be considered an option when metrics have already been established rather than a precursor to launching an operational excellence program.

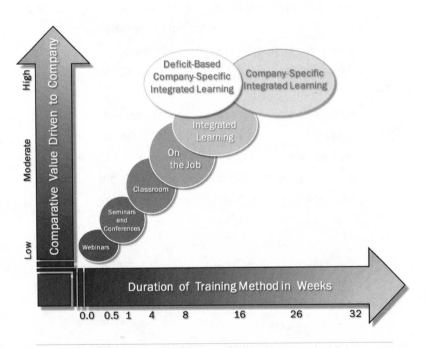

Figure 16.1. Education and training: Value received and investment requirements.

Even within these content and delivery options, there are factors that must be considered in creating a company-specific education program, such as who is responsible for the program development and delivery, including the curriculum, education, training, coaching, and mentorship.

Regardless of approach taken, your company should standardize the curriculum used for all trainees being trained to similar levels. This will allow for the establishment of metrics to compare students and their outcomes to what they have learned. In this manner, you can also determine if a trainee didn't properly absorb the material or—if enough trainees show a similar weakness—that the curriculum itself needs improvement.

The development and deployment options can be defined in one of four ways:

INTERNAL

With the *internal* approach, the company tries to build its own operational excellence program from the ground up. Usually, the company will seek existing resources from within the company as the foundation and then augment these resources with new hires who might have special skill that are found to be lacking.

The challenge with developing a team internally, and why almost all of these initiatives fail to realize their potential, is that the efforts, energy, and talent required to successfully develop and deploy such a program are noncore to the company. For instance, an aircraft manufacturer knows how to engineer and build an aircraft, but they know far less about building an operational excellence program. Although there are a lot of street smarts as a result of hiring from within, there will also be a high risk of the approaches being inbred—less inclined to see opportunities or approaches from different perspectives—which will stifle innovation and inhibit transformational change.

But the biggest challenge and risk is, by far, time. Finding and onboarding the people, creating education and training curriculum, and building all of the infrastructure necessary to launch will take a very long time—years. This will cause the company to start working on improvements before they have structured a program, and the efforts will never mature into being a program.

The result is usually an initiative that is a hodgepodge of assorted tools and materials for improving disparate processes. The efforts will lack coordination, and the creation of synergies and the form of the efforts will never be proactive but reactive instead—see the crisis, fight the crisis. Since the efforts of the program are at best loosely aligned with the company's strategies, the company leadership's support and commitment wanes along with the possible results.

EXTERNAL

With the *external* approach, the company subcontracts out the development and deployment of the program to resources external to the company. These external resources will almost never have experience with the industry, much less the company, especially when compared to the homegrown resources allocated in the internal approach.

Although the teachers will be empathetic and have book smarts, they will lack the street smarts—how the company works and how to apply what is being taught. The education and training materials will almost always be standardized and generic and may not be specifically relevant to the company or its operations. This will require the trainee to use their imagination to relate what they are learning to how it might be applied within their company.

In addition, the trainee will face challenges retaining the knowledge. Most external training programs require that the trainee goes off-site to receive instruction. But many studies have shown that the average student can only absorb approximately four hours per day—anything more is wasted time. Furthermore, if the trainee does not immediately apply the knowledge they have learned, it will atrophy, and, after six months, it will be as if they never learned it at all.

The end result is usually greater than that of the underfunded and underrespected efforts in internal development, but the lack of application knowledge means the trainees, once their training is complete, will be wondering, *what now?* And soon after, so will the company.

HYBRID

A *hybrid* approach pairs internal and external program development approaches: A partnership is created between the internal resources (who have the street smarts and intimate knowledge of the business's strategy and their industry) and external resources (who have book smarts and a command of the tools, have developed professional curriculum they keep current, and are expert educators and mentors).

This approach allows a company to maintain concentration on its core value proposition while leveraging its business and industry knowledge into a program framework and delivery mechanism that does not have to be created from scratch.

My experience has been that this is the most successful approach in the development and deployment of a program, and it yields the greatest net benefit to the company. By pursuing this approach, each and every party brings to the program their core competencies, with the result being rapid design and launch, low and flexible ongoing investment requirements, clearer metrics that are easier to monitor, a focus on the company strategy and not nostalgia or relationships, a vested interest realizing (and reporting) results, and momentum.

INTERNAL TURNED EXTERNAL

The *internal-turned-external* approach is the most complex, and—although potentially a very robust approach—it is wrought with challenges and risks. In essence, the internal-turned -external approach begins as an internal program or, alternatively, as an external program or hybrid program that became an internal program.

At some point, a decision is made to offer the services of the program so enjoyed by the company to other companies—the open market. They are relatively easy to spot because their names are usually a concatenation of the company name plus the word *consulting* attached to the end, such as Tata Consulting, Renault Consulting, and Porsche Consulting—or dedicated groups within companies like the consulting group within DuPont Sustainable Solutions.

The peril is that they become a victim of their own success. As semi-independent or completely autonomous business units—responsible for revenue generation and driving profit to the bottom line of the business unit's corporate master—who gets priority? Is it the paying customer, or is it the corporate master that gets the first draft pick for talent? Does the corporate master get the best resources and the customer gets the others? How is the conflict managed, and what are the protocols to ensure everyone gets the quality and professionalism they deserve?

I am not saying such a configuration cannot work, and I am not saying it does work—my personal observations are inconclusive. But the risk is real enough, and it's not a risk that is necessary to take. So why take it? Why would I want to create an organization that might compete with my own organization someday? And why would I want to hire an organization that I might someday have to compete against for the best resources and attention? I wouldn't.

If the company has enough bandwidth and diversity, and if there are strong protocols for resolving conflict and competition for attention and resources, then there is a strong chance the program can be as successful as the hybrid approach.

———

In the end, sponsorship and support for the program from the highest levels of leadership in the company are necessary for the program to be successful and meet the expectations mutually set and accepted. Perhaps the program efforts and employee training might be integrated into the human resource functions of the company (tied to positive reinforcement mechanisms) and ultimately become part of the fabric of the company.

Continuing education is critical to any professional who wants to remain on top of their game, but, as an operational excellence professional, you already know that. The questions remain: How much is there to know compared with how much you need to know? And how much do you actually know compared with how much you think you know?

CHAPTER 17

LESSONS FROM MT. STUPID

"Experience is a hard teacher because
she gives the test first, the lesson afterward."

—Vernon Law

We have all exceeded our capabilities at one time or another and probably more than once. Sometimes, we purposefully exceed our known capabilities to see how far we can go. You might call these *stretch goals*. Other times, we do not know what we are capable of until we do something to find out. Think, "look ma', no hands!" or "here, hold my beer and watch this!" Welcome to Mt. Stupid.

Human nature, being what it is, causes us to take our time before we make a decision about anything—somewhere between instantly and never. However, once the decision is made, we are eager to start. Sometimes, we are too eager. Oftentimes, in our haste and our hubris, we overestimate what we can do or what can be done, or we underestimate the time or effort it might take. Sometimes we get swept up in the moment of some early successes and let them set an expectation for the future that ultimately proves to be unsustainable.

Consider every "bubble" that has eventually burst; think about the stock-market crash of 1929, which found shoe-shine boys recommending company shares whose valuations were forever going to increase, or the housing crisis, which caught people thinking house prices would endlessly increase in value at a rate of 5 percent or more. Too often, people think recent results will trend indefinitely into the future, forever.

Well, forever is always much shorter a time than we imagine. But there is a model for this reasoning that applies to the initial launch of any new initiative, and operational excellence is no exception to this model. Understanding this and how it will apply to you and your company's efforts, and knowing what the symptoms are so you might see the warnings, will save you a lot of grief and increase your chances for success.

THE HEGELIAN DIALECTIC

The Hegelian dialectic is a form of argument and reasoning that is named after Georg Wilhelm Friedrich Hegel, a German Philosopher who lived from 1770 to 1831, who is credited with its formation and development. Not to be confused with a debate, a *dialectic* is a much more analytical engagement based on rational discourse and designed to discover a truth—at least as much as a truth can be discovered.

The Hegelian dialectic is usually described in three phases:

⇨ Thesis: a new paradigm, usually a transformational challenge to the status quo

⇨ Antithesis: what contradicts or negates the thesis

⇨ Synthesis: the reconciliation of the thesis and antithesis

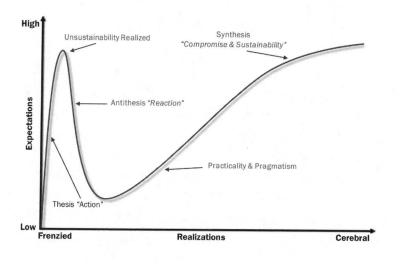

Figure 17.1. The Hegelian dialectic.

We see this pattern repeat itself throughout history. A glaring example in contemporary times came with the introduction of the Internet—when the "dot-com" bubble resulted in the "dot-bomb" bust.

Thesis (Upstroke)

In the late 1990s, the Internet was the next undiscovered territory—a technical Wild West, where everything and anything was possible, without boundaries and without limitation. Soon, the hype turned into a frenzy as start-up after start-up promised great fortunes in the new economy of dot-coms and scoffed at those companies still dependent on the brick-and-mortar form of business.

It did not matter that these cyber–*Young Turks*[1] and their fledgling companies were losing money by the barrelful. In their "new economy," cash didn't matter. What mattered was eyeballs on their websites. And the CEOs of these new-economy companies, when challenged, would scoff arrogantly at the ignorant old-timers who just didn't understand. Investment money kept pouring in, chasing revenue and profitability numbers that had no basis in reality. At one point, a company called e-Stamps, which sold stamps over the Internet, was valued at more than the United States Postal Service. How can that possibly be?

The mantra of this thesis became, *If you are not an Internet company, you are a dinosaur business and about to become extinct.* The euphoria drove the stock prices of the dot-coms to unrealistic and unsustainable levels: the dot-com bubble.

Antithesis (Downstroke)

Suddenly and spectacularly, this bubble exploded in 2001, and the companies whose fall from grace was so swift and remarkable became known as *dot-bombs*. Billions—if not trillions—of dollars were lost in a very short time by investors across the spectrum, from the institutional investor to the investment novice. The once-mighty CEOs of these companies, who had demonstrated such hubris, were exposed for the arrogance in their ignorance.

Afterward, business models that relied on the Internet were

anathema by the investing community. The opinion on business changed overnight from, *If you are not an Internet business, you are soon to be extinct* to *If you are an Internet business, you are not a real business.* The pendulum of paradigm shifts swings from the extreme of euphoria and aspiration to the extreme of detestation and dismissal.

Synthesis (Sustainability)

But, over time, more pragmatic eyes looked beyond the hype of the Internet and focused on the realistic potential and power it held. The market matured, and so did business models, giving us innovative companies like Google and social media companies like Facebook and LinkedIn and transforming the travel industry in its entirety. And although users and eyeballs to the websites are still important, they are secondary to Earnings Before Interest, Taxes, Depreciation, and Amortizations (EBITDA) and cash flow generated from operations—you know, the boring "old-economy" stuff.

THE DUNNING–KRUGER EFFECT

> "Pride goeth before destruction,
> and a haughty spirit before a fall."
>
> —Proverbs 16:18

In 1999, Dunning and Kruger[2] released a study on what came to be known as the *Dunning–Kruger effect*: For a given challenge, people who do not realize the limits of their competence will pursue a path with great but misplaced confidence until it is glaringly apparent they have exceeded their capabilities and the path they have chosen is wrought with peril. Ultimately, the expectations far exceed their ability to deliver and they fail in spectacular fashion. This failure will result in either a terminus or a rebirth tempered with the newfound wisdom from lessons learned.

As we will see, the Dunning–Kruger effect is a variant of the Hegelian Dialectic. Therefore, knowing the predictability of the path and the symptoms (including expectations set on false trajectories, our own ignorance of what we don't know, and hubris), if recognized, can help you avoid (or minimize) the pain and casualties of the inevitable downstroke.

Choosing the Team

> "Remember: upon the conduct of each
> depends the fate of all."
>
> —Alexander the Great

Embarking on a new venture, breaking new ground (even if it's not necessarily new, just new to the participants), is very exciting. Everyone "psychs" themselves up to face the challenge and the unknown. They take on the attitude of a conqueror. But does excitement for the opportunity result in the right individuals being chosen to complete the task? Are the people who are selected, or who volunteer, actually up to the task?

The selection process is the most critical step when formulating the members of the team—especially those initial members who will form the core, the leadership, of the group. During the interview, you will want to select individuals whose credentials and experience satisfy the prima facie requirements, but you may gravitate toward selecting the most confident and gung-ho individuals you can find—those who possess a *can-do/is-done* attitude—over those who are more cerebral, contemplative, deliberate, and modest. In allowing excitement to overshadow the selection and acting too hastily to achieve your objectives as quickly as possible, you risk selecting the unsound and unproven performers (who are uniquely unaware of their own inability and the inherent hazard that goes along with it) over more capable people (who are consciously cognizant of the reality of the challenge and therefore more reserved).

Naturally, you selected gung-ho over cerebral.

The Ascent of Mt. Stupid

> "Ignorance more frequently begets
> confidence than does knowledge."
>
> —Charles Darwin

And so our ambitious—but unlearned and unprepared—adventurer finds himself on the team and begins his ill-conceived journey up the slope of Mt. Stupid. Subtle warnings he might not be on sound footing go largely ignored. Instead, he either overestimates his own skill because he doesn't know any better or fails to recognize genuine skill in others because he doesn't realize his own personal shortcomings.

Reaching the Summit

> "Real knowledge is to know
> the extent of one's ignorance."
>
> —Confucius

More often than not, and directly related to his level of confidence and the size of his ego, our adventurer becomes self-aware that he lacks the skills or knowledge when the decisions he has made, or course he is on, are found to be incontrovertibly wrong or severely inadequate. At this point, he has reached the peak of Mt Stupid. He is finally faced with—and must acknowledge—the fallibility brought by his own lack of skill and capability.

Falling Off the Cliff

> "The only real mistake is the one
> from which we learn nothing."
>
> —Henry Ford

Depending on how high our adventurer has climbed and the magnitude of mistakes he allowed his misguided confidence and ego to drive him to, the fall from the peak can be a gentle roll down a hill or a long plummet off a cliff. It is at this point that the misalignment of expectations with the results is glaringly apparent. He and the operational excellence program are deemphasized or outright terminated. But this failure, although it is predestined, is not derived from nefarious intent. Indeed, it subscribes to Hanlon's razor: "Never attribute to malice that which is adequately explained by stupidity." (Folks would be wise to remember this when reading posts on Facebook.)

Valley of Despair

> "Every adversity, every failure, every heartache carries with it the seed of an equal or greater benefit."
>
> —Napoleon Hill

Eventually, our adventurer completes his fall and finds himself at the bottom. He has lost all confidence in himself and his beliefs. At this point, he has to make a decision. Does he reassess his circumstances and begin to take corrective action? Or does he give up and decide to sell spirit stones in Sedona?

And what about the company? Does it assess its experiences and reengineer and redeploy the operational excellence program? Or does it eliminate it to reduce costs?

STEVE JOBS'S CLIMB AND FALL FROM MT. STUPID

Probably the best example of a visit to the valley of despair is the story of Steve Jobs and the company he cofounded with Steve Wozniak, Apple Computer. Soon after Apple Computer went public, its board of directors became uncomfortable with its leader being rather inexperienced in business—especially a publicly traded company looking to transition from an entrepreneurial start-up to a mature enterprise.

(Continued...)

After Jobs was responsible for a few product failures that were the result of his unabashed hubris (such as the Apple LISA), he was unceremoniously discharged from the company he helped to create.

But Jobs did not wallow in self-pity for long. First, he took his fortune and started NeXT Incorporated. With the help of Ross Perot, NeXT Incorporated was eventually sold to Apple. Afterward, Jobs bought the Graphics Group from Lucasfilm, which he renamed Pixar, and helped to make the company a huge success. He parlayed his investment into his being the largest private investor of the Walt Disney Company (7 percent) and a seat on its board of directors.

In 2000, with Apple Computer facing a life-and-death struggle, Apple's board of directors asked Steve Jobs to rejoin the company, and he eventually became president and CEO.

Slope of Enlightenment

"Ignorance has always been the weapon of tyrants; enlightenment the salvation of the free."

—Bill Richardson

Let's assume our adventurer does not give up his career as a change agent to live off the land and start a head shop (marijuana dispensary) in Seattle, but, instead, he decides to reflect on his experience and discover the way forward.

In this phase, he performs a self-assessment of his beliefs and capabilities. He compares them with what is needed to achieve his goals. And he acquires the capability (either personally or by proxy) he lacks.

Plateau of Sustainability

> "One of the painful things about our time is
> that those who feel certainty are stupid, and
> those with any imagination and understanding
> are filled with doubt and indecision."
>
> —Bertrand Russell

In this final phase, real sustainability is achieved. There is no fanfare. There is no panic or talk of a "burning platform." There is just cerebral and methodical forward movement in a continuous and deliberate manner.

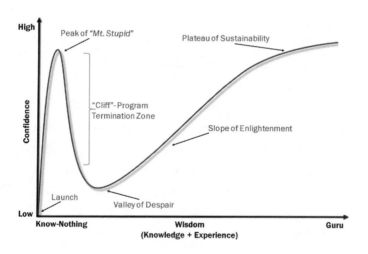

Figure 17.2. Dunning–Kruger Effect: The journey on Mt. Stupid.

The Humble Servant Leader

> "A fool thinks himself to be wise,
> but a wise man knows himself to be a fool."
>
> —William Shakespeare

There is something magical that also happens to our adventurer. His experience has taught him he does not know nearly as much as he thought he did and—striped of hype and hubris—his confidence has been set to be more aligned with reality. Over time, even as he learns more and more, he realizes his knowledge in absolute terms is less and less. He has become humble and wise. The transformation from being a Luke Skywalker to an Obi-Wan Kenobi is complete.

And now, a true mentor, he can be a positive and indelible force within the world.

———

So what can we learn from this? And how can we apply it to our operational excellence programs?

⇨ If this is your first attempt at operational excellence (or continuous improvement or Lean Six Sigma), make every attempt to set pragmatic goals. Hire the cerebral and the deliberate over the emotionally supercharged. Listen to them and give them the support they need. Realize everyone's expectations will probably not be met.

⇨ If you have climbed and fallen from Mt. Stupid—or are about to—brush yourself off and take a moment to reflect on the journey. What was good? What was not so good? How can we build on the successes? How can we ensure that failures do not recur? After all, the only alternatives to moving forward are to stand still or go backward, and you know your competitors (and the marketplace) are not going to follow suit.

⇨ Get going again. Move forward with your newfound expertise and wisdom.

⇨ Achieve a sustainable program in both pace and impact.

In all things, in all initiatives, and in all great aspirations, you should evaluate critically, consider cerebrally, prepare calmly, and act deliberately.

CHAPTER 18

TURNING A VISION INTO REALITY

"First comes thought, then organization of that
thought into ideas and plans, then transformation
of those plans into reality. The beginning, as
you will observe, is in your imagination."

—Napoleon Hill

What does it take to get from the idea to the realization of that idea? How do we get from a dream or the scribblings on the back of a napkin or some vivid imagery that is concocted in our mind's eye—perhaps the result of a peyote-induced haze—to something tangible we can deliver to our customers or our colleagues? What does it take, what is the process, to get from contemplation to completion? How do we turn our visions into a reality?

LESSONS FROM THE EARTH TO THE MOON

When I was younger, the space race was in full swing. There was no International Space Station (or any space station) and no Space Shuttle, and Neil Armstrong had not yet set foot on the Moon. I am too young to remember any of the Mercury or Gemini missions, but I do remember many of the Apollo missions. And I remember that each and every launch from Cape Canaveral was watched with intensity from every television in the nation, perhaps the world.

Vision

Vision is the image of the future that you have for your company.

The key to success for any initiative is to be able to know what the vision is—in its most simple and raw form—and to effectively communicate what that vision is to the team in clear and concise language so everyone can understand what the company stands for and what it strives to be. You must align the team so they know their roles in pursuit of this vision and what they are expected to accomplish.

In the case of our heroes at Mission Control, their vision began in 1961, when President John F. Kennedy proclaimed,

> **"I believe that this nation should commit itself to achieving the goal, before this decade is out, of landing a man on the Moon and returning him safely to the Earth."**[1]

Make no mistake in the boldness of this statement, especially the latter part. It's far simpler to put a man on the Moon than it is to put a man on the Moon *and* get him safely back to Earth. But no matter how bold a statement it was or how complex it would actually be to fulfill, the elegance of its simplicity made it all seem plausible and possible.

Kennedy had motivation. The Soviet Union had just put the

first man in space,[2] which showed the world that the United States was behind the Soviets in aerospace technology—and, by inference, maybe many other technologies. But Kennedy had a gut feeling, based on the accomplishments of the first half of the century—a century that saw the invention of flight, the harnessing of electricity, the automobile, submarines, space flight, and the splitting of the atom—that his bold gauntlet was achievable.

The very first step in achieving any future state is to define, as completely and as simply as you can, what it is you want to accomplish: What are the goals? Every sport has a means of calculating success or levels of success. Football has the aptly named goal line. Golf counts strokes. Even synchronized swimming has a manner of obtaining a score, however subjective it might be. (And don't get me started on cricket.) How will you know if you have accomplished your objectives if they are not defined?

Visions of the future do not have to be complex. In fact, the best visions are simple, succinct, elegant, and understandable. This is necessary because you will never be able to describe your vision to someone with as much clarity and detail as it is in your mind, unless you distill it down to its raw essence as Kennedy did. From a practical perspective, this is a requirement because you will need a cadre of people with their diverse talents and expertise to make your vision a reality. If you find your vision is complicated, chances are you don't understand it well enough yourself—never mind trying to explain it to others. Go back and do a better job. Revise your goals until they are clear, concise, and achievable.

Strategy

Once you have defined your vision, it's time to start figuring out how you are going to realize it. And to do that, you need to start mapping and planning the path to your vision, beginning at the highest-level view, the macro level. This is the essence of forming a strategy.

When President John F. Kennedy shared his vision of the Moon landing with the world, he also understood what it would take for its successful achievement. He might not have had a clue as to how it was going to be accomplished, but he knew it was going to take treasure and talent—and a lot of each—to realize this ambition. Things that were not even thought of yet would have to be invented, even materials that didn't yet exist. It was going to take a lot of real estate, and there were going to have to be a lot of people involved. It was also dangerous; the risk of people dying was very real.

Tactics

Tactics are how things get done. You have to be able to develop the tactics in alignment with your strategy in pursuit of your vision. These tactics have to be developed, then chunked down into manageable aspects (projects or missions). Once the commitment to the vision across the organization is understood, the actual hard work of pursuit can start.

Close cross-departmental collaboration is critical; you will need the commitment of those who will ultimately make the dreams a reality. However, you will never obtain commitment from everyone, and there is no such thing as the perfect plan. Here, gaining trust is a prime objective. People are more likely to support a plan they might disagree with but were given a fair say in than they are to follow a plan that is thrust on them dictatorially.

For the moonshot, this required the creation of an entity to lead the program, which resulted in the formation of NASA (the National Aeronautics and Space Administration). Then, concepts on how to achieve the ultimate vision had to be developed and vetted, along with a multitude of waypoints that needed to be accomplished as precursors to finally realizing the end goal. All manner of engineering had to take place to either prove or disprove the viability of the various approaches—and new materials and technologies had to be created. Then they had to plan, build, test, refine, and, finally, implement these innovations into working product. They also had to acquire knowledge, experience, and wisdom by working with the innovations through a series of evolutionary exercises such as launching a man in a space vehicle and safely recovering him to Earth (the Mercury and Gemini programs), Extra-Vehicular Activities (EVAs)— or as they are more commonly known, *space walks*—detaching then redocking two vehicles each traveling at seventeen thousand miles per hour, and countless other necessary achievements before a mission to the Moon could be attempted.

Logistics

To support the tactics in pursuit of the strategy to achieve the vision of sending a man to the Moon and returning him safely back to Earth required a lot of everything, including manpower, materials, innovation, invention, real estate, and commodities. And all of this was going to require money, lots and lots of money. All of these resources, and the management of the entire supply chain, are the necessary *logistics*.

By most accounts, the Apollo program employed 400,000 people and involved over 20,000 businesses and universities across the United States at its peak. It cost $42 billion in 1960s money—over $300 billion in 2016 dollars. It was, and still is, the single biggest peacetime program ever undertaken by any government in history.

Execute

Finally, you have to execute, take action.

I was fascinated by the scenes from Mission Control in Houston, Texas, as the time to launch approached. Mission Control was a huge room that looked almost like a theater. There were big screens and projectors at the front, with several rows of stations and monitors. Each row was a bit higher than the one in front of it and set in an arc facing the screen. Each station represented a system and was manned by at least one person monitoring that system, looking at the values being displayed and what the system was telling them.

Prior to the launch, the flight director polls the person in charge of each of the systems and asks whether they are a go or no-go. The person in charge of each system would respond, verbally, whether they are either a go or a no-go—shrugging shoulders and responding "Ehhh, maybe" is not an acceptable response. This is demonstrative of alignment, commitment, and accountability.

It is only after this all-systems-go confirmation that the launch can commence. Because the flight director knows that when he pushes the button, whatever else happens, the vehicle will not remain on the launch pad. The mission will either be a complete success or incremental levels of less success. The flight director is alone in the final decision. If it goes horribly wrong, the astronauts will die, and the flight director will have to live with his decision to launch for the rest of his life. Which is worse?

STRATEGIC, TACTICAL, OR LOGISTICAL— WHICH ARE YOU?

I have met countless operational excellence professionals over the course of my career, and I have become acquainted with their roles and efforts in regards to driving value to their organizations. Although they possess great passion for and take great pride in the value they drive within their companies, these professionals often express frustration at the lack of proper support from their company in their efforts.

Interestingly—perhaps even tellingly—although almost all of them consider themselves and their efforts "strategic" to the company, very few of them actually are. In examining the level of (*actual*, not *stated*) support given by the company to the operational excellence efforts and the net-benefit impact those involved in the operational excellence initiatives drive within their company, I have concluded that there are three levels of organizational maturity: logistical (the lowest), tactical (the middle level), and strategic (the highest). Of course, the operational excellence efforts at any given time, and within any given company, will possess characteristics of all three. It is the level of organization, structure, consistency, pervasiveness, and orientation to the company vision that determines what level of maturity actually exists.

First, you need to know what your company vision is. This is not to be confused with a mission statement, which are almost always far too vague and filled with so much drivel—empty phrases and buzzwords—as to serve no useful purpose. Rather, this is a simple statement (a *vision* statement) with specific objectives to describe the future state of the company or business unit. It might have to do with products or market share (even for specific markets) or how the company might bring products to market or even mergers and acquisitions. The objective here is to align the efforts toward the realization of this vision.

Next, you have to understand the importance of the prioritization of these efforts. It is vital to understand that priorities, once they are set, should not change often (and should do so only for very good reason). There is nothing that can diminish the results of these efforts more quickly than resetting priorities,

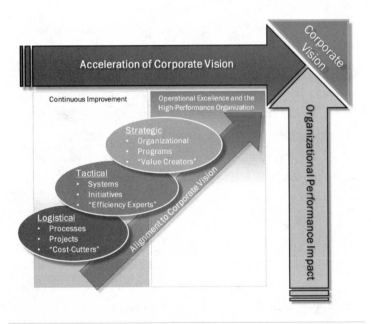

Figure 18.1. Operational excellence maturity model.

and it is imperative to realize not everything can be the highest priority; if everything is of the highest priority, then nothing is. It is vital that you understand that the single most critical responsibility of executive leadership is to achieve the vision for the company; anything that does not help in that effort is of secondary importance at best. Therefore, it is wise for you to take the time and make the effort to understand what is of value to the executive leadership and align your efforts accordingly. Only then will you gain the support and respect you need for your program.

Below, I detail the three maturity levels of continuous improvement and operational excellence efforts and some of their characteristics.

Logistical

Logistical is the lowest level of continuous improvement maturity. It is most likely found in organizations that are in the early and unproven stages of their journey or in an organization where the results of previous journeys have been a disappointment.

Organized Around Projects

A characteristic at this level of maturity will be that the efforts are organized around individual projects that are not related. The efforts are largely reactive with resources being deployed when and where problems manifest themselves. If there is any capturing and replication of improvement efforts and lessons learned, they are minimal.

Emphasis on Optimizing Processes

As one might expect with an emphasis on processes, the field of view for the efforts is usually linear, and the efforts are largely dedicated to eliminating variants and increasing the velocity of the throughput.

Little Alignment to the Vision of the Company

It is highly likely that the deployment resources have little real knowledge of what the vision (future state) of the company might be, and the efforts are not deliberately designed with the pursuit of the vision.

Incremental Performance Impact

The benefits of the company's efforts are certainly real, but they are made incrementally. After all, I have never seen or heard of a continuous improvement effort that resulted in a worse situation than when they started. Normally, disappointment occurs because the benefits realized are not what was expected or promised.

The Continuous Improvement Team's Role Viewed as Cost Cutting

The continuous improvement team is often seen only with the goal of cutting costs through the reduction of inventory, waste, or even personnel. As a result, the team is not embraced by the rank-and-file and, in fact, will most likely face significant resistance. Spies and assassins are never trusted or loved by anyone.

Priority Level 3

As your efforts begin to mature and there is more structure, opportunities for improvement that have the above characteristics should be given a priority level of 3, the lowest level. These are the efforts that are completed by the newly assigned or otherwise indoctrinated resources to hone their newly learned skills or when there are no opportunities with higher levels.

Tactical

The tactical level is intermediary. Organizations at this level have made progress in the development and deployment of their continuous improvement program, but it is not yet an operational excellence program.

Organized Around Business Smokestacks

As the continuous improvement efforts become more mature, they will become more structured and organized, becoming initiatives. These efforts will look at the value-stream map within business smokestacks inside the organization, such as production, logistics, sales, and so on. Accordingly, the efforts will become less reactive and more proactive.

An Emphasis on Optimizing Systems

Instead of focusing the efforts on individual processes, the continuous improvement team will begin to consider the vast number of processes that constitute a system within the business smokestack and will begin to examine the impact of improvements throughout the entire value stream.

Increasing Alignment to the Company's Vision

Even if it is not completely conscious and deliberate, at the tactical level of maturity, there is growing awareness of the desired future state of the company by the continuous improvement deployment professionals, and their efforts become increasingly aligned with this vision.

Growing Performance Impact

The magnitude of the benefits realized by the company when the improvement goals are placed on optimized and balanced systems (a collection of related and integrated processes) rather than on individual processes will be significantly greater than optimizing processes alone.

The Continuous Improvement Team Viewed as Efficiency Experts

The continuous improvement team that has achieved a tactical level of maturity is increasingly viewed as efficiency experts and not just cost cutters. But since they are usually working on processes within business smokestacks, observers will perceive the benefits in the form of increases in efficiencies within those smokestacks.

Priority Level 2

Opportunities that possess the above characteristics should be assigned a priority level of 2, the middle level. As the continuous improvement capacity and capability mature within an organization—and along with it, an increase in confidence— the emphasis will be on seeking opportunities to address more complex business systems. This will be the goal of those efforts maturing from tactical to logistical maturity and will be used extensively in the support of those efforts that have matured to the strategic level.

Strategic

The strategic level is the highest form of program maturity— the point at which the program is no longer just continuous improvement but is now considered an operational excellence program. Organizations at this level are well on the path of becoming a high-performance organization.

Organized Around the Enterprise

The hallmark of a continuous improvement program that has become an operational excellence program is when the program has evolved to the point where it is structured around the enterprise as a whole, the entire value chain—from the vendor's vendor to the customer's customer. It is not necessary that everyone in the value chain is onboarded with the program, only that there exists the structure and the intent (backed by deeds) to include everyone.

Emphasis on Building Programs

An operational excellence initiative, which has matured to the strategic level, is dedicated to creating a culture of excellence across the organization in an engineered manner. That is, it is deliberate and guided by planning. When the company builds capacity and capability by investing in its people, it is driven by an actual need in the company for a specific purpose. The company does not train individuals just to have trained individuals. This is seen as waste—the same as building inventory that sits idly on the shelf, waiting for a purpose.

Aligned to the Vision of the Company

The operational excellence program is first and foremost dedicated to accelerating the realization of the company's vision; that is its primary mandate. Cutting costs and increasing efficiencies throughout the organization will be a by-product of the efforts, but they are not the principal motivation.

Maximum Performance Impact

By organizing the team around the mission and having those missions aligned with the company's vision and dedicated to the accelerated achievement of the vision, both top-line and bot-tom-line benefits to the company will be as good as they can be. At this level of maturity, the emphasis is no longer confined to the cost of goods sold and general and administrative expenses but also placed on revenue and the effective use of assets (specifically, capital, plant, and equipment). At the highest level of strategic maturity (and in addition to accelerated vision realization), the company will also be able to more readily recognize and respond to opportunities or threats in a rapid and decisive manner.

The Operational Excellence Team Viewed as Value Creators

When the operational excellence efforts have matured to become a primary driver of the company's strategy, the oper-ational excellence team will no longer have to seek recognition and support from the executive leadership; the executive lead-ership will seek them out instead. At this point, operational excellence has evolved to fulfilling a key role in strategy execu-tion and has become instrumental in the company becoming a high-performance organization.

Priority Level 1

The opportunities to accelerate the realization of the compa-ny's strategy, and the threats that might inhibit it, are assigned a priority level of 1, the highest priority. And the company and its resources should naturally behave as one would expect for priority 1 situations and circumstances: Do them first.

———

If you want the efforts to evolve from the logistic or tactical level (continuous improvement), which is the present state of most efforts, to the strategic level (operational excellence), you need to align your efforts to the corporate vision. Become an accelerant of the vision. Take the time to learn it and to build your allegiances toward it.

Start looking at the big picture. Don't look at your shoes; look down the road. Evolve your perspective from processes to systems to the enterprise as a whole. Consider the impact of your efforts on the entire company. Seek to create an organization that works at an optimal state where all the efforts are working in a balanced and harmonic manner. Create cross-functional integration of your business smokestacks and enact the related communication and collaboration protocols.

Accelerate the decision-making process. Learn to see the opportunities and threats more quickly and to configure and deploy an effective and thorough response more rapidly and decisively. Here, understanding the capabilities and capacity of the resources available—and also their weaknesses—is of critical importance. Work toward achieving all of this, and you will gain a level of operational excellence, helping your company become a high-performance organization.

Now that we understand what it is that we are trying to accomplish, why, and to what level, we need to construct a framework to implement. It has to be a framework that will maintain alignment to the vision and must be able to measure progress made toward that vision.

PART 4

STRATEGY EXECUTION

"Take time to deliberate, but when the time for action comes, stop thinking and go in."

—Napoléon Bonaparte

The difference between *strategy* and *strategy execution* is the difference between dreaming and making dreams a reality. Success will be found only if the sequence for success is followed in the proper order: vision building, strategy development, tactical calculi, logistical organization, and, finally, strategy execution.

In a previous incarnation of my company, XONITEK, during the 1990s, we sold, consulted, implemented, and maintained Enterprise Resource Planning (ERP) systems. These systems were used to help integrate and run company operations and touched on everything from finance to customer service, procurement, logistics, and production.

The evaluation process with prospect companies was always long and arduous. It involved a tremendous amount of effort investigating how the company operated and what a successful solution would look like. This was followed by a series of presentations and demonstrations on how the company could use the systems and benefit from the proposed solution. Representatives from every business function would be involved, perform discovery, offer input, and otherwise participate in a meaningful manner in the process—including senior leadership.

All of this was performed before the contract was signed. But in nearly every case, once the decision was made and the contract was signed, the involvement of senior leadership would end. For whatever reason, senior leadership, having made the decision (established the strategy), would in their minds consider the project complete, leaving vulnerable the ultimate level of success realized. Making the decision is only the end of the very beginning; the system still needed to be implemented: strategy execution.

CHAPTER 19

THE ART OF BUSINESS

"Victorious warriors win first and then go to war, while defeated warriors go to war first and then seek to win."

—Sun Tzu

Have you ever wondered how and why so many military terms have made their way into the lexicon of business? Phrases like *We have won the battle for industry leadership,* or *We are fighting off threats* or *engaging in a price war,* or *We have successfully defended our market position* are commonplace. We talk about *gathering intelligence* on our competition and customers *making a preemptive strike, engaging the opportunity,* and even trying to *outmaneuver* the competition. War and business are both concerned with conflict—how to face determined adversaries and succeed. The most obvious difference between engaging in warfare and engaging in business is, in warfare, assets are physically destroyed and lives lost; if either of these normally occurs in your business, you're probably doing it wrong—very wrong. In both warfare and in business, a great deal of mental activity is expended in determining objectives, the means by which these objectives might be obtained, and the potential threats that might be encountered. In both warfare and in business, logistics and resources—such as physical or human assets, treasure, and time—are organized and consumed in the pursuit of the objectives.

In business school, we are taught that a solid strategy does not recognize the notion of victory: There is no end. Strategy is the way to gain and retain an advantage under the current circumstances and into the future but maintain the understanding that adjustments will need to be made.

Some important and useful approaches that have made the leap from warfare to business follow.

RED TEAM

Let's face it. Coming up with an idea is difficult. Depending on the nature of the idea, we might spend days, weeks, months, perhaps years developing the idea. We might put our hearts and souls into it. And the single most stressful moment we will have is presenting our idea to our peers—or worse, to a boss or a client. What might they say? Will they love it? Will they hate it?

As we should have learned by now, there is never a point where an idea is "done." There are only points where decisions are made, followed by a continuous series of refinements. This is to be expected.

But at the point the idea is presented, what words are used, by whom, and when are very delicate matters. Words are very powerful, and they should be wielded in a measured and deliberate manner. Failing to do so can lead to a variety of undesired outcomes.

One of the best techniques used to challenge and refine a hypothesis is to *red team* the ideas. I learned this practice while conducting a series of operational excellence workshops across Europe several years ago from one of my colleagues, Carey "Vixen" Lohrenz, a former carrier-based F-14 Naval aviator.

Red teaming is a method of peer review for an idea that is presented so it can be scrutinized for weaknesses, omissions, and even opportunities, in a nonthreatening and constructive manner. Since the presenter of the idea has an emotional investment, those involved in the red teaming exercise must remain cognizant of the wording they use, inflections and tone of voice, and body posture. You need to avoid provoking a "freeze, fight, or flight" response in the presenter. The purpose of leveraging the red team approach is to ensure that what is being presented has been thoroughly thought out so the desired outcome will be the very best possible.

In a red team exercise, the desired outcomes, challenges, and planned approaches are presented and discussed among the decision-making team and trusted outside advisors. After listening to the presentation, the red team will start asking questions to fully understand the idea. One important technique that is used is to begin the introduction of any argument or point with the phrase, *Have you considered . . .* This is so the presenter understands that the argument is not a personal challenge but a part of the discovery and refinement process.

In the end, if you don't question everything and if you don't foster an environment where others can question everything, instead of surrounding yourself with fools and yes-men, then the success of any decision will mostly be due to luck and relying on hope. And hope is not a strategy; hope is dope.

BRIEFING

Conducting a briefing is an efficient way to convey information among a specified audience. As the name suggests, a *briefing* is brief. It is not a Castro-esque diatribe lasting hours but, rather, a concise delivery of information distilled to its most basic elements. Briefings are used when information needs to be shared quickly and directly and when a decision needs to be made swiftly on the basis of that information. The briefing is intended to offer guidance and instruction just before action is taken.

During a briefing, it is important to keep in mind that communication is a two-way street. A briefing is not a simple download from a leader to a subordinate but an opportunity to ensure everyone understands what is expected and to offer clarity. As such, the audience is responsible for confirming that the information has been received and understood and that there are no questions.

There are four basic types of briefings:

⇨ **Information briefings** deliver information and knowledge in a form the audience can understand and use. Just the facts, an information briefing does not offer recommendations or conclusions. It does not require decisions to be made.

⇨ **Action briefings** have the goal of conveying the information necessary to describe an action and the various expectations involved. The goal is a unity of purpose and the coordination of efforts. It involves giving specific instruction to participants.

⇨ **Decision briefings** are intended to determine a solution through deliberation and the exchange of information.

The goal is to come to a conclusion on a matter and establish a recommendation of a decision for moving forward.

⇨ **Staff briefings** ensure alignment of the parties involved. The speaker discusses the current state of affairs to ensure everyone is aware of the latest circumstances in context.

The importance of briefing cannot be underestimated or undervalued. It is the opportunity for everyone to know and understand what is expected before the action is initiated. Redirects and mistakes after an action starts are almost always more disruptive and costly than taking the extra time up front to gain a clear understanding.

DEBRIEFING

Debriefing is a formal activity whose purpose is to review the facts and observations after some event has occurred. The debrief should be performed consistently after each engagement, project, or event within the company's value chain and should be part of your standard operating procedure.

Even if it's not convenient and there's pressure to move on to the next thing, debriefing is essential. The debrief should occur as soon as is reasonably possible after the event, while the memory of the event is still fresh in everyone's mind and there is an opportunity for those who were directly involved in the event to examine what occurred and to share their experience with others. An effective debrief is team-centric. There is no rank or hierarchy among the participants; everyone is considered equal. It is an opportunity to openly and honestly share one's feelings and observations without fear of recrimination or reprisals. Properly performed, a debrief is an excellent opportunity to build trust and understanding and is a pillar of team building. Anyone not directly involved in the engagement, even those in a position of authority, should be specifically excluded.

A proper debrief is not a haphazard meeting but, rather, is structured and formal and conducted in a professional manner. It is an opportunity for the team to explore and discover for themselves what happened, why it happened, what the various outcomes were, what worked and what didn't, opportunities for improvement for each individual and for the team as a whole, and how to best capture and leverage the wisdom gained for the next event. Its goals are to capture, distill, and disseminate the results of the event and the lessons learned.

The inputs involved in a debrief include reviewing events, assembling those events in a chronological order, clarifying confusion, building or mending relationships between teammates, and identifying and discussing the opportunities for improvement.

A debrief is a frank and intimate discussion of the engagement of an opportunity or threat and the team's actions and experiences. Each member of the team should purposefully strive for self-discovery and should hold themselves accountable for their actions—or inactions—as members of the team. You also need to reflect, both individually and collectively, on what could have been done better. This self-critique and honesty will build and reinforce trust among members of the team. Constructive criticism and guidance for professional growth are expected.

This can only occur if confidentiality is assured among the team members. What is said in the debrief stays in the debrief, and whatever is discussed should certainly not be reported to a person's boss or the circle of trust will be broken and the value of the debrief will disappear. Such interested parties will receive a report out of the engagement and may be separately debriefed later, as appropriate.

The conclusion of a successful debrief will include the development of a specific action plan to improve the performance of the individuals on the team, as well as building a knowledge base, which leads to wisdom. In this instance, wisdom is the sum of all applied knowledge.

The value of the debrief is to distill experience into lessons learned to be further converted into expertise. As such, it's important to highlight and celebrate individual successes, regardless of the overall outcome (not to be confused with rewarding stupidity or recklessness). The long-term value to the company is to convert a group of individuals who are experts into an expert team.

If that is what debriefing is, then knowing what it's not is equally important. For instance, a proper debriefing is not a stress-management or psychotherapy session, an opportunity to focus on emotions, an opportunity to humiliate or cast blame on other team members, or an opportunity for outsiders to play "Monday morning quarterback." A proper debrief is constructive, not destructive.

REPORT OUT

Confidentiality and team building aside, it is important to perform a *report out* after the debrief so others might learn from the experience. A good report out will include the basic details of the event, such as when and where it occurred, who was directly involved in the event, the intended objective of the event, the basic parameters and circumstances surrounding the event, whether the objective was obtained and to what extent (and if not, why), the lessons learned (without naming names or laying any blame), and what might be done differently and why next time.

Ideally, the results of the report out will be distributed through the organization's knowledge-management system so it can be easily retrieved and replicated when a similar need arises. Too often, I see redundant efforts, where an experience gained within a company is not leveraged elsewhere. Each time, they start from scratch. It is a colossal waste of time and resources. Take the time to know what you know.

SIMULATION

We need to practice before we perform in real life so that we can be as prepared as possible. This is even more true when it comes to efforts that involve teams over that of a single person. In training, an individual person can concentrate purely on improving their own abilities. But as a member of a team, the individual must not only hone their own abilities but also integrate into a group that will demand harmony and balance if the team is to perform in an optimal fashion.

As such, the principles of team building and teamwork can be learned individually, but the real test of understanding and effectiveness will be when the team gets together and practices. These practice sessions will be based on realistic situations under expected circumstances, as close to the "real thing" as you can organize so that the necessary team skills are learned and sharpened. But during the simulations, it is important to also introduce *injects*, those nasty little gremlins that unexpectedly appear during an action and whose sole purpose is to disrupt, perhaps cripple, your endeavors.

However, everyone on the team needs to understand that simulations are not reality but are merely approximations of reality. When reality does come, the individuals on the team, and the team itself, will have to rely on their training and the experience gained in the simulations, adapting and applying what they have learned to the reality.

EFFECTS CHAINS

I have had the opportunity to work closely with Matt "Boom" Daniel. Boom is a graduate of the Virginia Military Institute (VMI). After graduation, he became a Marine Aviator. He also graduated from the United States Navy Fighter Weapons School (also known as Topgun).

He and I have spoken at great length about how companies can take techniques for accelerating the decision-making process and establishing cross-functional integration that are used in the United States Armed Forces and adapt them to business. Some portions of the Operational Excellence Enterprise Readiness Model (see next chapter)—specifically, aspects of business readiness—are a direct result of those conversations and subsequent research and deliberation.

Every enterprise must have processes in order to conduct business. Processes are often combined and interwoven, creating more complex processes and systems. Complex processes can be difficult to track and manage without a concerted effort to horizontally integrate the people, efforts, and equipment across functional business smokestacks and divisions.

Simplistically, a widget-making business makes widgets. They must manufacture and sell their widgets. They must also package, warehouse, and distribute their widgets. They collect input from their customers, partners, and employees, and then they optimize their product and processes. None of these processes can stand alone; they are all interdependent. The company does not want to sell more product than they can make or make more than they can move.

Internally, the business collects payment on their widgets as they are sold. They pay their employees and partners, who make, distribute, and sell the product. They buy raw or processed goods to make their widgets. The business supports their workforce with infrastructure, facilities, benefits, and incentives because they want to be an attractive place to work. After all, they need people to make and move their product.

There are lots of processes that somehow nest together to ensure the business works well and makes a profit. It makes sense for the efforts to be horizontally integrated across the business to maximize efficiency, quality, and profit. Effects chains help to bin and manage such processes.

Horizontal Integration Across the Mission

An *effects chain* is a systems engineering tool that illustrates a sequence of events within a given complex process, called the *mission*. The effects chain systematically decomposes the mission, which is important for analysis. In order to identify areas of inefficiency or where the mission is working, a detailed understanding of each function's responsibilities and metrics is necessary. The effects chain also highlights the level of horizontal integration and interoperability (across the business smokestacks, from start to finish and back) of the components that accomplish the mission.

Effects chains are used to do the following:

⇨ Model, visualize, and simulate business process cycles for process improvement and optimization.

⇨ Understand business taxonomy for current and future operations development.

⇨ Horizontally integrate efforts within the business to enhance team awareness and team building.

⇨ Manage business resources, plans, and personnel to support the business leader's intent.

⇨ Analyze the mission's function and performance to identify key centers of gravity, high return areas.

The Four Actions (Bins):
Focus–Find–Fix–Finish:

The four actions identified in figure 19.1 are generic in nature, represent a nonspecific effects chain, and make up an iterative business mission loop. They illustrate the major muscle movements of a given mission. Similarly, mission-specific effects chain functions generally fall in these action bins.

⇨ **Focus.** Think of the *focus* action as surveillance. We are looking for broader areas on which to focus our efforts from past experience or from incoming intelligence. Our field of vision should be pointed in the right direction in order to identify problems and opportunities.

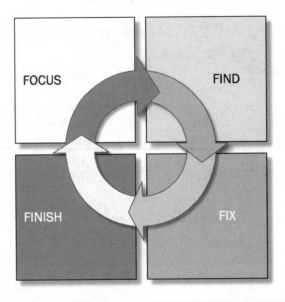

Figure 19.1. A basic effects chain loop.

⇨ **Find.** After focusing on a specific domain, our sensors have picked up a target. When we *find* it, we identify that it is worthy of more attention and it becomes a validated target.

⇨ **Fix.** Tracking a target is difficult, especially if it is moving. When we *fix* a target, we are finding and creating the solution for its precision engagement, and we are handing it off to the resource that will engage it.

⇨ **Finish.** We engage targets after they have been located, identified, and validated. When we *finish* the target, we engage it and then assess the mission for success, failure, or something in between. The assessment feeds back into the beginning of the effects chain and helps focus the effort with now-improved intelligence.

Enhanced Business Execution

The efforts of the first iteration continue in an ever-narrowing refinement of tolerances, using the results from the finish bin to feed into the next (and subsequent) focus bin, continuing the improvement or refinement process in an ever-tightening loop. Instead of a death spiral, a success spiral is created.

Effects chains are used to vet and pursue big decisions. They help identify roles, responsibilities, assumptions, limitations, and constraints. Accordingly, the use of effects chains includes all the right stuff to ensure optimal horizontal integration of decisions and actions with and among each other as they progress toward mission success.

Tailored Effects Chains

Having determined the *why* at the beginning of the effects chain when the mission was defined, by tailoring an effects chain to a business or department, the enterprise will be able to understand which resources are playing where within the chain and who is responsible for integrating with other resources. Now, we need

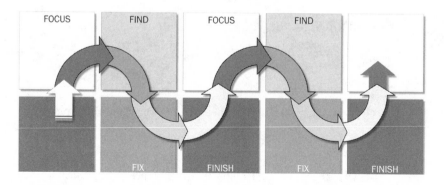

Figure 19.2. *Effects chains success spiral.*

to quickly decide who does what, where, when, with whom, and what resources are required. And we need to know how all of this affects the entire mission and how can it be evaluated.

Most businesses think of their complex processes in a way that is unique to themselves and their own organization. It is important for a business to be able to build their own effects chains at the division level where the functions of the effects chain can be binned into the basic actions: focus, find, fix, and finish.

Understanding what resources (e.g., assets, cash, time, equipment, personnel, activities, and investments) contribute to each of the functions of the effects chain allows for a mission-based analysis of those resources. How well do the resources serve their effects chain functions and how well they interoperate are areas for analysis.

To determine your business processes and effects chains and to understand the value of these effects chains, ask yourself the following questions:

⇨ What are your corporate missions?

⇨ What are the business functions that must be completed to accomplish your business missions?

⇨ Who and what (the logistics) are involved in executing your corporate missions?

⇨ How do these logistics fit together?

⇨ Do the logistics know where they fit together in the plan?

⇨ How do you know if they are successful?

⇨ What are the consequences of their individual successes or failures?

⇨ Can we efficiently and consistently complete business effects chains?

⇨ Where are we tripping up?

Although there are similarities between the effects chain and the OODA loop (chapter 9), the effects chain is designed to consider the capabilities and capacity across the entirety of the enterprise, identify the appropriate assets and resources necessary to support the mission, assess their readiness for deployment, and mobilize accordingly (strategy execution), but the OODA loop is designed to accelerate the decision-making process (strategy development).

CHAPTER 20

THE OPERATIONAL EXCELLENCE ENTERPRISE READINESS MODEL

"Excellence is an art won by training and habituation.
We do not act rightly because we have virtue or
excellence, but we rather have those because we
have acted rightly. We are what we repeatedly do.
Excellence, then, is not an act but a habit."

—Aristotle

The Operational Excellence Enterprise Readiness Model (OpEx-ERM) is, in essence, the framework for a business operating system whose primary objective is to facilitate the achievement of an appropriate state of readiness in a company so that the company has the capabilities and capacities to recognize, pursue, and engage—in an expeditious, meaningful, and decisive manner—all opportunities and threats such that success is as preordained as possible.

But having a framework is not enough, because understanding how an operational excellence program is engineered and constructed is one thing but rolling the program out is quite another. This is no small undertaking; it commands a considerable amount of respect, reflection, planning, and attention to detail. My experience has been that leadership might spend a considerable amount of time developing, discussing, and examining various frameworks (including this framework for operational excellence) and not enough time on what matters—defining success and the people who will become involved.

For instance, I was at a well-attended conference on change management. And many of the speakers were from Fortune 500 companies—household names we would all recognize. And, one by one, each speaker shared the change management framework for their organization with the audience. What struck me most during the deliberations was that none of the speakers addressed how to change the individual employee.

My role at the conference was to moderate a panel discussion at the end of the day; all of the day's speakers were the panelists. Since it was burning in my brain, my lead-off question was, "How do you get the individual to change?"

The response was as surprising as it was telling. Each speaker looked at me, rather gobsmacked—like they didn't understand what I was talking about. They then proceeded to revert back to the change management frameworks for their organization as a response. Even with my pressing and leading them, I could not get them to offer any ideas on how to get the individual to change. They all seemed to overlook the point that organizational change is impossible without change at the individual level. Without a strategy for changing the individual, a change management framework for the organization is useless.

What we have to remember is that when it comes to operational excellence—or for that matter, any business initiative—it's people first. The people you have on the team and the capabilities they have are the single most important component of any operational excellence program. They will determine whether the program is successful and to what degree it flourishes.

Here is a word of caution, as I stated in the introduction of this book: If you do not believe your operational excellence program will require investment or all this program preparation work is unnecessary, you should put this book down and go back to doing things the way you have always done them. Operational excellence and becoming a high-performance organization are not in your future.

PROGRAM DEFINITION AND PREPARATION

"Fascinations breeds preparedness,
and preparedness, survival."

—Peter Benchley

As with any construct, the first thing that needs to be done is to envision what the final results would look like. If you were to accidentally stumble upon success, would you be able to recognize it? What does it look like? Only when the desired outcome is defined and established can you begin the process of determining how you might organize its construction and actually build it.

This first phase is the most critical phase of the program and requires a considerable amount of time, effort, collaboration, and thought. Program success is defined, detailed, and determined in this phase by the company insiders. Although the fresh eyes of an outsider, peer, or consultant might help snap your vision of success into focus and determine how it might be measured and achieved, no outsider or documented best practices should define what success is for you and your business; the responsibility for what success looks like needs to be owned by you. Taking the time to define success here and now will drive the other pre-execution exercises necessary for program launch.

There are a near-infinite number of variables that can measure a program's success and an even greater number of permutations of these variables. I won't provide the details here because their importance, weight, and configuration are unique to each organization and its own desired outcome. Suffice it to say, it is necessary for you to spend the time defining what is important and what the goals are for your company, your program, and yourself.

The Executive Briefing

In an *executive briefing*, the senior leadership of the enterprise is introduced to the value proposition and concepts of operational excellence, the leadership techniques, and tools necessary for success. The meeting is also used to ensure leadership buy in and commitment to the program. The program needs to be owned by the executive leadership to succeed, and they need to be thoroughly and completely vested and onboard with what is expected of the program, what is needed for the program to succeed, what their role in the program will be, and how they can effectively engage and support the program's participants. In essence, they must become the *Chief Program Advocates*.

It doesn't matter as much where in this phase the executive briefing occurs. It can happen at the beginning of the process, the middle, or the end. But it must occur, and you must get the support you need, before you launch the program.

When the meeting does happen, it most certainly should occur at a time when the leadership can all meet face-to-face and in a place with minimal distraction. Preferably, the venue and environment will be subdued and relaxing (like a corporate retreat) rather than noisy and distracting (like a conference in Las Vegas). The idea is to be able to engage in cerebral discourse, digging deep into the company's soul to create the vision for the future and the path to get there.

Vision Building

Why do you want to do this at all? What does the goal line look like? What is important to your organization? What do you want the output of the program to be? Do you just want it to be reactive, driving value through the completion of projects, or do you want to go large and create a full-blown program that spans the entire value chain? If you were to read a newspaper dedicated to the success of your program, what would the headlines read?

There is no right answer to these questions, only your answer. Keep in mind, whatever your answer is dictates the outputs (expectations) and drives the inputs (resources). You can't order a cheeseburger and expect a rib eye.

Defining Success

An anticipated future state of the enterprise must be developed in which the definition of success is established. This is a hyper-critical step in the process that is too often overlooked or otherwise given short shrift. Every endeavor must have goals that serve to provide a measurement of progress and also to ensure alignment toward those goals. It is here, the first step of the first phase, when we establish what constitutes success.

These goals must be specific and not filled with platitudes and clichés. It's not enough to say "We are going to be the best" or the "biggest" or "number one in customer service." Nor is it good enough to pull numbers out of the air, as in, "We are going to increase sales by 10 percent" or "We're going to cut costs by 15 percent." I often wonder in meetings why these numbers are so round. Vaguely round numbers usually indicate a lack of real thought and research. The goals have to be real, they have to be tangible, they have to be understandable, and they have to be realistically achievable. Otherwise, the success of the program is jeopardized before it even begins.

It's okay to have *stretch goals*, but make sure everyone knows they are stretch goals. Never confuse them with realistic targets, because you will see the enthusiasm for the program evaporate before your eyes. (Nobody likes to be set up for failure.) And never propose goals that are not achievable; they are, by definition, unrealistic, and you will lose credibility as a leader with all of the stakeholders.

Just think back again to the vision statement Kennedy offered for the moonshot: "I believe that this nation should commit itself to achieving the goal, before this decade is out, of landing a man on the Moon and returning him safely to the Earth"—a simply stated goal, elegant, clear, and concise.

Strategies

What is the assessment of your present state? What capabilities do you have and to what capacity do you have them? And what capabilities need to be reallocated, built, or acquired? When determining the strategies are completed, you should have a detailed definition of the program, the expected outcomes, and what the approach to deployment will be on a grand scale.

Assessment of the Present State

Performing an open, honest, and thorough assessment of the present state establishes the baseline and starting point of your operational excellence program. How can you begin the journey to the future state if you do not have an accurate representation of the present state? However, the challenge in this step is that leadership often does not want to be open, honest, or thorough, because this would mean illuminating the good, the bad, and the ugly. And there will be a lot of bad and a lot of ugly that people would rather not face. It is similar with thorough, because thoroughness entails work and a considerable amount of work. There is no easy way. There's just a lot of hard work, but you cannot truly improve without it.

Whenever someone tells me they know where they are without having performed a proper assessment and without being able to produce sufficient documentation to justify their claim, I can guarantee they have little, if any, idea at all of the actual current state of their organization. Doom awaits.

Tactics

Planning the program creates the roadmap for deployment. It maps the vision through the strategies to the plans to realize the vision. It should be a clear roadmap to the future state, not a series of disjointed, unaligned projects. What are the particular plans your strategies require? What needs to be accomplished in

what order and to what level of completeness? Are there prereq-
uisites? What are the waypoints?

You must define the operational excellence metrics: the KPIs,
the program operating parameters, project development, establishment of audit points, and pass or fail criteria. And detailed
resource requirements necessary to support the plan should be
specified (e.g., the scope, talent, time, and money), as well as when
and where they might be required (budgeting) and any waypoints
that make sense to monitor the progress of the program.

Logistics

Based on the details of the tactics, what are the necessary logistics to support the plans that are created? What are the source,
lead time, and cost? Are backups to the primaries necessary, and,
if so, are they secured?

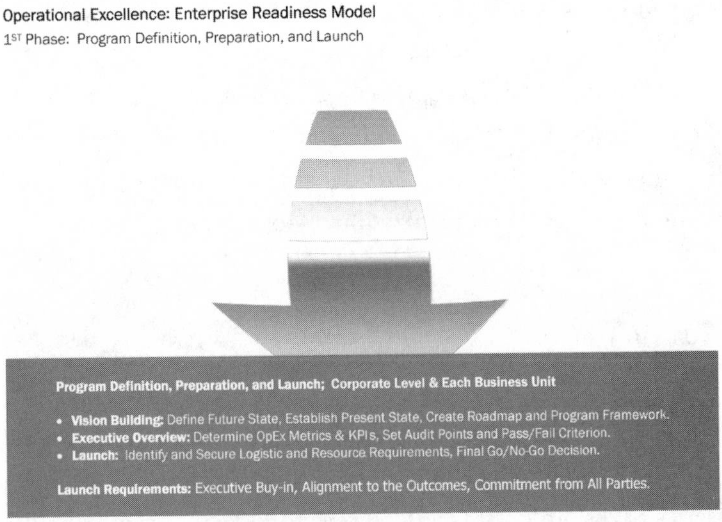

Operational Excellence: Enterprise Readiness Model
1ST Phase: Program Definition, Preparation, and Launch

Program Definition, Preparation, and Launch; Corporate Level & Each Business Unit

- **Vision Building:** Define Future State, Establish Present State, Create Roadmap and Program Framework.
- **Executive Overview:** Determine OpEx Metrics & KPIs, Set Audit Points and Pass/Fail Criterion.
- **Launch:** Identify and Secure Logistic and Resource Requirements, Final Go/No-Go Decision.

Launch Requirements: Executive Buy-in, Alignment to the Outcomes, Commitment from All Parties.

Figure 20.1. OpEx-ERM Phase 1: Program definition and preparation.

Countdown to Launch

In addition to not defining success, many postmortems performed on improvement programs that have failed (whether operational excellence, continuous improvement, or Lean Six Sigma) indicate a program's failure to maintain momentum as a primary cause.

Program momentum can be lost in a variety of ways. Remember that time is your enemy, and it will sap the program of momentum if you allow it. The following are some of the factors which will slow the progress and which you need to guard against or otherwise mitigate:

⇨ It takes time to define the program.

⇨ It takes time to identify the people involved in the program.

⇨ It takes time to determine their capabilities, capacities, and roles.

⇨ It takes time to organize the training and to coordinate people's schedules.

And there are risks to effectiveness:

⇨ How much is being taught in what period of time? Is what is being taught being comprehended and retained by the trainee?

⇨ Is there opportunity to quickly apply what is being taught so the new knowledge does not atrophy? Is the investment getting lost? As they say, use it or lose it.

All of these are real risks and, if not mitigated, will result in slow progress and diminished benefit. It won't be long before executive leadership does not see the expected results. Commitment to the effort will erode, and the program will eventually be considered a cost as opposed to a benefit, until the program is finally terminated.

How can these dangers to your program be averted?

The People

What we have to remember is, when it comes to operational excellence, it's all about the people. The people will determine whether an operational excellence program is successful and to what degree. Make sure to place your focus and efforts on the people first. The framework, the curriculum, or anything else doesn't matter if you don't start off by having the right people sitting on the right bus and on the right seats.

People are predisposed by their psychological, intellectual, and emotional traits to excel in some roles, to be average in others, and to fail miserably at still others. Therefore, the first step in selecting a candidate for each team is to establish their psychological predispositions so they are assigned to the role in the program that best suits their natural tendencies.

To do this, you need to perform a detailed assessment of the candidate. Although there are several such methods, the Myers–Briggs Type Indicator (MBTI) is one of the more common and one you might have heard of or otherwise be familiar with. (Although, it's maybe not the best.) The MBTI evaluates an individual to determine their native personality traits along four different dichotomies: valuing, visioning, relating, and directing. Even within these four dichotomies, there are opposing character traits. The individual character traits are:

⇨ **Extroverted vs. Introverted.** Types identified as being extroverted learn best by speaking or otherwise interacting with others; they organize and process information through interaction. The opposite of this category is introverted. Types identified as introverted learn best by reflective internal contemplation in private surroundings.

⇨ **Sensing vs. Intuitive.** Types identified as sensing need to establish a baseline before they can project into the future or to the abstract. They trust concrete information they can directly perceive. Types identified as intuitive tend to observe and place greater emphasis on relationships, associations, and patterns.

⇨ **Thinking vs. Feeling.** Types identified as thinking seek truth through the use of logic, objective analysis, and deductive reasoning. Those identified as feeling tend to be empathetic and focus on human elements, people and their motivations and issues (including their own).

⇨ **Judging vs. Perceiving.** Types identified as judging work best when the information on which they rely and the environment in which they work is structured and organized. They are highly motivated to complete tasks and to come to conclusions. Those identified as perceiving prefer a flexible environment, with few rules and little structure, where they can be motivated by foreign and exciting ideas.

What the MBTI does is suggest a person is likely to have the character traits of their classification; it claims to predict an individual's strengths and weaknesses and in what roles the individual may excel and in which they may be less suited. This knowledge is helpful in determining the likelihood of a candidate being a teacher of others, someone who excels at project execution or project planning and management, or a good fit for some other role. This is not to say one classification is better or worse than another; it's not subjective but, rather, objective. Nor is this to say a person who has one character trait or another is better or worse in absolute terms within your organization— only where they might be best utilized.

CAUTION: BE ESPECIALLY AWARE OF THE PETER PRINCIPLE[1]

The Peter Principle states that a capable person in an organization is evaluated based on their performance in their current role and not whether they will be successful in their new role. As such, "Managers rise to the level of their incompetence."

For instance, a star salesperson is promoted to manage all the salespeople with the thought that his "magic" will be instilled in the others and they will all become star salespeople under his leadership. What is more likely to occur is that the magic does not transfer to the other salespeople and they don't become stars, the star salesperson turned manager fails in management and severs from the company (being either fired or having quit), and the company is worse for the efforts.

A Standard Curriculum

It is important for your company to realize they are not in the curriculum-development business. Thinking otherwise will doom the program from the beginning, crushed under the weight of the investment requirements and soon forgotten because of development delays with no value to the organization realized. Instead, the curriculum should be licensed from some source that largely satisfies the desired outcome of your company. The curriculum should allow you to update as needed to reflect your actual company experience and the application of the knowledge gained through projects. Over time, this will evolve the curriculum from a state that is more general to a state more specific to your company. In essence, this process creates your company's curriculum over time.

Classes of Approximately Twenty-Five Individuals

Classes should be large enough to maintain energy and inspire collaboration among the trainees and be cost effective. Given the coaching and mentoring resources required, my experience has been that a class size of approximately twenty-five trainees is optimal (similar to standards found in education). If the class size is much smaller, the amortization of the delivery costs becomes a challenge. And if the class size is much larger, management of the trainees by the instructors, coaches, and mentors becomes unwieldy and less effective.

Building the Theory: Online and Offline Lectures and Materials

The instructors may or may not be a resource from within the company; they are subject matter experts and teachers. It is optimal to deliver as much of the theoretical as is appropriate, leveraging the Internet wherever possible. Here, the instructor will deliver live lectures via the Internet and in a structured manner similar to a university course. Depending on the technology used for delivery, the trainees should be able to see the instructor and the content being presented, as well as the other trainees during interactive sessions. In essence, the delivery system should approximate a cyber-classroom. In the case where a trainee might miss a live lecture, it might also be possible to record the lectures and archive them for later reference—perhaps even share them with similar classes within the company, which could reduce future instruction costs.

In addition to the live lectures, the trainees will be given offline reading assignments and exercises from books, videos, online content, or other sources as structured within the curriculum. This offline content is organized and integrated into the overall class in a meaningful manner and woven throughout the course.

The trainee will also engage in assessments at key waypoints in the curriculum to ensure satisfactory progress and to identify areas of weakness, either in the trainee's abilities or in the curriculum itself.

RISKS TO AVOID

The challenge with building capacity is how to organize and implement the conveyance of knowledge such that it is retained by the trainee and applied to the benefit of the company. Some risks include the following:

→ The appropriateness and qualification of the selected trainee

→ Building capacity without a clear need for the investment, such as enrolling trainees into learning opportunities where there is no immediate and defined requirement for, or benefit to, the company

→ Trying to organize trainees' schedules so they can meet in a specific location for an extended period of time, with the risk of the program quickly reaching stall speed because of delays in coordinating schedules

→ Relevance of the content being taught to the company

→ Atrophy and attrition of skills and investment because of a lack of opportunity to use these newly learned skills in a timely manner

All of these challenges can be overcome by building the knowledge and experience in the trainee using an integrated-learning approach (see more details on integrated learning in chapter 16). Integrated learning combines the delivery of the theory (in the form of instruction given in live lectures via the Internet, online self-study presentations and videos, and offline readings and exercises from select textbooks[2]), with the delivery of the practical or applied. These are provided in the form of practical application of the materials because they are being learned on a project that is of benefit to the company with the face-to-face support of the assigned coach and mentor.

Building the Practical: Applying the Theory on a Project

The trainee must not be assigned a class or start the curriculum without having a project to work on first. The purpose of this is twofold: First, the trainee gets to apply the theory they are learning, thereby increasing the retention rate of the knowledge, and, second, the approach will yield a net benefit to the company because a project will be completed at the conclusion of the course.

The financial benefit to the company from having completed a project should more than offset the investment required to train the trainee. Accordingly, if this approach is properly followed, the program will not only have no cost burdens on the company but should also immediately return a net financial benefit (as well as future benefit from subsequent projects completed).

In addition to having a project, the trainee will be assigned a coach and mentor who is internal to the company. The internal mentor is experienced in the company operations and the manner in which the company will invoke the theory that has been learned. The mentor helps the trainee apply the theory they have learned to the project they are working on and is responsible for the success of the trainee in their project.

Deploying a program in such a way should result in all investments in the candidate being fully recovered (and more) from the benefits realized by the completion of the candidate's project. If properly deployed, the rollout of the program should have no net costs to the company, only resulting in a positive impact on cash flow—operational excellence for free.

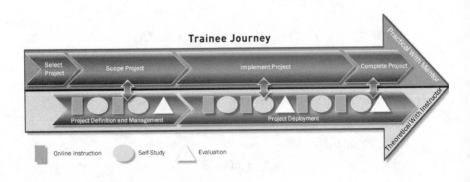

Figure 20.2. Trainee journey, integrated learning.

A LOGISTIC IN SEARCH OF A STRATEGY

I was coaching one of the national oil companies in the Middle East, offering mentorship to the director of their operational excellence program. He was frustrated he had invested considerable funds building a team of sixty Lean Six Sigma Black Belts over a nine-month period, and they had not yet worked on—much less completed—any project nor had they realized any benefit to the company (never mind the fact that a person should not be considered a Black Belt without completing at least one project). Worse, some of those who had been trained had left the company, taking the company's investment with them.

My coaching advice was twofold: Get the existing resources working on projects, and don't build any more resources unless you have projects for them to immediately work on. And preferably, they should work on these projects during training. I also suggested that there might be a disconnect within his organization, because it seemed those who claimed to have a demand for the resources actually did not (or perhaps they did not actually buy into the program), even as the considerable supply was being built. This is the danger in "having a logistic in search of a strategy."

All Systems Go

> "The time to take counsel of your fears is before you make an important battle decision. That's the time to listen to every fear you can imagine! When you have collected all the facts and fears and made your decision, turn off all your fears and go ahead!"
>
> —General George S. Patton

Before deployment of the operational excellence program, the executive leadership team and the deployment leadership team must meet face-to-face to review the results of program preparation in detail. It is at this audit point—before the launch of the program—when all fears and uncertainties are openly discussed. The go/no-go decision should be reached at the conclusion of this meeting, with everyone involved understanding the overall goals of the operational excellence program. They should have clarity of purpose for its achievement, and the company should have unreserved commitment for its deployment.

Consider an aircraft taxiing toward the runway and preparing for takeoff or a sailing yacht preparing to leave the safety of the harbor. In both cases, the crew is preparing the craft for a transition from a relatively safe state to a state fraught with hazards. These preparations are critical to ensure the safety of the craft and all souls who are onboard. If anything is not in line with specification, an evaluation must be made as to how critical the issue is and how it will impact safety. If non-critical, the defect is noted, counter-measures (if necessary) are deployed, and the journey commences. If the defect is critical, then the journey is postponed (or even abandoned).

An operational excellence program is similar. The launch, or deployment, of the program cannot commence without the executive leadership and the leadership of the deployment team meeting face-to-face and approving the program. This demonstrates alignment and commitment in achieving the desired outcomes.

At the conclusion of this planning and preparation phase, and before you proceed to deployment, it is critical that there is a formal and demonstrable go/no-go commitment and support from the C-suite. If you get it, it's time to start the execution phase. If you don't get it, prepare for a mediocre outcome (best case) or outright failure. Proceed accordingly.

BUILDING CAPACITY AND CAPABILITY

"If I have the belief that I can do it, I shall
surely acquire the capacity and capability to do
it even if I may not have it at the beginning."

—Mahatma Gandhi

If the program preparation has been thorough, the deployment phase can be anticlimactic. Certainly, what will be missing— what *should* be missing—is any sense of urgency or panic. There is no talk of "burning platforms."

This is not to say everything will go according to plan; it won't. Because of the framework structure that has been created, challenges should be identified early, triaged for severity and downstream impacts, and processed through the established exception-management protocols that are a part of the operational excellence program.

The Corporate Team

Before capacity is built, it is important to redefine the roles and responsibilities of the operational excellence leadership team at the corporate level. No longer will the corporate team engage in projects—this activity will be performed by the embeds we are about to create. Rather, the corporate team's primary responsibility and value add will be to serve as the leadership, advocates, and stewards of the operational excellence program and as facilitators, coaches, and mentors to the trainees.

As such, the existing corporate team will need to be evaluated to ensure they possess the proper skill sets. Ideally, the evaluation of the existing members of the corporate team will determine that they possess the characteristics of an empathetic servant leader, because their primary responsibility will be to mentor and nurture those who will be onboarded into the program instead of being taskmasters and project managers. It is important that the servant leaders resist the temptation to take control of projects because it will diminish the building of experience in the trainees.

The evaluation might show some members of the existing corporate team are better suited to be facilitators, project managers, or project resources. Certainly, the operational excellence program is a big tent, and these team members are valuable and necessary to the success of the program and have a place, just not as part of the cadre of servant leaders. In this case, the corporate team might need an augmentation of staffing levels to have the capacity to fulfill their purpose. I would strongly suggest you look to fill these roles from within your organization first.

It is also important that the corporate team not scale in size to form some new corporate bureaucracy; rather, the corporate team should remain nimble, agile, and responsive to the needs of the project teams. Speed is a factor for success, and it cannot be achieved effectively if the corporate team becomes too large.

Once the corporate team is established in accordance with the resource build-up parameters detailed in the program definition and preparation phase (phase 1), capacity building can begin.

Building Capacity

As mentioned, you don't want to build an operational excellence program that becomes a big corporate bureaucracy—but you need to scale the resources. Where will these resources be found?

The answer is simple: within your organization, at the business units, in the offices, in the warehouse, and on the shop floor—right there in front of you.

This is not to say you are going to hive off your staff to form a new department within the business units either. A distributed bureaucracy is not much better than a consolidated one. Rather, you are going to select specific individuals and build these additional skills in them. These skills will result in their taking on roles that are an extension of their core job function and responsibilities—remaining where they are, doing what they do, but as embeds to the operational excellence program.

The purpose of building capacity is not to train the core functions of a position, but rather, for the trainee to take what was learned and further hone their skills working in the position they hold and roles they fulfill. For instance, during the program, you should not expect to teach a salesperson the soft skills associated with selling or a design engineer how to be more creative. But you could expect the salesperson to improve a method for funnel management and the design engineer to improve the process for introducing changes into the production line.

Take the role of the sales forecaster, for example: When the sales forecast is not perfect (and it won't be), you don't want to teach the sales forecaster how to make better guesses. Instead, you teach them the skills to analyze the miss as a defect and then investigate the sources of the defect (weather, supply chain issues, currency fluctuations, and so on). This will make their forecasts better with the ability to incorporate the effects of injects as they happen in real time.

The trainees, as with all members of the program, will be evaluated to determine their personality traits so that they can be positioned to leverage their strengths. The importance of this cannot be underestimated. The successful trainee will possess an ability to lead and to realize projects but will also possess the empathy of a servant leader to properly onboard and coach their project team members. They need to have expert communication skills to effectively share situation reports upstream and downstream and to maintain alignment with the strategies of the company.

In the OpEx-ERM, the base level of capacity is referred to as *foundations* and is where trainees learn and incrementally apply a broad range of basic skills and disciplines. By leveraging an integrated learning approach (see chapters 16 and 18 for further details), you will build the knowledge in the trainees as efficiently and effectively as possible. This maximizes retention of the materials being taught and accelerates the realization of benefit to the bottom line.

Later, these skills can be further refined and constructed to focus on specific vertical disciplines (organizational smokestacks) within the organization. However, even within foundations, the trainees will be stratified on the basis of the level of expertise intended for them, their placement within the organization, their communication skills and psychological traits, and their alignment with the organization. The levels of indoctrination into the program are—

⇨ **Foundations Competent.** The trainee pursuing certification as *competent* will possess, as the outcome of their onboarding into the program, a broad understanding of the various philosophies, tools, and techniques of operational excellence and will have mastered an understanding of the OpEx-ERM and its objectives within your company. The takeaway of a successful *foundations competent* trainee will be that of fully trained foot soldiers capable of carrying out projects led by others. As such, their orientation and level of contribution will be largely as a logistic in support of the larger efforts.

⇨ **Foundations Proficient.** The trainee pursuing certification as *proficient*, in addition to possessing the skills at the *competent* level, will also have the ability to identify both opportunities and threats—and to engineer, deploy, and lead project teams. Their role and contribution will be tactical; they will be the primary on projects.

⇨ **Foundations Expert.** The trainee pursuing certification as an *expert*, in addition to possessing the skills at the *competent* and *proficient* levels, will emphasize leadership, communication, and larger-scale program leadership skills. As such, they will be stewards of the program and will ensure alignment with the realization of the organization's strategies.

At the successful conclusion of phase 2 of the OpEx-ERM, building capacity, the operational excellence program reaches a logistical level of maturity and should be in an increasingly excellent position to recognize and realize opportunities and threats at the process level within the business smokestacks. The people in the program are now viewed as cost cutters, and the program is akin to having implemented a beginner to average continuous improvement or a Lean Six Sigma program. But you can't stop here.

Operational Excellence: Enterprise Readiness Model
2ND Phase: Building Capacity

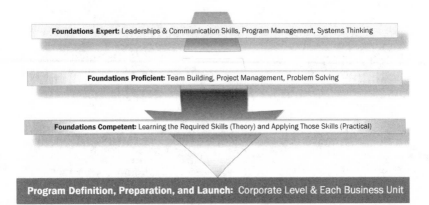

Figure 20.3. OpEx-ERM Phase 2: Building capacity.

Building Capability

Once a level of capacity is built, as prescribed during the program definition and preparation in phase 1 and achieved in phase 2, the program will have matured to the point where it is ready for the next level of achievement, which is to extend the capacity within the functional smokestacks of your company by *building capability* to integrate with immediately related functional smokestacks. It is meant to improve the employees' efficiency and effectiveness in using their training and education in foundations as an integrated resource of the enterprise as a whole, in an orchestrated approach and always in alignment with the company's strategies.

For the purposes of this model, we will organize the functional smokestacks of the business in groups that will closely track to the financial statements with the following:

⇨ **Balance Sheet, Finance.** The financial category includes all supporting activities primarily contained in the balance sheet, such as leverage, mergers and acquisitions, returns on equity, cash and funds flow, capital expenditures, and the like.

⇨ **Profit or Loss Statement, Revenue and Cost of Sales (COS).** The revenue category includes supporting activities related to revenue realization, including marketing, sales, and product design and development.

⇨ **Profit or Loss Statement, Cost of Goods Sold (COGS).** The cost of goods includes supporting activities related to some of the more traditional applications of operational excellence methodologies (including Lean Six Sigma and the rest) to such business functions as the supply chain, production, manufacturing, service delivery, customer service, and logistics.

⇨ **Profit or Loss Statement, General and Administrative (G&A).** General and administrative activities are those related to servicing and supporting the business entity as an ongoing enterprise, including asset and facility management, information technology, and human resources.

Follow-Through and Audits

It is very easy for any program to become untethered. So, to ensure the planned waypoints are achieved and the program remains aligned with the strategies of the organization, periodic audits of the operational excellence program are necessary and should be performed with a high level of thoroughness and intensity.

At the successful conclusion of phase 3 of the OpEx-ERM, building capability, the operational excellence program will have reached a tactical level of maturity and should be in an increasingly advantageous position to recognize and realize opportunities and threats at both process and systems levels within and across naturally related business smokestacks. The people in the program are now viewed as efficiency experts, and the program is akin to having implemented an above average continuous improvement or Lean Six Sigma program. But remember, this is not the end goal.

Operational Excellence: Enterprise Readiness Model
3RD Phase: Building Capability

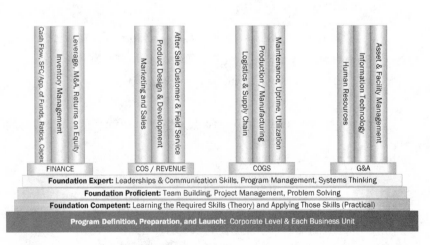

Figure 20.4. OpEx-ERM Phase 3: Building capability.

CREATING READINESS

> "The art of war teaches us to rely not on the
> likelihood of the enemy's not coming, but on our
> own readiness to receive him; not on the chance
> of his not attacking, but rather on the fact that
> we have made our position unassailable."
>
> —Sun Tzu

So far, we have built capacity and capability. We have the resources, and we have the talent. Our processes and systems within the smokestacks of our business are working in an optimized and balanced fashion, and we continue to see opportunities for improvement and realize those improvements.

But the main limitation of a traditional continuous improvement program is its emphasis on process optimization and not systems integration and optimization at the enterprise level. The net result is that the activities within functional smokestacks operate largely independently of the activities in other functional smokestacks, leading to miscues, miscommunication, a lack of alignment, poor synchronization and timing, and business blunders.

This fourth and final phase of the program deployment, business readiness, is the ultimate value proposition of the OpEx-ERM and is the reason we have successfully performed all the phases prior to this one. Without phase 4, the company will only realize the benefit of a traditional continuous improvement program, albeit a very robust one. But what is *business readiness*?

Business readiness is having the resources and assets in a proper state of preparedness so that there is an advanced ability to observe and recognize challenges and to rapidly organize and deploy a response to meet those challenges in a meaningful and decisive manner. And you must do this while identifying changes in the circumstances and context and trusting in the capability of yourself and your organization to stay ahead of the situation and not lose the advantage.

Phase 4 concentrates on establishing interoperability between and among the various functional smokestacks of the business to increase awareness of the goings-on within the company and throughout the company's value chain, to establish more robust collaboration in order to eliminate redundant efforts and increase synergies, and to generally accelerate the business-decision-to -action cycle.

In the OpEx-ERM, the level of business readiness your company has attained is defined by three stages of achievement. These stages are independently earned at the corporate level and at each of the business units (however you define a business unit).

THE FIRE STATION

Think of a fire station. All of the apparatus are in good repair and the individual firefighters are well trained, with the veterans mentoring the newly hired. They are fully prepared to successfully engage in the purpose for which they were intended.

They are in a state of readiness.

When the call comes, they react and perform as they have been trained, and they perform in a proficient and professional manner. And they do it all with speed and accuracy—the result of their training.

Arriving at the fire, they find that it is nothing like their training exercises and simulations. The situation is fluid, different, and dynamic—it's real. They have to call upon what they have learned and adapt it to the current situation. They have to communicate and coordinate their efforts. Above all else, they have to trust their colleagues in their capacities and capabilities and make important, life-and-death decisions in real-time.

This is operational excellence. This is business readiness: working as high-performance teams in a high-performance organization.

Bronze-Standard Business Readiness

In the *bronze standard of business readiness*, functional smokestacks within the business that are related and should be naturally inclined to work together and collaborate (such as marketing, sales, and product design and development) engage in structured learning activities, simulations, and application exercises in order to gain awareness of the capabilities and value add of each of the other smokestacks, as well as the needs each might have to fulfill the deliverables expected by the others. It is key to understand the integration points and bridges where this support and communication transpire.

I love golf, but no matter how much I practice I will never become good enough to be on the PGA Tour. However, my understanding, appreciation, and respect of the game are sufficient for me to engage. Similarly, people within the business enterprise working in their functional smokestacks are not expected to become experts in another; that is not the best use of talent and energy. Each has their talents, and those talents should be developed, not diluted. The key to success here is to learn to work better—more efficiently and more effectively—as a team and, therefore, as a business.

Since the bronze standard of business readiness involves the delivery and understanding of a considerable amount of core material related to the skills associated with leadership, communication, collaboration, problem-solving, decision-making, and situational awareness—all with an emphasis on enhancing team performance—the building of these abilities could be performed using an integrated-learning model. However, it would be advantageous for this group to meet on a more formal basis and to engage in face-to-face business simulation exercises to determine the team's dynamics, strengths, and weaknesses.

Silver-Standard Business Readiness

In the *silver standard of business readiness*, we expand the simulation training and exercises beyond related functional smoke-stacks through the entire company and, if appropriate, to key players in the value chain. Every significant opportunity or threat that precipitates a strategy involves the entire enterprise.

Take, for instance, a new product launch: Marketing and sales are involved to determine who the customers might be, what the price point is, and what messaging might be attractive to them. Product design and development needs to engineer the offering. Finance has to evaluate the capital expenditure necessary to support the new product launch, as well as the financial analyses for profitability. Production has to determine how the product is to be manufactured, and purchasing has to establish the supply chain. Those responsible for facilities need to be involved to support any new production lines that might be required. In essence, the entire organization needs to successfully collaborate so the product launch is successful. Here, a strategic advantage is to have an emphasis on speed: rapid decision-making balanced against optimal outcome quality.

The same approach to building capability by leveraging simulations should be applied to threats as well as opportunities. For instance, for a product recall, marketing and sales are focused on controlling image and revenue damage to the business. Finance models the impact of the recall on the bottom line. Logistics and customer service try to determine what end users of the product might be involved, where they are, and how critical the recall might be. (Is it life threatening or just an inconvenience?) Product design, supply chain, and manufacturing will work diligently to fix the problem.

Whether the event is an opportunity or a threat, the entirety of the company is involved, and success depends on the level of capability, capacity, and effectiveness of the business *as a system*, not as disjointed and quasi-independent processes. And it all must be done with ever-increasing proficiency and speed. This is, in essence, the difference between an average company and a high-performance organization.

Since the baseline knowledge and skills associated with business readiness were built within individuals at the bronze standard, the successful achievement of the silver standard of business readiness is realized in a face-to-face workshop with all participants across all functional smokestacks of the business.

The form of the workshop will consist primarily of working through a series of simulations, where the trainees will be faced with business challenges—some opportunities and some threats. The trainees will evaluate the situations from their individual perspectives; learn to appreciate and integrate the perspectives of others; and learn to define the strategy, develop the tactics, identify and organize the logistics, and make the go/no-go decision to execute a response. Some of the key takeaways and skills built during these efforts would be effective *red teaming* (a skill where the participants explore for weaknesses in a proposed approach in a constructive manner), and the acceleration of the decision-making process through trust in the team and their capabilities rather than the massive data collection and analysis.

Once this initial solution is formalized, a series of injects and variables will be introduced that will challenge different aspects of the solution. These might include the loss of key talent, disruptions to the supply chain, an unexpected change in financial or economic conditions, geopolitical issues, engineering issues, changes in market conditions, and the introduction of all manner of unknown unknowns.

Gold-Standard Business Readiness

Finally, at the *gold standard of business readiness*, the company has experienced one of these transformational, or even life-threatening, challenges and has engaged the opportunity or threat using all they have learned in their journey to implement their OpEx-ERM.

As soon as possible after the opportunity has been realized or the threat mitigated, those directly involved in the formulation and deployment of the response will perform a debrief. And the successful completion of structured and formal debriefs as an indoctrinated and standard practice of how the company conducts business—becoming part of your corporate culture—signifies the achievement of the gold standard of the OpEx-ERM.

The reason that so much weight is given to the debrief—and

the reason a debrief after a significant challenge has been faced by your company is the pass or fail assessment of the gold standard—is that it reflects the cumulative results of the investment in your operational excellence program, its abilities and impact on your company. In essence, it is a live-fire assessment of your operational excellence program. How efficient was your response in speed to develop and deploy? How effective was your response in thoroughness and quality of the outcome? How well did you react to changes in the circumstances or when the unexpected was injected?

Was the debrief itself conducted properly? Was it performed in a professional manner? Were all involved in attendance, and

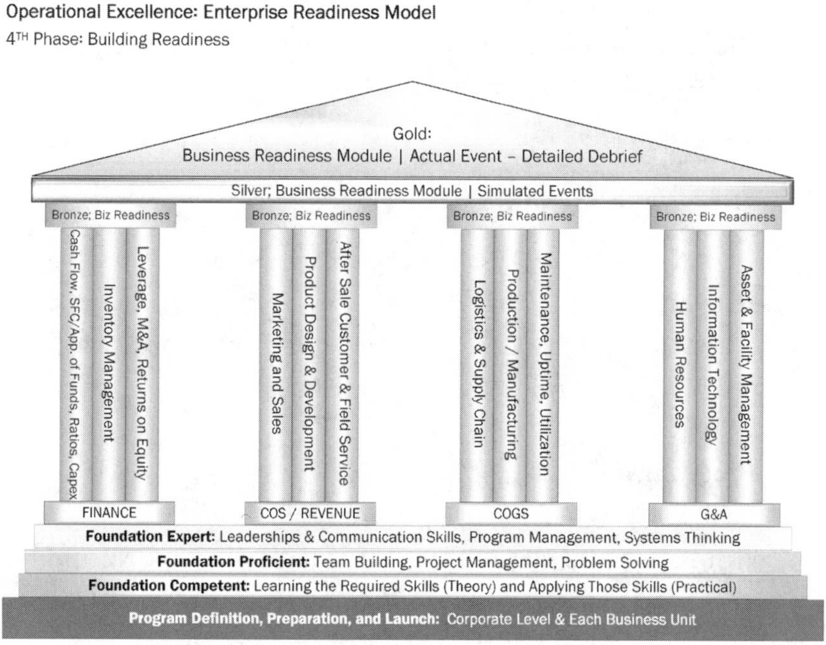

Operational Excellence: Enterprise Readiness Model
4TH Phase: Building Readiness

Figure 20.5. OpEx-ERM Phase 4: Building readiness.

were those not involved not in attendance? Was it open, honest, and collegiate? Did you look for opportunities for improvement and lessons learned? Did you do a report out at the end?

All of this is of critical importance and represents a culmination of all you have invested, and it is an indication of the health of an organization. That is why it establishes and defines the gold standard.

At the successful conclusion of phase 4 of the OpEx-ERM, business readiness, the operational excellence program will reach a strategic level of maturity and the company should be a high-performance organization. The people in the program are now viewed as value creators. And the company's ability to identify an opportunity or threat—and to rapidly formulate and deploy a meaningful and decisive response that pulls from across the smokestacks of the organization (perhaps from across the value chain)—gives it a considerable, if not crucial, advantage in the marketplace.

Enterprise Readiness

Once the OpEx-ERM is thoroughly understood, it is time to examine how the model can be the basis of an enterprise-wide operational excellence program and business operating system that will eventually involve your entire value chain.

Program Rollout

Achieving progress toward enterprise readiness and becoming a high-performance organization is the sum of all the incremental steps toward business readiness that have been achieved by the business units and the level of program penetration that is able to be made in the value chain.

With an emphasis on accelerated decision-making and a robust protocol for auditing the program for effectiveness and efficiency as measured against the program definitions at the business unit level and alignment to the corporate vision and strategies, in each instance of program expansion, the rollout will replicate the rollout at the corporate level, namely—

⇨ Program definition and preparation

⇨ Deployment: building capacity and capability

⇨ Creating readiness

As the level of operational excellence and the individual performance of your business units surpass that of their rivals—and the enterprise as a whole outperforms its rivals as a whole—your company will have become the high-performance organization, prepared to take on all comers.

But success today is no guarantee of success tomorrow. Once on top, you have to fight to remain on top and resist the seduction of complacency.

It would be wise to remember the triumphal march in ancient Rome. Upon returning to Rome, the victorious general would parade through the streets, showing the spoils of his conquests. As the grand procession unfolded with great fanfare and aplomb, a slave would stand behind the general and whisper a warning in his ear: "All glory is fleeting."

CHAPTER 21

CHANGING AN INITIATIVE INTO A GLOBAL PROGRAM

"It is not enough to conquer;
one must learn to seduce."

—Voltaire

The laws of nature are absolute. When we discover a supposed contradiction to one of these laws, it is not nature that is wrong but our understanding of nature and the law we have created. It was once believed that the Earth was flat and at the center of the solar system. Both of these beliefs were supported by our understanding of the science at the time—and both were eventually proven to be incorrect. Until the mid-1800s, the fastest man had ever traveled was by horseback. And when trains and travel by rail came to be, there were many who believed the human frame could not withstand speeds of over a hundred miles per hour. Even Queen Victoria, on her way from Slough to London, would have the engineer travel less than forty miles per hour because she found anything over that speed quite terrifying. In all of these cases, we evolved our understanding with increased knowledge. With each revelation of science comes a transformation.

The laws of man, on the other hand, are made by men and can be bent or broken by man as suits his ever-changing purpose. During the OPEC oil crisis in the mid-1970s, the national speed limit was set to a maximum of fifty-five miles per hour to reduce the consumption of foreign oil on which the United States was dependent. Many people disobeyed. In the mid-1980s, the national speed limit was raised to sixty-five miles per hour. Many people still disobeyed. In 1995, the national speed limit was eliminated and it was up to the individual states to determine what they would be. And still, people disobey.

It is similar with the various tools, frameworks, and methodologies associated with operational excellence. These are the laws of man, though based in formula and fact. For instance, the definitions and use of value-stream mapping, 5S, SMED, and PDCA are all universal. So why wouldn't the deployment of an initiative using these universal tools simply be a matter of cutting and pasting, with identical results no matter the application? Simply put, circumstances and context are variables.

When I travel from country to country talking about such programs and initiatives, the very first thing everyone says is, "I am sure it works that way in the United States, but things are very different in [insert country name], and many changes will have to be made for it to work here." Their immediate gut reaction is that it won't work; they are somehow unique, as if the laws of nature are somehow invoked differently in their home country than anywhere else in the universe. For some, it's their company or department that they feel is somehow unique. They are predisposed, even conditioned, into thinking this is so, but there is no prima facie basis for this in fact. And they don't even bother to look for the fact. If I wasn't so seasoned, I would think they are ignorant and they would think I am arrogant. Thankfully, I am seasoned.

When I moved to Europe to progress the international relationships of my business, I opened an office in the United Kingdom. No matter what country I visited in the European Union, they would say, "You have an office in the UK? That's nice, but if you had one here in [insert EU country name here], we could probably do a lot of business." So I opened an office in Germany and another in Poland, but this was not enough. When talking to a prospect in the Netherlands or in Switzerland or any other country, they would all lament that I should open an office in their country.

On the other hand, if I told them my office was in the United States, the tribalism would vanish, and there would be a much greater degree of openness and engagement. Certainly, the preference of the prospect would be to do business with a company who had an office in their home country, but approaching from the United States was always a close second place—especially if the prospect was a publicly traded multinational. So I decided to close down my offices abroad and just approach everyone from our offices in the United States.

Such is but one of the challenges—and the lessons—from my doing business globally. The reality is that the only major differences from country to country and from company to company are the culture and the infrastructure. So be prepared. Making changes to either will take considerable effort, imagination, investment, empathy, and a whole lot of patience.

PROJECTS ADHERE TO ADAPTATIONS OF TWO PHYSICAL LAWS

When we speak about projects and their characteristics, we can meta-phorically apply a few laws of physics to the way they are constructed and the manner in which we behave. The first is an adaptation of the *ideal gas theory*. Whereas an ideal gas will take up as much space as is given, a project will take up as much time as is allowed. Think back to college: How many times did we delay the start of a project until the last possible moment yet manage to still complete it on time and for a (reasonably) good grade? Do we also remember the effect on our stress level as the project deadline came near? Did we share our stress with gusto and bravado to all who would listen, even though they were enduring the same anxieties? Some things never change, even with experience.

The second is an adaptation of the *laws of fluid dynamics*. Imagine the construction of a pipe system consisting of three vertical pipes that are open at the top, connected, and partially filled with water. If we increase pressure in one of the pipes, the fluid will flow equally to the other two. And if we increase pressure in two of the pipes, the combined fluid will flow to the third pipe. As with fluid dynamics, every endeavor, every project, can be defined in terms of three variables that act as the pipes in our example:

→ *Scope* is the specifications of the final deliverable, the approach to be used, and the bill of resources required to support the approach.

→ *Time* is the duration from the project launch to its conclusion.

→ *Budget* is the cash necessary to acquire the materials required for the project.

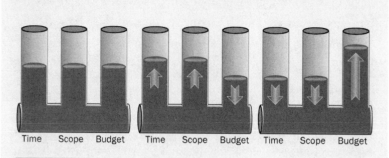

Figure 21.1. The law of fluid dynamics applied to project planning. The image on the left shows a static/balanced state. The middle image shows pressure on the budget, which results in less pressure on the time and scope. The image on the right shows pressure on time and scope, which results in less pressure on the budget.

When a client quizzes me about the parameters of a project, I often explain to them the nature of these three variables and how they are so closely interrelated, usually concluding by offering to give them control over two of the variables while I retain control over the third. It is unreasonable to expect that we are infinitely able to do more and more with less and less; the natural extension of this is the fantastical ability to do everything with nothing. For instance, if given the scope of the project and budget, I will tell them how long it will take. If given time and budget, I will define the scope. Or if given the scope and the time, I will determine the budget.

CASE STUDY: A GLOBAL LEADER IN THE PROCESS INDUSTRY

Let's examine the operational excellence journey of a publicly traded Fortune 500 company based in the United States. They are in the process industry, have over 100,000 employees, and have operations located around the world, as well as several partnerships with, and investments in, similar companies in their industry. Their value chain is as extensive as it is complex.

Initial State

The company's original operational excellence team consisted of twenty-seven professionals, almost all of whom reported to the company's world headquarters—though many did not actually physically work out of the corporate headquarters. Some had been promoted from other facilities and had considerable experience with the operations of the company, but many had been hired just for the purpose of being on the operational excellence team and didn't have any real experience with the company or its culture.

When the company designed their operational excellence program, the members of the operational excellence team were expected to be modeled after something that looked like a SEAL team, and they would operate in a similar manner: a small, agile team engaging in extremely critical missions. But they would be a reactive force, as opposed to a proactive program. Certainly, the company invested heavily in the team members' talents. The company even spent a few million dollars on a licensed curriculum. However, owning a curriculum is very similar to owning books: You don't get any smarter unless you open them and read them.

In addition to not reading the curriculum, the company had no structure or plan for educating the resources and building their capabilities, in what specific content or ability would they be educated, and how would their ability be measured. Neither were training and education standards established. There were no performance metrics at all other than to count the number of projects completed. The company forgot that their core competency was in designing and creating products, not building an educated workforce in noncore capabilities or in applying the related curriculum and the delivery vehicles necessary.

Even so, they launched their operational excellence program with great enthusiasm and fanfare. Early on, they enjoyed a series of big wins as the low-hanging fruit of opportunity was harvested. As that fruit became more scarce and harvesting the benefits required ever more effort, frustration began to set in. Although improvements were still in progress, the rate at which the benefits were realized—as well as the return on investment—decreased, adding to the frustration. Ultimately, the ability to effect improvements was limited to what those twenty-seven dedicated, capable, and passionate professionals could accomplish on an annual basis.

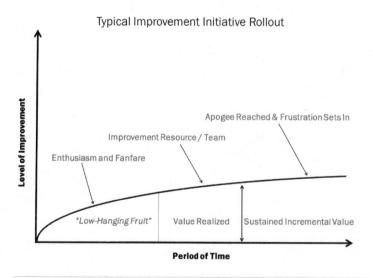

Figure 21.2. Operational Excellence Program rollout benefit realized over time.

Challenge: Overcoming Culture

People are tribal. They want to belong to a community of others with shared values, interests, beliefs, fears, and aspirations. This creates the community's culture, and its members will defend their tribe against all outsiders who would want to challenge the culture.

An unforeseen complication—and a flaw in the structure of the program—is that the team was based at corporate. They were effectively outsiders to the local offices they were trying to change. This meant they did not have an intimate understanding of the situations they were trying to address, the history, or the context. They had no real root-cause understanding of the actual problem faced by that particular facility.

Other than being acquired, there is nothing more threatening to the culture of a business unit than a visit from corporate to change the way they operate. When such a visit occurs, people at the business unit think a couple of things: The local leadership feels threatened because they feel the people at corporate don't believe they are doing a good enough job, or they think that corporate is sending spies. And the rank-and-file believe this is another visit from the corporate tornado, and all they have to do is hunker down and wait until it passes and then return to the normal way of doing things.

And since the operational excellence team did not truly engage the local workforce—not to mention take the time to involve the workforce other than as implementation tools—most of their improvements regressed toward the *before* state over time. The new knowledge and motivation to embrace the new and improved way began to atrophy as soon as the folks from corporate left.

Approach: Create Embeds—A Cadre of Leaders from the Business Unit

Most operational excellence initiatives within companies are conceived, orchestrated, staffed, and managed at the corporate level. This is a common blunder and will significantly squelch the potential benefit of the initiative because the improvements will be limited by their capacity to implement and ability to sustain.

For your consideration, instead of installing people from corporate at the business unit on a temporary basis (which will be seen as an invasion), better results will be achieved more quickly if corporate invests in building a team comprised of people from the business unit (winning hearts and minds) who learn the disciplines and become savvy in their use by accumulating experience. This ownership at the local level will ensure acceptance and assimilation of the new ways into the business unit's culture.

This approach will build alliances and convert resistance into alignment. The first step in this process is for the leaderships of corporate and business units to select, assess, and bring on board local individuals for education and training in the tools and techniques necessary to support the efforts and accelerate the realization of the corporate vision.

The next step is to ensure that the ownership and responsibility for success lies within the business unit and for corporate to take the role of mentor and support. The business unit should control the identification and prioritization of projects and should also be responsible for establishing the objectives and for evaluating their achievement and effectiveness. Here, it is important to pursue the low-hanging fruit early, so that the quick wins are realized, confidence and alliances are built, and the creation of a pull for the advancement of the program within the business unit is achieved.

And finally, but most importantly, corporate should not expect that what worked in one business unit will be identically successful in another. Rather, those improvement ideas can be replicated elsewhere, but you must take into consideration the context and circumstantial differences of local cultures and infrastructure. The program is the same, but you must customize the approach.

Challenge: Building Capacity and Capability

There are many types of people in an organization. The two most basic types are leaders and followers. Each of these types is dependent on the other to define its role. Leaders cannot be leaders unless they have willing (not compelled) followers, and followers need a leader they want to follow. It therefore stands to reason that a company must identify those who have the traits to be a good leader and then invest in those people so they can realize their potential. And they should keep in mind that it is equally important to build good followers.

As I mentioned above, these leaders should come from the local business units so their followers will perceive empathy for their local culture. The followers must believe that they are understood and respected and that their culture, values, and circumstances are being taken into consideration—and there is an implicit trust that is pre-established.

Another dichotomy in the types of people in a company are *systems people*, who tend to be the leaders, and *process people*, who tend to be the followers. Systems people have a tendency to take a macro view of an organization and how it works, but they have less capability with details. Process people, on the other hand, have a micro view, a command of the details, but they are less capable of seeing the big picture. My observations have been that there are fewer systems people than there are process people, which means the leaders need to take the time to effectively communicate to the followers the importance of their actions and how they are aligned with the company's strategies.

Approach: Identify and Build Leaders and Followers

One of the first steps in building a businesswide program, especially international programs, is to build a core team whose primary mission is to create and mentor additional teams and team members. Most likely, these people can already be found within the organization, and it would be a mistake to believe you have to hire an entirely new team to build and deploy an effective program.

As with any operational excellence initiative, the first steps here would be to define the future state of the operational excellence program, develop a plan for achieving it, identify the resources necessary to support the plan, identify any gaps or risks, and take action to fill those gaps and mitigate those risks.

It is also important to look across the functional smokestacks of the company and not focus only on supply chains, production, or logistics. Realizing a program's full potential requires the involvement and cross-functional integration of everyone—finance, sales and marketing, product design and development, human resources, information systems, facilities, and so on. The potential benefits cannot be realized using just a core of corporate resources.

Challenge: Program Stalls, Benefits Deferred

Too many companies make the mistake of believing that all of the efforts for building capacity and capability must be done face-to-face. This is a blunder that will result in the failure of the program to meet expectations or realize its potential. The challenge with this approach is to coordinate the schedules of team members, which causes sessions to be spaced further and further apart, resulting in significant delays for realizing the benefits of the program.

In addition to the delay in time to benefit, the delay in applying newly trained skills results in atrophy of the knowledge or a complete loss if team members leave the company or are transferred out of the program. Enthusiasm wanes. The entire program loses momentum and, ultimately, stalls, risking outright failure.

Another primary cause of program stalls is a lack of a structure and base curriculum for training the intended program participants. Training cannot be performed on a one-off basis; this is neither cost effective nor conducive to building deployment velocity. Better to have a cadre of trainees (at least twenty per class but no more than thirty) being brought through the program at any time, with the ability to run multiple cadres simultaneously.

Approach: Increasing Velocity, Sustaining Momentum

Deploying a solution that increases velocity and sustains momentum is the single most critical factor in realizing the benefits of your program. Not doing so will result in suboptimal results. The following simple steps can guide you toward that solution.

Create a structured program for onboarding, training, and

graduating program participants. Define the desired focus and capability outcomes for each level of participants in the program.

As mentioned earlier and adapted at the company in this case, unless you already have a very robust curriculum that satisfies multiple levels of employee engagement, procure an existing curriculum, which will become your company's training guide. Do not attempt to create this from scratch; it is not your company's core competency. It will take far too long before benefits are realized, and there is no possibility of it being cost-effective—dooming your program to failure before it begins. However, make sure to structure the program so that only trainees from your company are in the class and the class is using the company curriculum, materials, and protocols. Sending trainees to different classes delivered by different educators with other trainees from different companies will destroy any opportunity to establish metrics on performance and proficiency and eliminate the opportunity to make someone else's program your own.

As suits their capabilities, personalities, and dispositions, turn the existing operational excellence team at corporate into mentors and facilitators of the program or coaches to the trainees.

Identify, vet, and select employees at the various business units to be the trainees indoctrinated into the program. It is critical to the success of the program that the knowledge be disbursed throughout the organization and at the point of presence so the improvements—in the context of the unique environments, traditions, and circumstances at each business unit—are considered and a sense of ownership is established.

Leverage technologies to increase the velocity of the program and accelerate the realization of benefits. Nothing will slow the program faster than requiring all efforts related to the program be done face-to-face. Scheduling will add considerable unnecessary friction. It is far better to leverage an integrated learning model that separately teaches the theory and the practical. The teaching of the theory involves a robust curriculum, consisting of online and offline content (presentations, videos, books, and articles) and exercises (projects, homework, and assessments). The theoretical knowledge is delivered by live lectures via web conference and supported with cyber office hours. The training of the practical is accomplished by the trainee working on a project supported by one-on-one coaching from a mentor from the business unit. This results in the trainee's total understanding of the material and the additional benefit of the company receiving value from the completion of the project.

Ensure that the program sustains momentum by continually moving forward in both the number of successful trainees and the continued involvement of graduates. Failure to keep moving forward will result in skill atrophy, reduced capacity through attrition, and diminished long-term benefits of the program.

Results After Five Years: The Net-Net

Although the corporate operational excellence team of our case study company has grown marginally (from twenty-seven to thirty-two professionals), the biggest structural change to the program is that the roles of this team have changed from facilitation to program direction, coaching, training, and mentoring.

They have licensed a standardized base curriculum, which they are incrementally customizing over time to reflect their own experiences. This is so that all operational excellence resources are educated in a consistent manner, progress and ability can be assessed, and improvement realizations are more predictable.

They have implemented an integrated learning education

structure, which accelerates the trainee through the curriculum. They learn the theory, but the trainees are also assigned an internal mentor to apply their knowledge as learned (the practical). The vehicle for the practical is a project approved and evaluated by the company. The benefit of this approach is the investment in the program of building capability in the trainees and capacity across the company is immediately returned to the company by the successful conclusion of a project.

Over the course of five years, the number of operational excellence practitioners has grown from twenty-seven to over three thousand (increasing by between five hundred and seven hundred practitioners per year). This represents an increase of over 11,000 percent in the capacity and capability to effect improvement over the original team.

It is important to note that these are the numbers for this particular company and its case study. There is no magic ratio

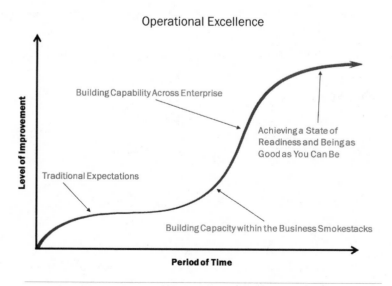

Figure 21.3. Operational Excellence S-Curve showing stepped realization of benefit.

or number of people who are involved in the program. How any company has defined the success of the program will determine the number and type of resources necessary and where they are needed to achieve that success.

Also understand that these practitioners do not occupy new full time positions; their roles in their existing positions have simply been expanded. The practitioners' primary function and responsibility at the company remain the same.

The new operational excellence practitioners are recruited from the individual business units, put through the program, and returned to the business units as embeds. They are then able to see opportunities and threats as insiders and are welcomed and comfortable in their home business unit or facility. They identify the potential of opportunities or threats and engineer an approach in context. They complete their projects with a pride of ownership; the natural result of which is increased sustainability of progress. They also capture their own best practices and replicate them across the entire organization, adapting the deployment to local circumstances.

Over the course of five years, the net bottom-line benefit to the company in raw terms—in either cost savings in production (elimination of waste) or revenue enhancement (accelerated deliveries and increase in revenue realization)—as a result of the program has been almost $1.25 billion. And this amount is (thus far) limited to cost savings in their production and logistics operations. The next implementation phase will look at streamlining their administrative functions and supply chain and getting the entire enterprise aligned and operating as one.

Of particular note and importance, the program was net cash-flow positive from the moment it was launched. All investments (and more) in building the program and its capabilities and capacity were recovered by the company in the short term through the benefits the company realized by the trainees' completion of the project they were assigned as a part of their training.

But remember, the transformational change you are making in your organization is like water on the rock; the rock will succumb and surrender to the water, but it takes constant pressure and it takes time.

CHAPTER 22

IT'S A MARATHON, NOT A SPRINT

"Dans la Légion étrangère, c'est marche ou crève"

"In the Legion, you march or you die."

—Unofficial motto of the French Foreign Legion

We have often heard improvement initiatives described as "a journey, not a destination"—meaning the pursuit of an optimal business condition is what is important and a perfect state is never to be realized. So how is it then that so many journeys are abandoned or fail to realize their potential? And what can be done to achieve a satisfactory result or even a level of success? How can an operational excellence program be sustained over time?

In my experience, most programs are in jeopardy from the very start because nobody defined what success looks like. And this leads to a lack of alignment between leadership and the deployment team in their mutual expectations (assuming the expectations had ever been set and made mutual). In this regard, more time should be devoted to honest communication.

Specifically, I have repeatedly seen leadership set expectations that are beyond the deployment professionals' ability to deliver, given the resources committed and the time allocated. And I have equally witnessed overcommitment on the part of the deployment team, given the resources allocated by leadership. The conversation goes something like this:

Leadership

"We need to drive an additional 5 percent EBITDA over the next year. Can you do it?"

Deployment professional

"Absolutely, it can be done."

Leadership

"Excellent. What do you need?"

Deployment professional

"We need to hire several more seasoned deployment professionals to act as facilitators and a few coaches and trainers to onboard the business units."

Leadership

"There isn't any budget for that. I need you to deliver with the resources you have. Maybe we can get the business units to allocate some of their budget to the initiative. Can you still do it? We are all counting on you because this is critical for the company to achieve its strategies."

Deployment professional

"I can certainly try."

Leadership

"I am not comfortable with your saying you will try. I need a commitment. I need to know whether you can or can't deliver. If you don't think you can do it, I will give it to Jones."

Deployment professional

"Of course. I will get started right away."

And so it goes . . .

Unfortunately, most operational excellence programs—and continuous improvement initiatives in general—are launched in response to some threat that has become imminent to the business (but rarely a surprise because human nature is such that we always wait too long to respond, hoping it will not materialize) or other disrupter (such as a merger or the onboarding of a new C-level executive). As a result, the initiatives are launched under strain and with a sense of urgency.

Would you be surprised if I told you the single biggest revenue day each year for fitness centers and exercise equipment is January second? This is the day we all realize we thoroughly enjoyed ourselves over the holidays and have the additional weight to show for it. We resolve to lose that weight and a few pounds more, and we are going to do it by spring.

For the first week, maybe two, we spend all of our extra time exercising. We even reallocate time intended for other activities so we have more time to exercise. We really want to lose that weight by spring. But after a couple of weeks (perhaps even less), we become tired and discouraged. We see we lost hardly any weight (probably none), we find other important things are starting to be sacrificed, and we see the real investment involved—until we just give up. So the question becomes, *Which is more important: losing the weight, or losing the weight by spring?*

The same holds true with the launch of an operational excellence program. You have to plan for it to be a long-term campaign, with the pace set for a marathon, not a sprint. And make sure you train, outfit, and otherwise prepare yourself accordingly.

Then, how can an operational excellence program be designed and launched in a manner that maximizes the opportunity for its success? I offer the following for your consideration.

⇨ **Define and communicate the vision.** What do you want your future self to be and to look like? Can you explain why it's important to achieve this vision of your future company? Can you articulate the risks and rewards? Can you explain it in the simplest terms (no MBA jargon) so even the employees who are most junior and most distant from leadership can comprehend it? Remember, it's not only the analysts on Wall Street who have to understand.

⇨ **Create a roadmap.** Do you know where you are now? Are you having serious conversations that are open, honest, and frank with the people who you need to help get to where you want to be? Are you actually listening to them? Are you establishing checkpoints along the way to incrementally assess how you are progressing on the plan?

⇨ **Plan and prepare.** As you begin the journey, have you established a culture that will embrace the changes necessary? You have to trust that your team is capable to engage the tasks at hand. How are you going to overcome those individuals or structural issues that are a threat to success? If you can't overcome (or it's too difficult), are you ready to make the hard decisions so the risks are mitigated or neutralized? Are your resources aligned so the right people are onboard and in the right positions?

Before you launch the initiative, have you attained the proper level of preparedness?

⇨ **Engage the pursuit.** Have you set a sustainable pace, or are you setting up for failure? Do you have enough of the proper resources (talent, time, money) allocated? How are you progressing against your checkpoints? Are you harvesting wisdom—the sum of all applied knowledge—so you can replicate what is learned? Or are you realizing benefits, then hermitizing so you have to rediscover the knowledge time and again?

Like a rocket leaving the launch pad, the first stage of a program is going to be very disruptive and will consume a lot of energy. It is critically important to be strapped in and ready. But the subsequent stages will be smoother as momentum builds and a rhythm is established.

⇨ **Continually reassess.** Pursue your plan, but don't be so blind in your pursuit that you fail to see changes in the business landscape. Maybe there is a new opportunity or threat that should be considered. Make sure you have your eyes open. In this respect, the process of planning is more important than the plan itself.

Remember, people will see benefit in an operational excellence program from a menagerie of lenses, each from their own perspective. They have to know the WIIFM (What's In It For Me). The people in finance will evaluate the benefit from a financial perspective, whereas the people in production will evaluate it on the basis of production velocity and quality, and the people in sales will evaluate it on the basis of increased revenue. This one effort will have many benefits that can be measured.

For instance, we had one project with a major oil producer in the tar sands of Calgary, where we were engaged to examine ways of reducing carbon emissions. The primary motivation for the engagement was to build and demonstrate the company's sustainability credentials and to establish themselves as a good corporate citizen of the world and the environment. After all, oil production is a dirty business, particularly in the tar sands of Calgary.

Our approach was to create value-stream maps of the various processes, with the added variable of the amount of carbon being produced at each of the process steps. It didn't take long to realize that carbon was a waste product and the production of carbon was an indicator—a genetic marker—of fuel consumption. Somewhat unexpectedly, one of the biggest sources of carbon was the tens of thousands of diesel electric generators being used to power portable lighting and other temporary apparatus. By reducing the number of smaller units and replacing them with larger and more efficient units, we reduced the amount of fuel consumption. We were able to accomplish the primary objective of reducing carbon emissions but with the added benefit of saving on fuel costs, which are quite significant in and of themselves.

In addition, we reduced the number of runs the big earth-movers were making. The reduction in costs associated with running the equipment (labor, fuel, repairs, and maintenance) was obvious, but soon, others were seeing related benefits. The safety people observed that, with a reduction in runs of more than thirty thousand annually, the opportunity for injury from operations was significantly reduced. And the people monitoring greenhouse gas generation observed that the carbon emissions as a result of this change were reduced by more than seventeen thousand tons annually.

So we accomplished our primary goal: reducing greenhouse gas emissions and establishing the company's credibility in sustainability and image as a good citizen of the world. But, rather unexpectedly, we also drove considerable savings in the cost of operations. Seeing what is in front of you is important, but don't ignore what you might see in your peripheral vision; you never know what opportunities or threats might be there, waiting.

And this is why it's a marathon and not a sprint. Each person within each department of each business unites within the organization and will have their perspective as to what is important and what is not. More often than not, these perspectives will be contradictory and competing. Sometimes, new opportunities and challenges will be discovered. But the wise leader will consider all and maintain the alignment of the organization to its objectives. They will be able to sift through the mud to find the gold flakes. And they will be able to prioritize what is most important so that the achievement of the overall objectives are met with predictability, velocity, and maximum impact.

CHAPTER 23

A STATE OF READINESS

"Consult not your fears, but your hopes and
your dreams. Think not about your frustrations,
but about your unfulfilled potential. Concern
yourself not with what you tried and failed in,
but with what it is still possible for you to do."

—Pope John XXIII

All new companies start small and possess an entrepreneurial
spirit where vision, ambition, and innovation intersect with risk
and reward. It is in these early times when the employees are
few and relationships are close. It is a time when debate is robust
and decisions are made quickly, driven more by gut instinct
than detailed analysis. For the company to succeed, it needs to
have the capacity and capability to grow from its nascent state
through its present state on the way to its future state. Accomplishing this requires the total alignment and commitment of its
energies in the pursuit of the company's vision if the company
is to be successful.

At the very beginning of the company's history this is simple because all of the decision-makers are in the same office, perhaps even a garage or a Starbucks. If there is a need for a brainstorming session or if a decision has to be made, all that everyone in the company needs to do is turn their chairs around and start collaborating. The team has been built and it is a tight team. Any laggards or those who otherwise don't fit move out and move on very quickly. And it is in these early moments in the company's history that the company's culture is established, adopting the values and traditions of its founders as the basis for its own.

But as the company grows, the resources and supply chains get stretched further afield. The tightness of the team that existed at the founding of the company loosens as the company expands and with the addition of so many unfamiliar faces. There is a corresponding loss of the intimacy that existed in the early years of the company, and coinciding with this loss of intimacy is a reduction in trust. Not that there is suspicion of nefarious intent, but a lack of trust that is the natural result of not having worked closely together for an extended period of time under the extreme stress that exists when launching a business—the camaraderie and bonds that are created by being Brothers in Arms. The need for team building becomes increasingly acute.

Over time and assuming the company survives its launch phase, the successful company charts an expected evolutionary course: progressing from entrepreneurial and innovative, through mature and stable, to institutional and predictable. And the energy in the company follows a similar path converting from highly kinetic into momentum as the use of speed and agility converts to that of brute force. We can see this transformation, evolving from entrepreneurial to institutional, occur sequentially in contemporary times with the companies Microsoft, Google, and then Facebook.

One of the more stark examples of this evolutionary transformation can be found at Google. When Google first launched their Initial Public Offering (IPO) in 2004, the founders of Google, Larry Page and Sergey Brin, highlighted the idea of 20-percent time in their IPO letter. They wrote, "We encourage our employees, in addition to their regular projects, to spend 20 percent of their time working on what they think will most benefit Google. This empowers them to be more creative and innovative. Many of our significant advances have happened in this manner."

By 2013, managers had reduced the availability of 20 percent time to the employees who reported to them because of the negative impact this time had on the productivity KPIs on which the managers were measured. This, in turn, resulted in a negative impact on the employee performance reviews where employees were found to be not giving 100 percent to the project, only 80 percent. Now, if an employee wants to work on a 20-percent-time project, they have to propose the idea and gain approval before they could start. Creativity and innovation had given considerable ground to institutionalization.

The challenge is this: How does a company, which must be a high-performance organization at its beginning when it's at its most vulnerable, balance the need for protocols and controls as it grows with its need to remain innovative at high-velocity?

Like a rowboat that can quickly spin in circles versus an ocean-going vessel that requires more time and space to maneuver, as a company grows, its ability to remain nimble similarly erodes. Escaping this erosion is not possible, but limiting it is.

Therefore, a key to sustainable success can be found in planning for the scalability of the company in its entirety and putting in place the proper support infrastructure.

⇨ **Learn from the past, build for the future.** The twenty-first century company should not expect to do business like a company of the twentieth century and still be cutting-edge. The most successful companies will be disruptive, the ones that break from the old and traditional ways of doing business into known marketplaces and, instead, create new paradigms. Certainly, the implementation of historical business management methods and protocols should be considered for your business to the extent that they can add value, but with the understanding that there are limitations. The contemporary company needs to press beyond what was, through what is, to what will be. Modernization, even futurization, is key. And not just in the products or services you offer, but in the way your business operates.

⇨ **Create and cultivate a leadership culture.** Whether an employee or participant in the value chain, start with building trust, integrity, respect, and transparency within each member of the organization. Do not use fear or drama to compel people to do your bidding; motivate them instead. And no mention of "burning platforms." Remember that leaders are only leaders because people are willing to follow. As such, you can tell the capability of a leader by the caliber of their followers. The best leaders will be mentors to those they lead and to whom they are responsible, and they are stewards of the company's vision and assets.

⇨ **Communicate the vision, then align and commit to its achievement.** People will follow only if they know where they are going. Therefore, be clear and succinct in describing your vision for the future. Remember, if you can't explain it simply, you don't understand it well enough yourself and people will be less inclined to support you in your quest. What is success? People need to know. Connect the dots to the vision to gain alignment. Everyone needs to believe in the vision, know how the vision will be achieved, and know what their roles will be its pursuit. Then establish a pact for mutual commitment—with their committing to the pursuit of the vision and your committing to support them in their efforts. Set a course for the destination, but also establish waypoints so that progress might be assessed along the way. Adjust as prudent and necessary, communicating all the way.

⇨ **Become set-up for success and not set-up for failure.** Having accountability and responsibility is nothing to fear. Without it, you don't have a business, you have a clubhouse. But accountability and responsibility without authority will only set you up for failure and doom. Don't micromanage; let the big dogs eat. Delegate as you are able. Let those to whom you delegate do their job. After all, that is why you hired them. But do follow through and follow up in support. Understand that there are goals, stretch goals, and peyote-induced hallucinations. Avoid the latter.

⇨ **Innovation is a requisite for long-term viability.** While innovation is no guarantee you will be successful, a lack of innovation is a near guarantee that you won't be successful. What is the cost to the organization of missed opportunity? Maintaining velocity is a requirement for your company in preserving a competitive edge. Wisdom comes with experience. It is the sum of all applied knowledge. Your company culture needs to expect there to be failed attempts, so there should never be a fear of failure, only a fear of not trying. Fail quick, fail small, learn, and move on. Speed of development and innovation must never be slowed by the scaling of a company. Instead of planning for change as if it's something new and to be approached with trepidation, ensure that operating through and with change is the native state of the company.

⇨ **Construct a program for rebuilding capacity and capability.** You will need to construct a program designed to recapture some of the velocity, decisiveness, and efficiency that existed when the company was entrepreneurial and nimble. The starting point to any program will be to define what success looks like, for today and into the future. Then you need to identify the types of talents, skills, and resources your company will need to succeed, as well as when and where they will be needed. You will also need to build leadership, decision-making, and communication skills throughout your organization so that others can quickly orient themselves and follow.

It is important to know what you know, but even more important to know what you don't know. Take the time to understand and detail the skills necessary and build your education and training regimen to meet that need. Work hard at finding and filling the gaps. Hire and retain the best, and build the rest. Identify key personnel from across the organization who will play key roles in the design and deployment of the program. If you don't have the talent, you will need to acquire the talent. Create a structured framework for delivering the education of the theoretical and the training of the practical so that, as this talent is built and on boarded, it is aligned to generate the outcomes necessary for success. Build the proper capacity and capability where they are needed and as they are needed. Be sure to accumulate and disseminate the collective wisdom of the organization so that you discover your best practices and replicate across the enterprise.

⇨ **Prepare for the long haul and sustainability.** It took a long time for your company's entrepreneurial can-do/is-done attitude that existed at the time it was founded to atrophy and for the bureaucracy and bloat to build to the points they are today, so you can't expect miracles overnight. The journey will be long, it will be difficult, and you need to prepare accordingly. Don't be seduced by the early victories that are easy to accomplish and whose rewards are large. That pace won't last long. This is only the harvesting of the low-hanging fruit and there is only so much of that before the work gets harder for the rewards that are realized.

For your company to have a competitive advantage, it needs to regain the ability to quickly evaluate a situation and to formulate and deploy a decisive response using all of the appropriate abilities from across the business smokestacks. Obviously, the company needs to cut the waste and friction in the supply chain and in the production and delivery of its goods and services. But it is also imperative that the company constantly strive to shed the burden of bureaucracy and protocols.

Acquiring some bits of technology might accelerate the process, but it also might not. It's better to build a rock-solid process, then increase the through put and accuracy by introducing the right technology where it makes sense. Remember, making the decision to acquire a technology is only the end of the beginning of the process. The benefits will only be realized after a lot of work is done in the technology's implementation. Don't believe the two greatest canards of the technology salesperson, which are "It's easy" and "No problem." It's never easy and there is always a problem. Also, don't discount the rigidity that comes with technology or the on going cost of ownership.

A better means of accelerating the realization of positive results is to capture your own best practices and replicate them across your company—to actively accumulate and disseminate the wisdom you already own and leverage this wisdom across the enterprise to increase capacity and build capability as you eliminate waste in processes and optimize systems.

———

For all of this, you will need to have patience and persistence. You can't become a high-performance organization without first having high-performance systems comprised of high-performance processes developed by high-performance teams.

As I wrote in the introduction, this journey will not be easy. There is no button to push or pill you can swallow that will make it easier or happen faster. It's damn hard work, and it's going to take time, effort, investment, gumption, and stick-to-itiveness.

You must move the ball down the field in a deliberate, continual, pragmatic, and measured manner—day by day, week by week, month by month, and year by year.

One misstep will not kill a company. If that were ever true, the company was already near death and just put out of its misery. What kills a company is the illusion—becoming a delusion—that all is well and they are untouchable. This sense of entitlement leads to internal conflict, and the company rots from the inside. The arrogance in which they hold their ignorance is what kills them.

The corporate funeral pyre has consumed many rock-star companies whose complacency killed them. We need look no further than companies like Research in Motion (Blackberry), Tandy (Radio Shack), Delphi, and Kodak (to name a few). Even General Motors and Chrysler (twice, once in 1979 and once in 2009), although they both had the good fortune of being reborn thanks to the Federal Government. And to this partial list, we can add the countless family-owned businesses that could not survive the transition to the next generation.

You don't have to start today. Everything will still be the same tomorrow. But how many tomorrows do you have before someone leapfrogs over you while you are standing still? And they will not have beaten you; you will have lost to them.

ACKNOWLEDGMENTS

"De l'audace, encore de l'audace, toujours de l'audace!"
"Audacity, more audacity, always audacity!"

—Georges Danton

I remember one of the first conversations about leadership and operational excellence I had some years ago with Matt "Boom" Daniel, an F/A 18 pilot for the United States Marine Corps and graduate of the United States Navy Fighter Weapons School (Topgun). I commented on how impressed I am with the performance of aviators in the United States Armed Forces—especially those who are carrier-based.

His immediate retort was, "The reason we look so good—the reason we perform at the level we do and are as successful as we are—is because the other five thousand people on the carrier, and the innumerable marines and sailors on flight lines around the world, do their job with the highest level of proficiency and professionalism. Even though we are at the pointy end of the stick and get the glory and accolades, our success is the natural culmination of all of their efforts. Without them, we would be nothing."

Wow... Just wow. . . .

My name is on this book—and I certainly did author it

(sometimes it felt like I was chiseling each word from granite, it was that difficult)—but it is the result of having a tremendous team behind me, encouraging, supporting, motivating, advising, debating, inspiring, sometimes even kicking. Their efforts were not always pleasant experiences for me and sometimes made me uncomfortable. But, without them, without my own high-performance team, I would never have written this book.

So I would like to do a callout to a few special people who were instrumental in my completing this book and my success. Thank you all.

My wife, Beata, for your encouragement and persistence in pressing me forward. I am very happy to *finally* be able to answer the question you have been asking me for the past few years: "Yes. Here it is. Thank you. I hope you like it. I love you, Honeybunny!"

Carey "Vixen" Lohrenz, for keeping me focused and motivated, especially when I was struggling, and for being my Sherpa through the publishing process. You sharing your publication experience saved me from having to pay as much tuition to the University of Publishing as you did; it is greatly appreciated.

Matt "Boom" Daniel, for offering your keen, experience-born insight into accelerated decision-making (and introducing me to the OODA loop), building cross-functional teams and high-performance organizations, and being humble. In fact, I can safely say that I am now the most humble man anyone will ever meet because of you.

My parents, especially my father, for being my early mentors and for giving sound advice in my early years that has carried me through today—even if you sometimes didn't know you were giving me advice at the time (my very own Yogi Berra).

And it doesn't really matter much that you still don't understand what I do after thirty years of my doing it. Perhaps after you read this book, you might—but, then again, maybe not.

Francis "Pogo" Paolangeli, for being my business mentor in my early days as an entrepreneur. My father taught me a lot about growing up and becoming a man, and you taught me so much about running a company and being a businessman. I know you are a very modest person, and you always say I would have made it without you (which may or may not be true), but you certainly did accelerate that success by years.

All of the people who helped me with the construction and development of this book, especially **Donna O'Leary; Benjamin Taylor; Wilson Faure; John Ryan;** my illustrator, **Allen Hall; David Deutsch; Loretta Fendrock; Joseph Terrell; Larry "Invictus" Hynes;** and my substantive editor, **Nathan "The Metzger" True.**

Rick Hulse, for nudging me along in your Socratic way.

The **untold number of sages and seers** on the various subjects who, throughout the ages, have incrementally added their thoughts and wisdom to the vast and ever-growing body of knowledge—and the many **academics, industry leaders, practitioners, and people** from around the world who have generously shared their opinions, insights, and experiences with me over the years. All the conversations we have had were invaluable to me in forming my own thoughts and hypotheses.

NOTES

Chapter 1

1. A derivation of Peter Drucker's quote, "Doing the right thing is more important than doing the thing right."

2. Alan Gropman, ed. *The Big 'L'—American Logistics in World War II.* Washington, DC: National Defense University Press, 1997. http://www.ibiblio.org/hyperwar/USA/BigL/BigL-1.html

3. The term sigma comes from the use of the Greek lower-case letter (σ) that represents standard deviation in statistics. The number comes from the idea that if one has six deviations from the standard between the process mean and the nearest specification limit, then almost no items will fail to meet specifications.

4. These smokestacks are also often referred to as stovepipes or silos.

5. Bigelow, Madeline. "How to Achieve Operational Excellence." American Society for Quality 35 (2002), http://asq.org/data/subscriptions/qp/2002/1002/qp1002bigelow.html

6. United States Coast Guard. "Coast Guard Auxiliary Operational Excellence Program." Washington, DC: United States Department of Homeland Security, 2003. http://www.uscg.mil/directives/ci/16000-16999/CI_16794_4.pdf

7. Economist Intelligence Unit. "Strategy Execution: Achieving Operational Excellence." The Economist: New York, 2004. http://graphics.eiu.com/files/ad_pdfs/Celeran_EIU_WP.pdf

8. DuPont. "Delivering Operational Excellence to the Global Market: A DuPont Integrated Systems Approach." Wilmington, DE: DuPont, 2005. http://docplayer.net/2045056-Delivering-operational-excellence-to-the-global-market-a-dupont-integrated-systems-approach.html

9.   Kreutzer, Idar. "Growth, Capital Efficiency, and Operational Excellence."
     Lysaker, Norway: Storebrand, 2006. https://www.storebrand.no/site/stb.nsf
     /Get/getc8b1e9f3d48cfc4a2c35ec30edee27a7/$FILE/1_Idar_final.pdf

Chapter 2

1.   Toyota. "The Origin of the Toyota Production System." http://www.toyota
     -global.com/company/vision_philosophy/toyota_production_system
     /origin_of_the_toyota_production_system.html

2.   Dr. W. Edwards Deming (1900–1993) was born in Iowa. In addition to being
     an expert in many fields, Deming's contribution to Six Sigma was in the field
     of statistical quality control.

3.   Joseph Moses Juran (1904–2008) was born in Romania. He imigrated to
     the United States and became a pioneer of quality management. He is
     credited with refining the work of Vilfredo Federico Damaso Pareto and
     the Pareto Principle and being a founder of Six Sigma.

4.   It is widely accepted that the term Lean Manufacturing was coined by John
     Krafcik, from the Massachusetts Institute of Technology (MIT).

5.   Carl Friedrich Gauss (1777–1855) was born in what was to become Ger-
     many. He was a mathematician who made significant contributions to the
     field of statistics.

6.   Walter A. Shewhart (1891–1967) was born in Illinois. He was an engineer
     who made considerable contributions to the field of statistical quality control.

7.   Vilfredo Pareto (1848–1923) was born in Paris, France, but was an Italian
     national. He was accomplished in many fields, but his contribution to Six
     Sigma was his work in statistics and the development of the 80/20 rule (after
     discovering that 80 percent of the land in Italy was owned by 20 percent of
     the people), later referred to as the Pareto Principle.

8.   Homer Sarasohn (1916–2001) was born in the United States. He was an
     engineer who was recruited by General Douglas MacArthur to help rebuild
     the electronics industry in post-war Japan and contributed to the quality
     control body of knowledge.

9.   Bill Smith (1929–1993) was born in New York. He is often referred to
     as the Father of Six Sigma. Working with the leadership of Motorola, he
     helped to establish Six Sigma as a formal discipline for quality management
     and improvement.

10. Bob Galvin (1922–2011) was born in Wisconsin. He was the son of the founder of Motorola, Paul Galvin, and became president of Motorola in 1956. He strongly supported the work of Bill Smith in Six Sigma.

11. John Francis Mitchell (1928–2009) was an electrical engineer who became the president of Motorola. He lead the establishment of Motorola University and the Six Sigma Institute along with Bill Smith.

12. Everett McKinley Dirksen (1869–1969), Senator (R-Illinois) from 1951–1969

Chapter 3

1. All figures are Per-Capita (PC) converted to US dollars. There is also a column for GDP in Purchasing Power Parity (PPP) that shows the buying power of the Japanese economy versus the United States economy. This is done so that an apples-to-apples comparison can be made, with other variables equalized.

2. GDP per capita based on purchasing power parity (PPP). PPP GDP is gross domestic product converted to international dollars using purchasing power parity rates. An international dollar has the same purchasing power over GDP as the dollar has in the United States.

3. Irrational exuberance is a phrase coined by Alan Greenspan, who was chairman of the Federal Reserve Board, during a speech given at the American Enterprise Institute. It is now considered a code phrase used to convey the message that a market is overvalued.

4. In financial markets, the graphing of corrections (especially dramatic corrections) starts with a severe decrease in value, which is represented by a sharp downstroke on the graph and is followed by a similarly severe increase in value which is represented by a sharp upstroke on the graph. Together, the two slopes look like the letter V.

5. The phrase *dead cat bounce* is widely used in finance. It is used to describe a small and brief recovery in a stock that has fallen significantly in value. The metaphor is derived from the idea that even a dead cat will bounce if it falls from a considerable height.

6. The G-7 is an informal group of modern industrialized nations and includes: Canada, France, Germany, Italy, Japan, the United Kingdom, and the United States.

7. Abenomics is the name given to the economic policies of the Japanese government under their prime minister and architect of the policy, Shinzō Abe, and is a concatenation of the words Abe and economics. It involves the liberalization of the economy, increase in government spending, and the loosening of monetary policy to foster economic growth.

8. Ernst and Young, "Study: Could trust cost you a generation of talent?" Ernst and Young, 2016. http://www.ey.com/gl/en/about-us/our-people-and-culture/ey-global-study-trust-in-the-workplace

9. National Highway Traffic Safety Administration (NHTSA), "2012 Vehicle Recalls by Manufacturer" (NHTSA, 2012), www.nhtsa.gov /staticfiles /communications/pdf/2012_Vehicle_Recalls_by_Manufacturer.pdf

10. NHTSA, "2013 Vehicle Recalls by Manufacturer" (NHTSA, 2013), www.safercar.gov/staticfiles/safercar/pdf/2013-recalls-mfr.pdf

11. NHTSA, "2014 Vehicle Recalls by Manufacturer" (NHTSA, 2014), www.safercar.gov/staticfiles/safercar/pdf/2014-recalls-mfr.pdf

12. Tribune Media Wire, "The 10 Car Manufacturers with the Most Vehicles Recalled" WGNtv.com, March 24, 2016. http://wgntv.com/2016/03/24/the-10-car-manufacturers-with-the-most-vehicles-recalled/

13. As reported on the Toyota website, http://toyotanews.pressroom.toyota.com/

14. http://www.epi.org/publication/the-decline-and-resurgence-of-the-u-s-auto-industry/

Chapter 4

1. The Kobayashi Maru is a fictional space freighter from the movie *Star Trek II: The Wrath of Khan* used in simulations to train cadets at the Starfleet Academy. The simulation resulted in a no-win scenario in that there was no winning outcome possible.

Chapter 5

1. For a deeper dive into this phenomenon and the dynamics, I would highly recommend you read *Blue Ocean Strategy* (Watertown, Massachusetts: Harvard Business Review, 2005), written by Renée Mauborgne and W. Chan Kim.

2.   Margaret Cronin Fisk, "What Will Faulty Ignition Switches Cost GM?"
     Bloomberg Businessweek, March 10, 2016, http://www.bloomberg.com
     /news/articles/2016-03-10/what-will-faulty-ignition-switches-cost-gm

3.   Linda Sandler, "GM Nine-Month Recall Costs Total $2.7 Billion on
     Repairs" Bloomberg, October 27, 2014, http://www.bloomberg.com/news
     /articles/2014-10-27/gm-nine-month-recall-costs-total-2-7-billion
     -on-repairs

4.   Means to arrive at a final decisive contest. Originates with Napoleon Bona-
     parte's (of France) battle engagement against the Duke of Wellington (of
     England) and Gebhard Leberecht von Blücher (Prussia) the at the Belgian
     town of Waterloo. Bonaparte lost the battle and his empire.

Chapter 8

1.   There is a method in Lean Six Sigma called 5 Whys. It is a technique for
     discovering the root cause of a result. Of course, the actual discovery of the root
     cause might take greater or fewer asking of the question why. But the idea is, if
     you ask why enough, you will (eventually) discover the root cause of the result.

Chapter 9

1.   The details on the OODA loop, PDCA cycle, and DMAIC contained in this
     book are intended to be summary explanations used to compare and contrast
     each at a high level. There are many fine reference sources available on the
     subjects if you wish to do a deeper dive.

2.   Colonel John Richard Boyd (1927–1997), a fighter pilot with the
     United States Air Force, is credited with inventing the OODA loop deci-
     sion-making cycle.

3.   William Edwards Deming (1900–1993), who is credited with defining the
     PDCA, was an American engineer and statistician who specialized in busi-
     ness management. Deming himself often referred to PDCA as the Shewhart
     cycle, named after Walter Andrew Shewhart (1891–1967), who was an engi-
     neer and statistician; this earlier cycle was Plan–Do–Study–Act (PDSA).

Chapter 10

1.   Please, it's a general rule—and there are exceptions to the rule and they are
     even made to be broken. I get that. No need to cite them all to me.

Chapter 11

1. The Marquess of Queensberry rules are the general code of conduct accepted in the sport of boxing. They are named after John Douglas, the 9th Marquess of Queensberry, who sanctioned the code.

Chapter 12

1. Called the Shingo Price for Excellence in Manufacturing until 2007, when the criterion was updated and renamed the Shingo Prize for Operational Excellence in 2008, then merely the Shingo Prize in 2010.

Chapter 13

1. The Nash Equilibrium is a cornerstone of game theory formulated by Nobel Laurate John Forbes Nash, Jr. (1928–2015).

Chapter 16

1. Full disclosure: The Operational Excellence Society is a "Think Tank"—not a consultancy—I founded several years ago. It is a creator and aggregator of content related to the various disciplines of operational excellence and also a creator of a framework and curriculum for companies wanting to implement an operational excellence program.

Chapter 17

1. Young Turks was a political movement in Turkey during the early 1900s. It favored the replacement of the Ottoman Empire's absolute monarchy with a constitutional government.

2. David Dunning and Justin Kruger of the Psychology Department at Cornell University in Ithaca, New York.

Chapter 18

1. President Kennedy's address to Congress on Urgent National Needs, May 25, 1961.

2. Yuri Gagarin, on April 12 1961, took a 108-minute orbital flight aboard a Vostok-1 spacecraft.

Chapter 20

1. The Peter Principle was developed by Laurence J. Peter and published in 1969.

2. The technology for delivering education via the Internet on a grand scale is referred to as Massive Online Open Courses (MOOCs). Institutes of higher learning such as the Massachusetts Institute of Technology (MIT) and Harvard and Stanford Universities and companies such as Apple and Dell deliver education to their constituents using this technology.

INDEX

A

accelerated decision-making,
259, 306, 310, 313. *See also*
OODA loop
accelerated strategy execution,
138–42
accountability, 14, 93, 188, 268, 345
Achieving Competitive Excellence
(ACE) program (UTC), 171
action bins, 273–75
action briefings, 267
Adams, John Quincy, 89
ad hominem, 159
adjustment, 98, 129
Agile, 130
Alexander the Great, 236
alignment
    effective communication and, 90
    levels of organizational maturity,
      254–58
    reaching state of, 11
    as requirement for leadership, 98
    with strategies, 110–11, 194, 226,
      248, 300, 303, 325
    with vision, 11, 165, 260,
      313, 345

ambiguity, 161
AME (Association for Manufactur-
    ing Excellence), 214
American Society for Quality
    (ASQ), 15, 18, 214
Andretti, Mario, 7
Android, 66
anecdotal arguments, 161
antithesis phase (of Hegelian dialec-
    tic), 233–35
appeals to authority, 160
appeals to emotion, 160
appeals to nature, 161
Apple Computer, 19–20, 239–40
arguing from fallacy (arguing from
    ignorance), 160
Aristotle, 279
Armstrong, Neil, 245
ASQ (American Society for Qual-
    ity), 15, 18, 214
assessment of operational excellence,
    169–76
    external, 172–73
    hybrid, 173–76
    internal, 171–72

ABOUT THE AUTHOR

Joseph F. Paris Jr. is a recognized thought leader on the subject of operational excellence; an international entrepreneur; a prolific writer; and a sought-after strategist, consultant, and speaker with engagements around the world.

With over 30 years of experience in international business and operations, he is routinely called upon to offer guidance to C-suite and senior executives and to business-operations and -improvement specialists who wish to improve the overall efficiency and effectiveness of their organizations. He is highly valued for his ability to provide strategic insight and tactical analysis—and to convert these thoughts into reality by successful engagement and execution.

Although he is an expert in the more granular facets of the discipline, he places a special emphasis on the cornerstones for success: the engagement of people and instilling a leadership culture as part of the company's DNA. His end-goal is to help create high-performance individuals working in high-performance teams for high-performance companies.

Paris's vehicles for change and delivering the promises of operational excellence include the following positions:

⇨ Chairman of the XONITEK group of companies, a management and operations consultancy helping companies located around the globe

⇨ Founder of the Operational Excellence Society, a think tank serving professionals in the field of operational excellence and its greater ecosystem.

⇨ Publisher of the *Operational Excellence by Design* newsletter, with over 30,000 subscribers.

⇨ Owner of the Operational Excellence LinkedIn group, with over 60,000 members.

⇨ Producer and cohost of *The Outliers Inn*, a podcast that examines typical business issues from atypical perspectives.

In addition, Paris serves on the editorial board of *The Lean Management Journal* and the advisory boards of the Systems Science and Industrial Engineering Department at the Watson School of Engineering at Binghamton University, the Institute of Industrial and Systems Engineers' Industry Advisory Board, and the New York City Chapter of the Association for Corporate Growth.